Read What Others Are S

A Housekeeper Is Cheaper Than a Divorce

Every once in a blue moon, a book comes along that will literally change your life. This is one of them. Sherman's passionate mission to live a more fun, productive, and engaging life with her family is every parent's secret desire, and her well-researched solution to get over the guilt and hire household help is convincing and, yes, even practical. Through this book, all working parents can unite—whether Mom, Dad, "Entrepreneurial Parent," or nine-to-fiver. *A Housekeeper is Cheaper Than a Divorce* is not just a must-read, it's a must-do!!

—Lisa Roberts, author of
How to Raise a Family and a Career Under One Roof **and**
editor/publisher of *The Entrepreneurial Parent*, **www.en-parent.com**

Bravo to Sherman for a well-argued, important book which encourages every parent to reevaluate priorities and hire the help they most need.

—Arlene Rossen Cardozo, Ph.D.,
author of *Sequencing* **and** *Woman at Home*

In an easy-to-read manner, this book covers every possible question or concern you might have about hiring household help. Especially welcome is the comprehensive section covering the legal and tax obligations that need to be considered.

—Jan Zobel, EA, author of *Minding Her Own Business:*
T¹ Self-Employed Woman's Guide to Taxes and Recordkeeping

Delegating tasks such as housework is an essential part of balancing work and family—especially when you run a home business. This efficient book shows you how.

—Ellen Parlapiano and Patricia Cobe, authors of *Mompreneurs®:*
A Mother's Practical Step-by-Step Guide to Work-At-Home Success

This book is practical and so insightful. It's an ethical and caring guide to the nitty-gritty details that make hiring help in the house truly helpful, so that parents can free up time for themselves and each other and have a calm, well-ordered house. It will save marriages, and many women's sanity. I'm going to follow her tips on getting my groceries delivered right now.

—Rhona Mahony, author of *Kidding Ourselves:*
Breadwinning, Babies, and Bargaining Power

Time is money. But money well spent can also save you time—time for your husband, family and the fun things in life. From hiring a housekeeper to other "time freeing" tips, Kathy Sherman is right on with advice for modern women.

—Jennifer Openshaw, CEO, Women's Financial Network, WFN.com

A Housekeeper is Cheaper Than a Divorce may be just the "permission" you've been seeking to shatter the "shoulds" of the Perfect Mother/ Housewife, and to become the person, mom and wife that is buried underneath housework.

—Kimberley Converse, co-author of *The Myth of the Perfect Mother* and *God's Comfort Food for New Beginnings*

I'm convinced more couples today quarrel over housework than over money. This book is indispensable to the large majority of us from a generation that did not grow up with household help.

—B. Meredith Burke, Ph.D., author/columnist, economist, past president of the National Women's Political Caucus of San Diego

A Housekeeper Is Cheaper Than a Divorce is the first book to explain the "nanny tax" laws in plain language. The tax information in this book is crucial for anyone who employs household help, as well as their tax preparers.

—Ellie Luker, JD, LLM, CPA, Tax Director with a "Big Five" accounting firm

My husband didn't understand why I wanted to hire help because my standards are so high. But once you taught me how to sell him on the idea and I hired a team of housekeepers, I had the time to launch a new career.

—Paula Shuer, BSN, graduate student in marriage and family therapy and mother of three

After my divorce, my children needed extra attention from me. The principles in this book helped me to hire and manage a terrific housekeeper, freeing my time for the really important things in life.

—Alison Mark, program marketing manager and mother of two

I am so happy to have household help. If it weren't for you, I don't think I would ever have considered it. It truly improves the quality of life for my whole family!

—Beth Myers, marathon runner and mother of two

A Housekeeper Is Cheaper Than a Divorce

A Housekeeper Is Cheaper Than a Divorce

Why You **Can** Afford to Hire Help and How to Get It

Kathy Fitzgerald Sherman

Life
Tools
Press

Mountain View, California

A Housekeeper Is Cheaper Than a Divorce
Why You Can Afford to Hire Help and How to Get It

Kathy Fitzgerald Sherman

Published by Life Tools Press

PO Box 390220

Mountain View, CA 94039-0220

(650) 428-0625

First Printing, June, 2000

Printed in the United States of America

Publisher's Cataloging-in-Publication
(Provided by Quality Books, Inc.)

Sherman, Kathy Fitzgerald.
    A housekeeper is cheaper than a divorce : why you CAN afford
to hire help and how to get it / Kathy Fitzgerald Sherman. -- 1st ed.
    p. cm.
    Includes bibliographical references and index.
    LCCN: 00-190606
    ISBN: 0-9679636-0-5

    1. Housekeepers--Selection and appointment. 2. Marital
conflict--Prevention. 3. Home economics. I. Title.
TX331.S54 2000   640'.46
                                                   QBI00-386

About the Author

Kathy Fitzgerald Sherman has employed household help of various kinds for nearly 20 years, successfully using management skills she developed during a high-tech career in Silicon Valley. Like millions of mothers everywhere, Kathy struggles to balance career, childrearing, and homemaking. She finds that delegating housework to a paid employee is the only workable solution to this challenge.

After earning a bachelor's degree in computer science and mathematics in 1978, Kathy worked in the computer industry, holding positions in engineering, sales, and management. In 1986, she formed Results Unlimited, a motivational speaking and seminar business specializing in personal effectiveness. She teaches others to define goals consistent with their values, interests, and priorities and to use their skills and resources to achieve those goals.

Taking her own advice, Kathy changed the form of her business after her first child was born in 1988. Instead of leading seminars on personal effectiveness, she began writing about the topic from home. An award-winning writer and speaker, Kathy has been published in newspapers including *The Christian Science Monitor*, parenting magazines including *Bay Area Parent* and *Big Apple Parent*, and business and computer magazines. She also moderates several on-line discussion groups for parents.

Kathy grew up in Utica, New York, and graduated from the University of Scranton, in Scranton, Pennsylvania. She lives in the San Francisco Bay Area with her husband and two children, ages 9 and 11.

To arrange for Kathy to speak to your group, please call toll-free (877) 543-3857 or email *publicity@LifeToolsPress.com.*

Disclaimer

Even great books have their limitations. This book is designed to provide information about the subject matter covered. It is sold with the understanding that neither the author nor the publisher is engaged in rendering legal, accounting, or other professional services. If legal advice or other expert assistance is required, the services of a competent professional should be sought.

Every effort has been made to make this book as complete and accurate as possible. However, there may be mistakes both typographical and in content. Therefore, this text should be used as a general guide and not as the ultimate source of household employee management information. Furthermore, tax law changes constantly. Some of the tax and legal information contained herein may be out of date shortly after the book's printing.

The purpose of this book is to educate and entertain. The author and Life Tools Press shall have neither liability nor responsibility to any person or entity with respect to any loss or damage caused, or alleged to be caused, directly or indirectly by the information contained in this book.

If you do not wish to be bound by the above, you may return this book to the publisher for a full refund. If you find mistakes, please send your corrections for the next edition to *corrections@LifeToolsPress.com*.

Notice: Some of the names used in this book are real and some are pseudonyms (for interview subjects who requested anonymity).

Acknowledgments

Hundreds of people helped bring this project to completion. I'm grateful for the enthusiastic support I've received from so many. Here is a far-from-complete list of those who have lent a hand:

- My husband, Michael, whose financial and emotional support made this entire venture possible and whose love and commitment never waver

- My children, Sam and Leslie, who bring me joy and whose very existence created the events that led to this book

- My good friends Mary Hudak and Jean Sutherland who are always available for a juicy gossip session or a satisfying heart-to-heart when I need one

- My parents, brothers, and sisters, especially my youngest sister, coach, and personal cheerleader, Margaret Beaton, who not only was our family's first published writer, but also made the first *Oprah* appearance

- My long-time friend and second mother, Rita Harken, whom I count on to provide often-unexpected but always just-right advice

- My writing group—Esmarelda Alderete, Irene Douglass, Grant Head, Melissa Houle, Owen Johnson, Rosalie Mangan, Grace Nilson, Judy Weiler, and Toni Whyte—who taught me how to improve my writing without ever making me feel like quitting

- My friends at the California Writers Club who were the best cheering section a writer could ask for

- The dozens of people who responded in writing to my nationally mailed questionnaire

- The dozens more who participated in formal and impromptu interview sessions, sharing their thoughts on household help

- My writing colleague Meredith Burke, who likes to remind me that she was my first fan

- John Schofield, who donated his HP 110 laptop, so I could sit in my car and write while my daughter attended preschool

- All of the housekeepers and housecleaners I've employed whose hard work allowed me to be productive and who taught me valuable lessons about what succeeds and what doesn't in managing household help

- Ellie Luker, attorney-at-law, who reviewed the tax and legal information in this book

- My literary agent, Linda Mead, who instantly understood what this book was about

- My copy editor, Pat Tompkins, who found more errors than I ever thought possible, while insisting that the manuscript was quite "clean"

- My cover designer, Peri Poloni, whose remarkable design captured the book's spirit

- My book designer, Mary Kantor Torban, whose generosity knows no bounds

- My photographer, Robert Weaver, whose persistence resulted in that "perfect" shot

- Friends and family members who read countless incarnations of this book and offered invaluable suggestions

- Hal Deering, Roselie Buonaro, and Kathryn Hoover, three people who saw my future before I did, held up a mirror for me, and set me on a path that I would previously never have considered for myself.

Table of Contents

Introduction
Why women don't hire the help they need ▪ Who this book is for   13
How the book is structured ▪ How and why the book was written

Part I — Making the Decision to Hire a Housekeeper
Understanding the problem ▪ Deciding to solve it ▪ Planning the   21
solution

It's Only Housework — How Bad Can It Be?
Size of the housework job ▪ Costs of not hiring help   23

If We're So Overloaded, Why Don't We Just Get Help?
Why sharing doesn't work ▪ Why housework is part of our identity
How gender roles were created ▪ Why our mothers seemed to do fine   31
Why hiring help seems elitist ▪ Why we believe household help is too
expensive ▪ Choosing standard of living over quality of life

Make Your Daydreams Real
Why daydreams are important ▪ Resurrecting old dreams ▪ Creating new   45
ones ▪ Making space for your dreams ▪ Committing to your dreams

Think Like a Manager
What a manager does ▪ The importance of creating a mutually rewarding   55
business relationship ▪ How to avoid exploitation

Know Where You're Headed
The importance of planning ▪ Analyzing your unpaid workload
Deciding between housekeeper, nanny, or cleaning service   63
Calculating how much help you need ▪ Researching the going rate

Boil It Down to Numbers
Calculating benefits and costs ▪ Finding ways to pay for help   79
Selling the idea to your spouse

Part II — Managing Your Housekeeper
Organizing your household ▪ Hiring the right person ▪ Following the law   95
Giving instructions ▪ Treating employees well ▪ Handling problems

Solve Each Problem Only Once
Eliminating decision-making ▪ Creating effective household systems   97

8 Decide on Benefits

Attractive benefits that cost little ▪ "Nanny tax" myths, misperceptions, and realities

121

9 Hire the Right Person

Finding good job candidates ▪ The hiring process—phone screening, reference checking, background checking, interviewing ▪ The job offer

135

10 Fulfill Your Legal Obligations

Tax requirements ▪ Fair labor practices

161

11 Share the Road Map

Creating a sense of ownership ▪ Training ▪ Ongoing communication Language, culture, and personality differences ▪ Setting emotional boundaries

179

12 "How Am I Doing, Boss?"

The importance of praise ▪ Using "I" messages ▪ Deciding whether a problem is attitude or capability ▪ Handling absences
Firing a housekeeper

191

Epilog

Some Final Lessons

205

A Appendix

Housekeeper Instructions

211

B Appendix

Housekeeper-Friendly Recipes

221

Resources

Understanding the problem ▪ Overcoming guilt ▪ Clarifying daydreams Negotiating with your spouse ▪ Getting organized ▪ On-line grocery shopping ▪ Offering insurance as a benefit ▪ Background checking Help with payroll tax paperwork ▪ Communicating with your housekeeper ▪ Establishing boundaries with your housekeeper

229

Notes

237

Index

243

Introduction

Imagine the following scenario: Leaving the office at the end of a busy day, you approach your parked car and unlock the driver's door. It's been a tiring but satisfying day, and as your sedan joins the mass of commuters, your thoughts turn to the family waiting at home.

Once through the front door, you're struck by the enthusiastic greetings of your children and the aroma of a hot meal in its final stages of preparation. After a quick check of the day's mail, you sit down at the family's computer with the kids for a 20 minute game of Tetris before dinner is served.

Your husband joins you and the kids at the dinner table, and you all share the news of the day over a tasty meal. After dinner, you supervise homework, baths, and the bedtime routine, mediating the nightly debate over stories versus board games.

Once the kids are tucked into bed, you change clothes for a ride on the family's exercycle, which is followed by a relaxing soak in a hot bath, some child-free spouse time, and a half-hour of recreational reading in bed before lights out.

Noticeably absent from your evening routine? Cooking. Cleaning. Laundry. Grocery shopping.

You consider yourself successful, but not exceptionally so. Yet you are special in one way: You understand that hiring household help allows you to be more effective on the job (because you're able to "recharge your batteries" off the job), enhances the quality of your marriage (because you are free of all-too-common resentment over unfair division of household labor), and enables you to be the kind of parent you want to be (teller of stories, not sorter of socks).

Although your husband is an involved parent who spends lots of time with your kids, he's a working professional, too. The hot meal that the whole family enjoyed was most definitely *not* prepared by him. Your evening, and your husband's, was free of household chores because you had delegated those chores to a paid employee.

It took a leap of faith the first time you hired a housekeeper. Maybe the family budget had to be tightened a bit. Possibly you had to increase your efficiency at the office so that you could bill a few more hours each week. You might have had to endure your mother's pointed comments. Maybe you had to learn a new set of management skills. You weren't sure the investment would pay off. But now that you've done it, you wouldn't go back to the way life used to be for anything. The tranquility that has allowed you—finally—to live the life you've dreamed of makes the trade-offs clearly worthwhile.

■　■　■

Does this scenario sound like an impossible fantasy? For most families, it probably *is* a fantasy. Studies show that in an average household with children, the magnitude of housework approaches that of a full-time job, women do the bulk of it, and few hire the help that would substantially relieve us of this burden. But the aim of this book is to show that the scenario is not impossible. Despite the cultural myths that would have us believe that household help is a luxury only for the wealthy, this book will show that, in fact, hiring such help can be an effective time-management tool for busy women (and men!).

"But Shouldn't My Husband Be Doing Half?"

Getting husbands to equally share housework is the impossible fantasy, not the scenario described above. Granted, some men are willing to pull their weight, domestically speaking, and have wives who insist they do, but they are few and far between. Despite wide-ranging press coverage of men who pitch in equally at home, studies show that the "equal sharing" is much more likely to occur with childcare than with housework. That shouldn't be too surprising. Given that housework alone is nearly a full-time job in households with children, men who share such a workload face the same unpleasant consequences their wives do: loss of sleep, leisure, income-producing opportunities, and time with loved ones.

If you and your husband share housework equally and that arrangement works for you, congratulations! But if you are looking for a pressure valve that will allow both of you to spend more time on what's most important, hiring household help can provide the release you seek.

"But I'd Feel too Guilty if I Hired Help"

Many of us don't hire the help we need because we fear condemnation for doing so, whether from ourselves or others. That's because our society sometimes makes inaccurate and unfair judgments of women who delegate some or all of their homemaking responsibilities.

For example, if a woman (as a mother) purchases childcare so that she can work, her actions are accepted as necessary, even admirable, and she receives sympathy and advice when she encounters difficulties such as high prices or low quality. Even if she hires childcare simply to give herself some child-free time, alone or with her husband, she is met with understanding.

If a woman (as a professional) hires help with administrative tasks so that she can be freed to do the highly skilled work for which she is best qualified, she is seen as an effective executive.

But, if a woman (as a homemaker) hires help with housework, she is often viewed, not as wise, but as self-indulgent or lazy, even if the household help she employs allows her to spend more time working in her profession or becoming a more involved parent. And while most people don't begrudge her the right to spend money on this "luxury," a few actually see her as a snob—"too good" to perform her own dirty work and willing to exploit the labor of others to get that work accomplished.

Some women wisely invest their time where their talents lie and shun any guilt feelings about doing so. But if guilt has gotten the best of you, turn to the first two chapters of this book, which will help you understand where your housework-related guilt feelings come from and how to give them up.

"But It's too Expensive"

A smart woman recognizes that, though the cost of hiring help is not insignificant, the cost of *not* hiring help may be much greater. In case you're not sure what those costs are, many of them are outlined throughout this book. Nevertheless, the costs of hiring help *are* real.

For many women, the decision to hire a housekeeper is an easy one: It is simply out of the question for financial reasons. (But you may be surprised by some stories in this book, since affordability is a very subjective issue.) For a few others, there *is* no question: Finances are not an obstacle, so they simply hire the best-trained, most-experienced, and (consequently) the highest-priced housekeepers available who, because of their qualifications, need little management.

The rest of us must think long and hard about hiring help. We must either find areas of our budget to shave or identify new sources of income to pay our employees' salaries. Since we probably can't afford to pay top dollar, the employees we hire will need careful management and training. And since we're short on time, we want our management to be highly effective, so that we can reap the full benefit of our investment.

If you fit into the "rest of us" category, this book is for you. Maybe you are a professional trying to balance the competing demands of career and family. Maybe you are a full-time homemaker with time-consuming responsibilities such as volunteer work, homeschooling, or a special-needs child. Or maybe you simply would rather not do housework. This book will help you spend your dollars wisely so that the way you spend your time will be equally wise.

"But I Can't Find Good Help"

This book aims to fulfill two goals. First, it will help you to make a well-informed decision about whether to hire household help. Part I, "Making the Decision to Hire a Housekeeper," examines and explodes the taboos against hiring help, clarifies *why* you might want to hire help, and shows how to quantify the amount of help needed, justify the salary expense, and, if appropriate, sell the idea to your husband.

Once you do decide to hire a housekeeper, finding, hiring, and keeping good help is easier said than done. Until now, there have been few books or magazine articles on the topic, and few of us have had mothers who taught us by example how to manage household help. The second aim of this book is to provide you with the specific skills needed to be successful once you decide to hire help.

Accordingly, Part II, "Managing Your Housekeeper," demystifies every aspect of employee management. You will learn to develop a job description and training plan, navigate the hiring process, comply with employment laws, deal with cultural differences, and motivate high-quality performance to get full value for your dollar. (Part II is filled with useful forms and checklists. Visit our website at *www.LifeToolsPress.com* to find them in downloadable form.)

The difference between a great household employee and a poor one is the difference between an effective employer and an ineffective one. This book will show you the simple steps to becoming an effective employer.

About Me

I am passionate about the topic of household help for a very good reason: hiring a housekeeper transformed my life. Although my current daily routine closely matches my values, interests, and priorities, it wasn't always that way. It took me five years of motherhood before I saw that the tasks of mothering are distinct and separable from the tasks of homemaking. I had fallen victim to a condition that I like to call "Motherhood Myopia"—difficulty discerning the difference between the role titles "mother" and "homemaker."

For the sake of my children, I had postponed my career, naively thinking that my years as an at-home mother would be a good time to launch a freelance writing career, a long-time goal of mine. I loved being home with my children, but my career plan wasn't working. I simply didn't have time to write.

My moment of clarity came one day when my kids were five and three. I wanted to experience life with full-time childcare, so I hired back-to-back teenage babysitters (it was summertime) from nine to six every day for a week. Not wanting to get behind on household chores, which piled up at a relentless pace, I devoted half of every day that week to writing and half to chores. For years, I'd employed a three-hour-per-week cleaning service. But now that I had a husband, a house, and two kids, the service barely made a dent in the housework.

On one of those afternoons, I was folding laundry at the kitchen table while I watched the babysitter laughing and playing with my kids. Then it hit me: childcare and housework were two different jobs. And I had it backwards. In my week-long experiment, I had delegated what I *wanted* to do—childcare—and kept doing what I *didn't* want to do—housework. Even though most professional women delegate childcare, I saw that we actually have a spectrum of options: delegate childcare, delegate housework, delegate both, delegate neither!

My insight excited me, but my subsequent decision to hire a 20-hour-per-week housekeeper seemed unique among the professional women I knew. I embarked on a crusade to find out why this "obvious" solution is so underutilized.

I became a self-taught sociologist, psychologist, historian, demographer, and economist. I collected reams of newspaper and magazine articles, read dozens of arcane books, tracked down obscure academic studies, and pored over mind-numbing government statistics. I conducted a nationwide survey of college-educated women. I interviewed friends, relatives, professional acquaintances, fellow parents at my children's schools, even unwitting repairmen who came to my house to fix an appliance and found themselves engaged in a conversation about housework! (The unattributed chapter opening quotes in this book come from the survey and interviews.)

Eventually the picture came into focus. I hope that what I learned and share in these pages helps you cure your "Motherhood Myopia" faster than I cured my own.

Overcoming Motherhood Myopia was only the first step in my transformation, however. I'd engaged cleaning services for many years, but employing a traditional housekeeper to also cook, shop, do laundry and ironing, and tidy up unleashed a new set of problems. I soon stumbled over guilt feelings, tax mysteries, language barriers, training challenges, and conflicts over quality standards.

Luckily, my high-tech management background and entrepreneurial experiences had taught me some valuable skills. I drew on that knowledge in managing my housekeepers (I've had several, and you'll hear about them later), and those management principles fill this book. Of course, there were a few bumps along the way, but I learned from my mistakes, and I'll share that knowledge with you too. I want to help you create a life that, like mine, closely matches your values, interests, and priorities.

All of my life, I've believed that each of us has some unique good to contribute to our planet and that it is a tragedy when we are limited, simply through ineffectiveness, in our efforts to make that contribution. My goal, in writing this book, is to help you make your unique contribution, whatever that might be.

So, whether you're considering hiring a cleaning service for the first time, ready to engage a housekeeper for many hours a week, or simply trying to understand why your Superwoman cape fits so tightly, make yourself a cup of tea and settle into your favorite chair. We've got some work to do.

Part 1

Making the Decision to Hire a Housekeeper

The chapters in Part I will help you do two things. First, they will help you cure your own "Motherhood Myopia." You will understand how you became, by default, your family's housekeeper. You will appreciate the magnitude of the homemaker job and recognize that you can't make it go away by reorganizing it or sharing it. And you'll see that for many, hiring household help is the best solution to the problem, despite myths and taboos to the contrary.

Second, these chapters will help you make your own decision about hiring household help. You will identify new opportunities that would open up to you if you delegated some or all of the housework to a paid employee. You'll figure out what kind of help you need, and how much. And you will calculate whether the benefits of hiring help will outweigh the costs of doing so. By the end of Chapter 6, you will know whether hiring household help is right for you and your family.

1 It's Only Housework — How Bad Can It Be?

My husband, Michael, hadn't seen his college roommate, Frank, for a couple of years. One Sunday afternoon, Frank was in town and stopped by for a visit. After greeting Michael at the front door, he bounded into the kitchen, where I was enjoying the morning newspaper. "Yo, Fitz! What's up?"

"Hi, Frank!" His enthusiasm always brings a smile to my face. "Want to hear about my new project? I'm writing a book."

"Cool! What's it about?"

"Housekeepers. I'm on a mission. I want to encourage women to delegate housework and teach them how to do it."

Like Michael and me, Frank comes from a middle-class background. With brains, hard work, and lots of education, he's achieved professional success. A pulmonologist with a thriving practice, Frank is often interviewed as an expert by TV journalists.

"Oh, that's great! Susan has a woman come in five hours a week who does everything! It's a good thing, too, because she's been putting in long hours on the job." Frank's wife had just become certified as a physician's assistant after spending a couple of years commuting 100 miles to receive her training. Their daughter is in elementary school.

"She does everything?" I asked, feigning surprise. "My housekeeper works 20 hours a week. She does most of the housework, but not all of it."

Frank's surprise was genuine. "Twenty hours! What does she do?"

I began listing my housekeeper's duties. "Not just housecleaning, but laundry, ironing, grocery shopping, cooking, baking, changing sheets, watering plants…"

With each new task I listed, Frank uttered an increasingly sheepish sounding "Oh." He admitted that his family's housekeeper did the housecleaning and ironing, but Susan did the rest. Even though she didn't like doing the remaining chores, according to Frank, she saw no other option.

A Nation in Denial

Despite Frank's professional success, his household, unfortunately, is all too typical. If you are an average American woman, you work 71 hours each week, with half of those hours devoted to unfulfilling, unpaid work.[1] What makes up the bulk of your unpaid work hours? Housework. And even though all objective measures say that those chores are time consuming and take away from more interesting pursuits, our national psyche seems to be in denial about the housework problem.

"Get a life!" retorted one well-established, single writer in her forties when I told her I was working on a book about housework. "Don't sweat the small stuff!" sniffed a 38-year-old childless college professor, even though happiness guru Richard Carlson, author of several "Don't Sweat the Small Stuff" books, advocates hiring a housecleaner.[2] "Get organized!" recommend countless magazine articles, as though good organization can make a nearly full-time job fade into the background. "Share the chores with your husband!" advise another crop of articles, as though men are eager to add to their already overloaded schedules by performing chores that they don't like, don't know how to do, and may not even care about.

Even our national bean-counters ignore the magnitude of household chores by failing to measure them.

Here are some facts about the size of the housework job:

- The average American mother spends 35 hours a week doing housework. And whether she is employed doesn't have much of an effect: employed moms spend 32 hours per week on housework, while stay-at-home moms spend 39 hours. These hours don't count time spent in childrearing.[3]

- The presence of children accounts for most household labor. The first child triggers an increase of 21 hours of chores per week, not including any direct childcare, while each additional child adds 6 hours of chores.[4] Children under six generate the greatest work-load.[5]

- Convenience foods, modern appliances, and changing standards haven't lightened the load for us. American women today spend just as much time doing housework as our mothers[6] *and* our grandmothers[7] did.

- The Gross National Product, which is the sum of the values of all goods and services produced in our country during a year, does not include the unpaid household labor performed by millions of Americans, most of whom are women. (If we don't measure it, we assume it must be insignificant.) Experts estimate that, if included in the calculations, unpaid household labor would raise the GNP by about 25 percent.[8]

How Do Men Fit Into This Picture?

Not to provide ammunition for the gender wars, but the disparity in the amount of time spent by women doing housework, compared to men, explains not only why we're tired but also why we're angry. Consider these facts:

- While the average American wife puts in nearly a full-time shift on housework, her husband spends only 8.7 hours each week on household chores.[9]

- Even though many women work part time to accommodate their family responsibilities, they still end up working more than their husbands. The average American work-week, including paid work and unpaid work at home is 15 hours more per week for women than it is for men[10], for a total work-week of 71 hours for women and 55 hours for men.[11]

- The size of a woman's earnings, compared to her husband's, has little effect on the amount of housework she does. One study even showed that the *less* husbands earn relative to their wives, the *more* housework the wives do.[12]

- The arrival of children affects men and women in different ways. While new mothers find their housework load significantly increased, men with children, whose help is badly needed at home, work longer hours than those without, on average, because of the increased financial demands of a family.[13]

Pay Me Now, or Pay Me Later

Do you think it's possible to squeeze a full-time, unfulfilling job into your "spare" time and not experience any consequences? Despite the Superwoman myth, most of us can't do it all, at least not without paying a price.

Oh, for an Extra Hour of Sleep!

For starters, we women are tired. In our macho, "I don't need much sleep" culture, most Americans cut back on sleep when in a time crunch. As a result, many of us, both men and women, are chronically sleep deprived. But women seem to be disproportionately shortchanged.[14] Perhaps, in cutting sleep, we've cut to the bone. Arlie Hochschild observed something curious about the working mothers she interviewed for her book *The Second Shift*. They talked about sleep the way starving people talk about food—fixating on it, apologizing for their need for it, talking about strategies to avoid waking fully when needed in the middle of the night.[15]

Our lack of sleep is uncomfortable. But even more importantly, it harms our ability to function in our daily lives. The irritability we feel when we lack sleep damages the quality of the family life our balancing act was designed to protect; our lethargy affects our ability to perform in our jobs. Lack of sleep depresses our immune systems,[16] too, leaving us vulnerable to illness.

Even worse, lack of sleep is downright dangerous. Employed mothers of young children risk an increased likelihood of on-the-job injuries.[17] Every year, 100,000 traffic accidents (including 71,000 injuries and 1,500 fatalities) are related to sleepiness.[18]

During 18 months when I had two children under the age of four and insufficient household help, I knocked the side-view mirror off of my car while backing out of my garage three times, in three separate incidents. Not only was this expensive (my power-adjustable mirror cost $250 to replace each time), it was an unheeded signal of how vulnerable my children and I were to injury, due to my sleep deprivation. It scares me now when I realize that, rather than facing the potential consequences of my work overload and hiring the help I needed, I continuously placed my children and myself in jeopardy.

Oh, for an Hour to Myself!

When we think of sleep deprivation, most of us think of too few hours in bed. But often our lack of sleep can be caused by insomnia that results from too little "wind down" time. Overwhelmed with responsibilities, our minds race at night, continuing the day's mental processing work when we should be sleeping. More leisure time would give us a chance to unwind, but, just like sleep, it is in short supply for American women, especially when compared to men.[19]

Experts report that, without a chance to "recharge our batteries" through sleep and leisure, we women are likely to experience high levels of stress, which raise blood pressure and cholesterol, cause hardening and constricting of the arteries, and leave us vulnerable to cardiovascular disease. Exercise that could help reduce this risk is often eliminated when leisure time is in short supply.[20]

I'm Mad as Hell...

Women's anger toward men has been rising steadily over the last two decades. The biggest source of resentment? The fact that men don't do their share around the house.[21] We women have been socialized not to express anger, but our bodies don't follow instructions.

If you feel sick and tired all the time, unresolved anger may be the real culprit. In a "damned if you do, damned if you don't" situation, our anger hurts us whether or not we express it. Unexpressed, our anger goes underground and creates psychosomatic illnesses or translates into depression. And, because expression of anger is socially unacceptable for women, when we occasionally lose control with an angry outburst, we feel guilty because we have failed in our self-imposed role as family peacemaker.[22] Worse, expressed anger can be dangerous. Studies show that arguments about housework are the ones most likely to precipitate domestic violence.[23]

Even our sex lives can suffer. One of the predictors of sexual frigidity in women is repressed anger.[24] Thirty-five percent of respondents to a *Working Mother* magazine survey reported that diminished sex drive was one of the ways they reacted to stress.[25]

The saddest casualty of our unresolved anger, though, is the state of our marriages. One survey found that almost half of couples have fought about cleaning, and 1 in 10 has separated over housework disagreements.[26]

Hochschild stated the problem eloquently in *Second Shift*: "If there is one truth that emerges from all the others, it is that the most important injury to women who work the double day is not the fact they work too long or get too tired. That is only the obvious and tangible cost. The deeper problem such women face is that they can not afford the luxury of unambivalent love for their husbands."[27]

Before the epiphany that led me to hire a 20-hour-per-week housekeeper, I had become so angry with my husband over my long, exhausting working hours that I seriously considered divorcing him. One evening near midnight, when I folded laundry while Michael read a magazine, I launched into an all-too-familiar tirade. My infuriatingly reasonable husband responded, "Fitz, I acknowledge that you have a miserable life. I wouldn't wish it on my worst enemy. But you *cannot* solve this problem at my expense. I barely have enough R&R time as it is. What good will it do if we're *both* overextended?"

He was right, of course, to protect his own leisure time. But I needed some too. In a perverse way, his stubbornness forced me to discover the perfect solution—hiring help—that allowed both of us to spend our time in productive, enjoyable ways. The story has a happy ending: Our marriage did recover. And now my husband has become a vocal proponent of hiring household help. As the saying goes, "If mama ain't happy, ain't nobody happy!"

Children—The Innocent Victims

Much has been written about the potential harm done to children who spend many hours a day in daycare while their parents are at work. While the arguments on both sides of the controversy are compelling, the crux of the issue is the time that children spend with parents. One side argues that "quality time" is sufficient, while the other side argues that both "quality time" and "quantity time" are necessary. But what neither side addresses, perhaps because it would be difficult to measure, is how time with children (either quality or quantity) is affected by their parents' second shift of household chores.

In 1995, I conducted my own nationwide survey. A recurring theme among my survey respondents who employ household help was the additional family time it gives them. In particular, the pressure point seems to be weekends. Those who hire help made comments such as, "I'm not willing to give up my weekends to clean when I'm trading off time with my young children," "With three active boys, we're constantly running to a sports activity and I'm able to enjoy all that without having to worry about cleaning the house," or "I employ a housekeeper so that I can enjoy more quality time with my family."

In contrast, comments from those who don't employ help revealed frustration about the difficulty of carving out "quality time." For example, "Since we both work, there doesn't seem to be enough time to complete housework and still have time to relax," and "We both get frustrated by how housework interferes with our other activities." One person expressed a bitterness that must certainly poison any time she spends with her family: "They are all slobs and lazy and I do not have time to work *plus* do bills, laundry, grocery shop, straighten up, etc.!"

I can attest personally to the positive impact that household help can have on family time. After I hired my first 20-hour-a-week housekeeper, I noticed that I began to enjoy my children much more, instead of just viewing them as another obligation. I did a lot less yelling and a lot more laughing. Weekend family time improved, too, as my increased leisure time allowed all of us to enjoy Sunday outings together.

Divorce and Other Financial Costs

Although financial independence is a primary goal for most women who enter the workforce, in an ironic twist, the work-family balancing act actually undermines women's financial health. Employed mothers often choose part-time or low-paid positions because those jobs offer more flexible working hours, fewer demands, or less travel. Then, in a vicious cycle, those lower earnings become the justification for women's ownership of household chores. Finally, conflicts in marriage arising from these events often lead to divorce; some women conclude that life would be easier with one fewer "child" to care for. But the financial compromises that employed mothers make almost guarantee financial difficulty after divorce.

Experts are beginning to view the stubborn disparity between men's and women's wages not as an effect of lingering discrimination, but as a result of work/family compromises.[28] Even differences in career success among women are better explained by variations in family responsibilities than by raw talent. While intelligence is the best predictor of a man's career success, researchers have found no such correlation for women.[29] Although no employee can ever be a third spouse, certainly household help can offer a woman at least some of the career flexibility her husband has.

Everyone's Loss—The Missed Opportunities

Beyond the pain (the anger, the sadness, the disappointment), beyond the damage (to our health, to our children, to our marriages, to our financial well-being) are the missed opportunities.

What could we be contributing, to ourselves and to society, if we weren't doing housework? What if Michaelangelo couldn't paint the Sistine Chapel because he had to get the laundry done? What if Louis Pasteur never figured out how to kill bacteria because he was too busy shopping and cooking?

Virginia Woolf, in *A Room of One's Own*, asserted that most of the great artists in history were men, not because they were more capable than women, but because they were free of the domestic responsibilities that burdened women.[30]

You may not be an Aristotle or a Christopher Columbus or even a Margaret Sanger. But what contributions can you make that are uniquely yours? What business can you launch? What patient can you heal? What story can you tell your child?

2 If We're So Overloaded, Why Don't We Just Get Help?

A 1996 *Working Mother* magazine survey found that most of its readers feel very stressed and suffer a strained relationship with their husbands or children as a result. Yet only 11 percent ask for help.[1] Why? Could it be that working mothers don't feel entitled to help?

One night when I was watching television, a commercial mesmerized me. It began with the camera panning over acres of lush, beautifully maintained lawn. The sun was low in the sky, the light the soft yellow of dusk, and the relaxing background music implied that this was the end of a tough but satisfying day. The voice-over began: You, the viewer, the voice told us, work hard at what you do… Although you enjoy gazing on everything you own, you are smart enough to let someone else take care of it.

Then the panning camera caught sight of a team of gardeners hard at work and it became clear why the lawn looked the way it did. Finally, the camera focused on a man in his forties reclining comfortably in a hammock, with a big smile on his face and a credit card in his hand (which he would presumably use to pay the gardeners).

The message was clear: You (a man) work hard during the day and deserve time to relax when you are at home. Your wisdom in delegating household chores and your financial savvy in finding a way to pay for it (hopefully with the advertised credit card) will provide you with the leisure you are due.

Where are similar ads targeted to women? Don't advertisers think we deserve leisure? Why does Miller Time seem to be an exclusively male entitlement?

Of *course* we women deserve leisure. But have you heard the joke about the hapless soul stranded in the flood who refuses help from the National Guard because he's waiting for God to save him? We women can be like that, too—turning down help that's staring us in the face because we think it's supposed to come in a particular form.

Looking for Help in All the Wrong Places

Conventional wisdom says that overwhelmed women should share household chores with their husbands. But, as sociologist Stephanie Coontz says in her book *The Way We Really Are*, "There's no nonstressful way to divide three full-time jobs between two individuals."[2]

As women's roles have changed dramatically in the last generation, most men still shoulder their traditional role: family breadwinner. So, while wives have taken on a great deal more responsibility, husbands' loads have not been correspondingly lightened. In fact, although men have not significantly increased their participation in housework, they have become enthusiastic participants in the task of childrearing.[3] Leisure time has been declining for all adults, not just women.[4]

Although it might be "fair" to ask men to take over more of the housework, it's not realistic. The same 24-hour day that limits what you can accomplish is a constraint for your husband, too.

When we fail to get our husbands to do housework, many stressed-out mothers turn to our children for help. Unfortunately, while teaching children how to do housework is an important parental task, it doesn't impact our own workload the way we'd like it to. For one thing, the time we spend teaching children these skills can consume the time we save by delegating the chores to them. Second, kids aren't mature enough or competent enough to perform household chores of any significance until they're halfway through their childhoods. And third, children have important developmental tasks of their own that take time. Given the time-consuming nature of housework, can children provide enough help to make a difference without interfering in their own age-appropriate work? Not likely.

By the way, once I hired our first 20-hour-per-week housekeeper, my husband began doing housework! How come? My theory is that, before we had the help we needed, the sheer volume of work was so overwhelming that pitching in was a no-win proposition for Michael. If he was still going to end up with an angry, unhappy wife, why should he give up his precious leisure hours? But afterward, the chores he did were a big share of the little bit our housekeeper didn't do and my positive reaction encouraged him to do more.

And my kids now spend much more time doing housework than they did in our prehousekeeper days. That's because I have the time and energy to devise age-appropriate chores, train my children to carry them out, and monitor their performance.

Housework Is Women's Work

> *I just can't get past the feeling that if I'm not the one doing their laundry and cooking their meals, my husband and kids won't know I love them.*
> —43-year-old beauty consultant and mother of two

Many of us are not even sure we want help with housework. That's because domestic labor has been fused in our minds with love. Our mothers were our first teachers and most important role models and, whether or not they were employed, were the ones who did the physical and emotional caretaking in our families of origin. To repudiate the domestic work that our mothers did may threaten our very identities as women.

Advertising for household products is directed almost exclusively at women and heavily reinforces the message that housework equals motherly love. Even biology plays a role in the way we view housework. Mother Nature dictates that gestation and lactation can only be performed by women, and household chores necessitated by the presence of children can seem like a natural extension of those functions.

But, although you may no longer be physically performing most of your family's household chores if you hire a housekeeper, it won't be necessary to give up the emotional work of caring for your family. After you've delegated the bulk of the drudgery (the most boring, repetitive, time-consuming chores), you may have more energy for the special loving touches that make the biggest difference to your family.

A desire to take emotional care of our families is not the only reason that we women do more than our share of housework. Some biological differences between men and women make us care more than our husbands about whether and how the housework gets done. For one thing, women, in general, are more perceptive in all five senses: We can hear and see better, are more sensitive to touch, and can identify greater subtleties of taste and smell. (We are more likely to be annoyed by the drip-drip-drip of a leaky faucet, the sight of smeared fingerprints across a picture window, the ripe odor of dirty laundry.)

Furthermore, not only do women perceive *more* than men, but in some ways we perceive differently as well. For example, while men have better depth perception within a very narrow field of vision, they actually have tunnel vision compared to women's wide field of vision.[5]

This last fact reminds me of dozens of times when I've sent Michael into the pantry for an item, but because it wasn't precisely where he expected it, he was incapable of seeing it without my assistance. Or the times I've come home to a hopelessly cluttered house, my husband blissfully reading a magazine in the middle of the mess, thoroughly unruffled.

Here is another reason that women are the ones who do housework: Wives develop a stronger sense of "ownership" toward the domestic realm than do their husbands. As soon as we create our first homes together, women's early childhood role-modeling and training lead us—in very subtle ways—to stake out our territory. (Who chose the china pattern when you got married? The linens? Who picks the brand of laundry detergent you use?) Then, during our pregnancies, with our hormones in overdrive, we begin to "nest."

During our maternity leaves, which can last weeks, months, or even years, we experience the home as the focal point of our activities. Once we return to work, we are much more likely than our husbands to work part time to accommodate family responsibilities.[6] More than half of all home-based workers are women, again, to better balance work and family, and our numbers are growing.[7] And, even if mothers work full time, we are more likely than our husbands to stay home to care for sick or vacationing children.[8] Thus, it should come as no surprise that we women typically care more about a pleasant home environment than our husbands do.

But when a man (or a woman) works in an office, janitorial services that maintain the workplace are considered a cost of doing business. Why don't we consider hired household help to be a cost of doing business as well, whether the "business" in question is a home-based business or the business of childrearing?

Have You Come a Long Way, Baby?

History and tradition also tell us that housework is women's work. The home has been defined as women's exclusive realm since the Industrial Revolution created the middle class. But it wasn't always that way. In the farming economy of colonial America, every family member worked on the farm according to his or her physical capabilities. The work of the farm*house* was a family effort, too, with the men and boys doing such strenuous housework as beating rugs and carrying firewood. Childrearing was a collaborative effort because both parents had extensive contact with their children all day.

When factory work sent poor farming families streaming into newly developing cities, every available family member went to work. But factories were dirty and dangerous and were no place for children (despite the all-too-common practice of using children as cheap labor). In families that could afford it, men worked long, hard hours in the factories while women stayed at home with the children who were too young to work.

As labor became more specialized and wages increased, more and more mothers could afford to stay home. Homemaking achieved recognition as an endeavor requiring talent and skill. Soon, this women's role answered a sacred purpose as well. The home that a woman created, filled with the aroma of freshly baked bread and the sounds of contented, well-mannered children, was just the sanctuary her husband needed after his toils and travails in what was viewed as the evil, corrupt outside world. Several generations of rigid gender-based division of labor firmly established the idea that housework was women's work.

But by the 1960s, many women were no longer content to limit their worlds to the domestic sphere. During the world wars, many had patriotically gone to work in munitions factories, giving them a taste of freedom and an independent income. Once back home, homemakers felt an increasing sense of isolation and discontent, fueled by the explosive growth of suburbia after World War II. And the widespread availability of household appliances and convenience foods, while eliminating most of the drudgery from the homemaker's day, also eliminated the creativity. In search of fulfillment, women began streaming into the workforce in record numbers.

Unfortunately, the reasons that most married women went to work in the 1960s and '70s—personal fulfillment, financial independence, a desire to give their families a better standard of living—were not enthusiastically embraced by their husbands. Many men considered these motivations downright threatening. As a result, most married women who embraced the newly available employment opportunities did so, not with the enthusiastic blessing of their husbands and an offer to share the workload at home, but with the understanding that "if the household was functioning, if she was not making too many demands on him, whatever she did was fine."[9]

So the married working mother of the '60s and '70s hired a babysitter for the children (or waited until they were old enough for school before joining the workforce) and worked a "second shift" at home every night to accomplish the housework she would otherwise have done during the day. Thus, an unfortunate precedent was established: A family could depend on two incomes, and mother would perform all of the household chores and do all of the childrearing, except for the childcare that was done by others while she was at work.

"I Must Be Doing Something Wrong"

My mother seemed to handle everything just fine and she had four kids and worked full time. There must be something I haven't learned yet.

—38-year-old employee relations specialist and mother of one

My own mother, a college graduate, had a short-lived career as a math teacher. Like most women of her generation, she quit her job after the birth of her first child (me) to become a full-time homemaker. Then she went on to have seven more children.

Apparently, the burden of housework in my mother's life impressed and horrified me because the bulk of my childhood memories revolve around it: the stacks and stacks of folded laundry (she was usually finishing up the third or fourth load as I arrived home from school), potato peels piled high on old newspaper (can you imagine cooking dinner for 10 every single night?), the piles of dinner dishes in the sink, and the occasional "last straw" spilled glass of milk that would send her sobbing to her room.

Even my academic studies were affected by this firsthand view of housework. My impression of the Industrial Revolution, as first presented to me in the fourth grade, was that it had its greatest impact on the homemaker. Although other inventions were undoubtedly mentioned, I only remember the discussion of household advancements (automatic washers, electric irons, miracle fabrics like Dacron) and the enormous improvements in the quality of life consequently experienced (or so the book said) by the American housewife. If my mother was a "beneficiary" of these modernizations, I shuddered to contemplate the lives of my foremothers.

So when I became a mother and homemaker myself and found myself commiserating with my friends about housework, I naturally felt confused. I had only two kids, compared to my mother's eight. How could it be that housework overwhelmed me? Was my fourth-grade social studies textbook wrong about the easy life of the American housewife? Had I not yet mastered the art (or science) of running a household? Or was I simply a spoiled brat?

Author and political scientist Susan Moller Okin observes that we women compare ourselves with other women, rather than with men.[10] We look around at the women we know, women we read about in the newspaper, or even our mothers and conclude that we're better off, or at least no worse off, than the others. If that is so, we conclude, we have no right to complain about our own situations.

Of course, the conclusion is silly: No advancement in any field (science, politics, medicine, education, architecture) would occur if we contented ourselves with the status quo. But standing in our own little slice of history, sometimes we miss the perspective of the big picture.

While it's certainly true that the changes in the home over the last century (indoor plumbing, washing machines, gas and electric stoves, and so on) have eliminated the drudgery and saved the homemaker labor, they haven't saved her time. That's because increased wealth and new technology always go hand-in-hand with increased living standards. And higher standards cost the time ostensibly saved by the new technology. Fine hardwood floors need more care than the rough-hewn floors of the colonial farmhouse. Tile bathrooms cry out to be cleaned more often than outhouses. And, with washing machines readily available, society now looks askance at those who change clothing only once a week.

Here are some more time-consuming improvements: Houses are larger—an average of 2,200 square feet for a new house today[11] compared to 800 square feet in 1949.[12] Compared to our parents, we own more cars—54 percent of households had two or more vehicles in 1990, compared to 29 percent in 1970. And we own more gadgets—microwave ovens, VCRs, computers.[13] All of these advancements, while making our lives more comfortable, also require more time for maintenance.

But increased standards alone don't account for the continued time-consuming nature of housework. Along with the modernization of the home has come a duty that we rarely think about when we compare ourselves with our foremothers: consumption.

Not only must we purchase our home's "labor-saving devices" and periodically have them maintained or replace them, we must also acquire, with frequent regularity, the necessities (food and clothing) that, prior to the Industrial Revolution, were produced at home. And with the explosion of new brand names and product varieties that are introduced to the marketplace every day, the job of consumption includes not only the physical tasks of traveling to stores and making purchases, but also the mental challenges of educating ourselves on what products are available, setting purchase criteria (price, quality, convenience), and deciding what to purchase. Although consuming goods is certainly easier than producing them, though far less creatively fulfilling, consumption can nevertheless be a daunting, time-consuming undertaking, for which we rarely give ourselves credit.

Our grandmothers spent much less time on the consumption task because there were fewer product choices and because home delivery was widely available. Grocery stores delivered phoned-in orders. "Milk men" (my grandfather was one) made regular deliveries. "Vegetable men" and "meat men" drove their trucks through town, making regular and unscheduled stops. Laundry services picked up and delivered. Even healthcare was easier to purchase: doctors made house calls when their patients were sick.

Although the average family size has decreased, childrearing is more time-consuming today than it was in the past.[14] The most noticeable difference is the number of hours we mothers now spend on chauffeuring: 11 hours a week for those of us with school-age kids.[15] As a child, I walked, took the bus, or rode my bike everywhere I wanted or needed to go. And if I wanted a playmate, I wandered through the neighborhood in search of one. No playdate was arranged for me. But mothers today depend on cars due to safety concerns and because of ever-widening suburban sprawl.

We have different ideas about parenting, too, compared to a generation or two ago. While our mothers may have read Dr. Spock, we study childrearing techniques with an intensity that was absent in previous generations. The advice manuals available to us today are legion and their numbers grow every day. And though our mothers may have found the playpen to be a handy and safe place to confine a toddler while they did housework, we aim to stimulate and challenge our children through a schedule of activities beginning with baby gym and continuing through their teenage years, a priority that makes housework a "second shift" even for full-time homemakers.

Paige, a 35-year-old medical assistant, grew up in a family of four children where both parents worked full time. She remembers a youth spent watching TV after school while her older sister supervised. No "quality time" was ever spent with her parents. Her father spent his evenings behind a newspaper and her mother spent hers doing housework. The contrast between the "benign neglect" parenting styles of our mothers and the more involved approach of today may best explain how our mothers were able to "do it all" a generation ago.

Isn't Hiring Help Elitist?

Quite frankly, I look down on my friends who use household help because they are not able to handle their household duties themselves.

—32-year-old homemaker, mother of two

I paid my dues when my children were young and you should too.

—My mother-in-law's reaction when I told her I planned to hire a housekeeper

Here's a curious fact: A century ago, there were an average of two servants per family of five.[16] My friend Florence, a retired psychotherapist, says, "I remember my years as a social worker, in the 1930s and '40s. Even the poorest of my client families hired household help for at least a few hours a week. It was viewed as a necessity. I don't understand how household help has come to be perceived as a luxury."

Florence's memory hasn't deceived her. *Good Housekeeping* magazine recently reminisced about an article published in February 1924, "Serving the Sunday Dinner When the Cook Goes to Church."[17]

Despite the widespread use of household help in generations past, the idea that hiring such help is elitist was at least partly the result of a successful journalistic effort. In the late nineteenth century, when few married women were employed, three prominent writers, Sarah Josepha Hale, Catherine Beecher, and Harriet Beecher Stowe, began a campaign to stigmatize the hiring of household help. By democratic custom, Beecher wrote, the virtuous of all classes must work; only aristocrats (a decidedly un-American concept) scorn work. By doing their own housework, women uphold the most fundamental American standards.[18]

But American women ignored this message when household workers were plentiful and easily affordable. After World War II, though, a shrinking domestic worker pool (due to a reduction in immigration earlier in the century) served a growing middle class (thanks to the GI Bill). And as families spent more money on "labor-saving devices" such as washing machines, they had less available to spend on servants. With fewer workers to go around and more of the household budget allocated to machines, the "do-it-yourself" mentality took firm hold among American women.

Unfortunately, as we finally followed Beecher and her colleagues' advice not to hire servants, we also internalized their characterization of that path as morally superior. At the time of the workplace revolution of the 1960s and '70s, the many married women entering the workforce had a genuine need for hired help. By then, not only had we fallen out of the habit of hiring help, but we'd also come to believe there were good moral reasons not to.

"I Can't Afford to Hire Help"

It's a stubborn myth that household help is a luxury affordable only by the wealthy. Believing it may prevent you from recognizing a good time-management tool when you see one. But this myth has a powerful hold on us for a compelling reason—because so few of us see ourselves as wealthy, many of us find hiring help unimaginable, no matter what the justification.

I first became interested in the question of how we view wealth after I began receiving responses to the four-page questionnaire I mailed to college-educated women, as part of the research for this book. The responses, for the most part, confirmed my early impressions of the issues surrounding hiring household help. But I noticed something that was particularly striking: There seemed to be little correlation between a respondent's income and her assessment of whether she could afford help.

For example, Deanna, a 37-year-old mother of a preschooler, is an accountant who owns her own business and earns a substantial income. Her husband, a high-tech sales professional, earns a matching income. Most of us would probably agree that their combined household income puts them in the wealthy category.

Both Deanna and her husband work long hours and Deanna expresses deep resentment over the fact that she, not her husband, performs most of the household chores. Remarkably, though, the only household help they employ is a weekly cleaning service. Why don't they employ more help? According to Deanna, they can't afford it.

In contrast, Jill is a full-time mother of two children, ages three and five. Her husband's income equals the combined incomes of Deanna and her husband. Jill's schedule, presumably, could more easily accommodate household chores than Deanna's. Nevertheless, Jill and her husband employ a housekeeper 32 hours a week. Jill's unapologetic explanation? "I don't have time for housework."

And Charlene, a housecleaner I employed several years ago for a few hours a week, once told me that she herself pays someone to clean her house. I found this news surprising and said to her, "But you clean houses for a living! Why don't you just do your own house as well?" She replied, "Because I'm a working mother. I don't have time to clean house when I get home from work."

Of course, it's impossible to tell, simply based on household income, what a family's total financial picture looks like. And for Jill and Charlene, their perceived need for household help seems to make any question of affordability moot. But Deanna's story, along with many others told by my survey respondents, left me wondering: Could our willingness, or unwillingness, to think of ourselves as wealthy affect our inclination to hire household help?

If you were to believe media headlines, you would think the current generation is struggling financially just to stay even. Wages are stagnant, we've been told. We now must work harder and harder to buy less and less. It now takes two incomes to support a family instead of just one. We are not wealthy, we conclude, we are working class, and we've got the hectic schedules and frayed nerves to prove it.

But something doesn't quite add up. Our standard of living has improved astronomically in the last couple of generations. We own more "stuff" than our parents and grandparents did (homes, cars, appliances) and, thanks to technological improvements, the quality is better now, too. Most of us rely on gadgets that didn't exist a generation ago: answering machines, microwave ovens, VCRs, CD players, fax machines, cell phones, personal computers. We're safer, we're healthier, we live longer, we're better educated, our environment's cleaner. All that and our net worths are higher, too.[19] Even single-income families are better off now than a half century ago. Single-income couples have seen their median cash wages increase 87 percent (adjusted for inflation) between 1949 and 1991.[20] Yet most mothers stayed home in 1949, when we were much poorer, and most mothers went to work in 1991, when we were much wealthier.

When sociologist Arlie Hochschild was researching her latest book (*The Time Bind: When Work Becomes Home and Home Becomes Work*), she spent three years studying employees of a Fortune 500 company, which she cryptically calls "Amerco," along with their families. Hochschild's interview subjects came from every level of the corporation, from the executive suite to the factory floor. Their household incomes covered a correspondingly wide range.

Interestingly, the most financially stressed couple Hochschild interviewed was also the wealthiest: one of the company's top executives and his wife. They were fretting, at the time of the interview, over whether they would have enough money to repave their tennis courts. The least stressed couple she interviewed was also the poorest: a worker from the company's childcare center and her husband, who worked in a box factory. They felt they were getting along just fine.

Hochschild further reported that, of the male assembly-line workers she interviewed, half had wives who were employed and half had stay-at-home wives. Those with employed wives cited financial need as the women's motivation for working, while the others stated that they were managing just fine on one income. Wages were presumably similar for both groups of men, so what accounted for the different perceptions? Hochschild theorized that economic need has a strong cultural component.[21] In other words, we select a desired lifestyle, then define that lifestyle as "need."

Standard of Living Versus Quality of Life

Hochschild's observations about how we determine what income we "need" can be applied to the way we spend that income, as well. It works like this: First we become acclimated to the lifestyle that we perceive our income allows. We commit ourselves to that income by creating a high-maintenance infrastructure that includes a big mortgage, luxury cars, and costly habits like expensive vacations and clothes. Then, we find ourselves locked in if our high standard of living fails to translate into a high quality of life; we have no room to adjust.

Sometimes this happens when we delay childbearing and enjoy one household supported by two professional salaries. Sometimes it's a simple matter of keeping up with the Joneses. We look at our friends' lifestyles and figure that something's wrong if we're not making the same acquisitions they are. In such situations, even though household help is needed, it can seem absolutely unaffordable.

So even though, as measured by our comfortable lifestyles, more of us are wealthy than care to admit it, the employment of housekeepers is still relatively limited among us. It's impossible to wake up one day and discover that you've employed a housekeeper the way that, thanks to creeping consumerism, we seem to wake up and discover that we own bigger homes, finer cars, new furniture, and so on. Housekeepers aren't available to us using the "more, better, sooner" method. Nor are we made comfortable with the idea of hiring a housekeeper by being bombarded with ads, the way we are for new consumer goods.

The unconscious type of financial decision-making facilitated by creeping consumerism does not always serve our best interests. Sometimes we choose standard of living over quality of life.

One of the most effective time-management techniques is actually a money-management technique: Pay someone else to do the tasks you don't want to do, so that you're free to do what really matters and what you're good at. Break the vicious circle of spending for luxury items that don't free up your time and then having to work harder and longer to pay for them. Instead, spend your money on tools that will help you build the life you've dreamed of.

None of us likes to see ourselves as manipulated robots, making decisions, both large and small, as though we were Pavlov's dogs trained to salivate on cue. But if we accept the idea that only the wealthy can afford household help, while refusing to see ourselves as wealthy, we might assume, without examination, that we can't afford to hire help. Maybe the right question is, can we afford not to? As Lily Tomlin once said, "If I had known what it would be like to have it all, I might have settled for less."[22]

3 Make Your Daydreams Real

What would you do if your fairy godmother granted you an extra 15 hours a week? Twenty? Thirty? How would you spend those extra hours? For example, would you:

- Earn (more) income?

- Continue your education?

- Start a business?

- Enjoy relationships—with spouse, children, family, friends?

- Exercise?

- Pursue hobbies?

- Perform volunteer work?

- Participate in church activities?

- Write a book?

- Remodel your house?

- Resolve long-standing health problems?

- Spend more time on the creative aspects of homemaking?

- Ensure that you have unstructured time every day to "recharge your batteries"?

In Chapters 5 and 6, you'll calculate exactly how many hours of household help you need each week and how many you can afford to buy. But in this chapter, let's explore the new possibilities that you could create if you suddenly had a significant chunk of free time.

Do What Only You Can Do

Author Alison Owings once worked for CBS News as a network news writer. When she left her job at CBS, she told Walter Cronkite, "I do not want to do that which will get done if I am not there to do it."[1] A well-trained employee can do housework. What is it that only *you* can do?

The incredible material wealth that our nation has acquired in the last 50 years stands in sharp contrast to the poverty of time that so many of us, mostly women, now experience. A survey conducted by *Working Mother* magazine found that what its readers want most is more time—to spend by themselves and to spend with their families.[2] Yet how many of us recognize our power to change how we spend our time?

To be truly effective is to accept that for every task you take on personally, there is a universe of other possibilities that cannot occur. The tasks that you choose should be the most meaningful and important ones. When you come to the end of your life and look back, what do you want to see?

You may already have a very clear idea of who you are and what your life is about (or would be about, if only you could find the time). You have a sense of purpose, and you know how your values, interests, and priorities fit in. Because of your clarity, you'll be able to easily identify the best uses for your newfound free time.

If your daydreams have gotten buried, however, in the busyness of your life, instead of being guided by your inner sense of self, you may be controlled by your "to-do" list, which you fill in response to the demands placed on you by others.

This chapter can be your chance to take a breather, to refocus on that inner sense of self. Maybe you simply need to remember and articulate the grown-up version of your childhood dreams. Or maybe your daydreams are buried so deeply you will need to do some major excavation work to rediscover them. (Extra help with this task is available through the books listed in the Resources section in the back of this book.)

Wherever you are in the process of creating the masterpiece that is your life, household help can be just what you need to prepare the canvas. Let's see what some others have done.

Resurrecting a Childhood Dream

Animals were a passion for Kathryn during her childhood in the Midwest. Her summers were spent tending to, and adding to, her at-home menagerie. She dreamed of one day becoming a veterinarian.

But when she entered college in the late '60s, her daydream was quashed. Her school's dean of students strongly disapproved of Kathryn's plans, stating that veterinary medicine, because of its long and unpredictable hours, was a poor career choice for a woman who would also ultimately become a wife and mother. He recommended engineering and she acquiesced.

Although a bright student who was capable of handling the engineering curriculum, Kathryn never fell in love with the field. Nevertheless, she did fall in love with Leo, a fellow engineering student who eventually became her husband. After graduation, they moved to California and soon joined with several others in founding a high-tech venture.

Because children are about the only creatures on the planet that Kathryn loves as much as animals, she retired from the business world when she and Leo started their family. Now at home with their three children, she has been able to manifest a revised version of her daydream, thanks to the success of the company she helped found and her family's resulting financial security.

Although veterinary school is an unattractive option at this stage, animals once again have taken an important place in Kathryn's life. In addition to the usual dog and a couple of cats, a variety of other animals have taken up long- and short-term residencies with her family: rabbits, chickens, mice, hamsters, even an iguana. Kathryn, of course, is primary caretaker for the menagerie, even providing medical care when needed. And when she has a yen for contact with large animals, she and her kids go to the local riding stable to ride and care for the horses there.

Because caring for animals (not to mention children) is time consuming, Kathryn depends on a housekeeper to help with most of the household chores. And she feels that the benefits of hiring help extend beyond getting the chores done.

"Elena, our housekeeper, has become our friend. She teaches the kids Spanish, cooks Salvadoran food for us to try, and suggests improvements around the house I would never have thought of. She is much more than household help. She's a shining example of a woman who works very hard to support her family. I have a lot of admiration for her and thank my lucky stars I'm able to employ her because I *hate* housework!"

Creating a New Dream

Like Kathryn, most of us have continued at least some of our childhood interests into adulthood. But we usually develop new interests as well, which incorporate our adult experiences and perspective. Often, our lifestyles need to be modified to incorporate them.

Paula, originally trained as a nurse, is married to a neurosurgeon who is also chief of staff at a major university hospital. After several years of staying home to raise their three children, she began working part time as a volunteer peer counselor in a women's ministry. Although she enjoyed her work, she found that her new schedule left her no breathing room because she hadn't eliminated any responsibilities, only added some. Delegating housework, the area of responsibility that least needed her personal touch, gave her the relief she sought. In fact, once her head was free of the clutter of household "to-dos", she realized that her love of counseling warranted earning a professional degree in the field, so she began graduate studies.

Finding Space for Your Dream

For a lucky few of us, life does go as planned. But we don't always anticipate the constraints imposed by the 24-hour day. Household help can loosen some of those constraints.

Jackie works full time as a technical specialist with a medical diagnostics company. Despite her heavy travel schedule, it never occurred to her that with two children, she might need household help beyond childcare. Luckily, her husband figured it out.

Jackie tells the story:

"The breaking point came when I was pregnant with my second child. I was traveling two or three nights a week and was experiencing *all day* nausea. I simply could not get out of bed on the weekends to cook meals and do housework.

"For my birthday that year, my husband gave me maid service. I was torn about accepting the gift. The Superwoman part of me felt I should be able to cover all responsibilities, both in my job and at home. The perfectionist part of me wasn't sure if anyone else could clean my house to my standards. But my body gave me no choice. I accepted the gift.

"The first time the maid cleaned the house I returned home, not only to a spotless house, but also to a note from my husband: 'Everything is taken care of, but you can still empty the dishwasher if you want!' Now that I have maid service, I wonder how I ever managed without it. The time I spent on weekends cleaning I now spend just having fun with my family."

Or Maybe Just Kicking Back . . .

Not all of us hire help so that we can do more important things or to avoid problems. Sometimes it just feels good to relax.

Christine is a childless accounting manager whose husband pitches in equally on household chores. But they pay a service to do the heavy cleaning.

"It's such a self-esteem boost to walk in the door after the cleaning service has been in our apartment," says Christine. "It feels wonderful! It's great to think about what's on my 'to-do' list and *not* think about cleaning!"

Why Dreams Are Important

Not only is updating your childhood daydreams the most fun part of hiring household help, but it's also the most important part. That's because you will inevitably confront challenges along the way: We already know you lack free time (why else would you consider hiring help?), so it might be a struggle for you to find time for the planning and organizing that are critical to your success. Despite your best efforts in hiring, you might encounter difficulties with your employee that you didn't anticipate. You might grapple with your conscience about complying with the "nanny tax" laws.

Updated, enticing daydreams will strengthen your resolve to clear these hurdles. If the future you envision is exciting enough, inspiring enough, important enough, any difficulties you encounter in delegating housework will pale in comparison with the new possibilities that you've created.

Redefining the Work/Family Conflict

Much has been written about the conflict between work and family that women and men face. But many of us are now discovering that, by dissecting "family time" into "relationships" and "housework," the conflict can be reframed. By delegating housework, we can find a meaningful balance (and enough hours in the day) for both relationships and paid work.

When I discovered, despite my career ambitions, that at-home motherhood was the only acceptable childcare option for me, hiring a housekeeper helped me create space for part-time professional work.

When Lotus CEO Mike Zisman's wife died of cancer, leaving him with three children to raise and a five-bedroom house to run, he hired a housekeeper, reduced his job responsibilities and working hours, and asked his mother-in-law for childcare help. As a result, Mike now has a better-balanced life (ironically, one his wife argued for in vain during her healthy years) and has minimized the trauma that the children have unavoidably experienced as a result of their mother's death.[3]

Nora met her husband while they were both students at Harvard's business school. In spite of her educational credentials and thriving career, she valued staying home with her children, a choice that was threatened when her dream marriage turned into a nightmare. After her divorce, Nora resumed part-time professional work and spent a significant portion of her reduced income (her part-time salary, plus alimony and child support) on a full-time nanny/housekeeper. Because her employee cares for the children on the days she works and does household chores on the days she doesn't, Nora is able to spend her days off mothering her children instead of catching up on chores.

Although my aunt, Sister Gratia, a nun, never explicitly hired household help, she discovered its benefits when my grandmother gave up her apartment and moved into an adult-care home. The fees of the home encompass all housekeeping services, including meals and laundry. Sister explains how her relationship with her mother changed after the move: "The amount of time I have available to spend with Mom is limited. After she moved into the adult-care home, I noticed that the time I spend with her is what some might call 'quality' time. I even do her nails now! In retrospect, I can see that much of the time I thought I was spending with Mom when she lived in her apartment was actually spent cleaning house and doing laundry."

Calling a Truce in the Chore Wars

Few of us eagerly anticipated the "joy" of performing household chores when we were creating our childhood daydreams. Yet the results that those chores produce—a well-cared-for wardrobe, nutritious, delicious meals, and a nurturing and attractive home environment—are a part of almost all of our daydreams.

Unfortunately, the "chore wars" that arise when husbands and wives fail to agree on who should do what and how they should do it create disharmony that threatens the very daydreams that those chores are supposed to support. Once again, a housekeeper can help to bridge the gap between daydream and reality.

As a licensed clinical social worker, Wendy has refereed many housework conflicts in her counseling work with married couples. As a result, she well understood the importance of household help when she herself married and expresses her gratitude that her husband led the way.

"Having a housekeeper is wonderful! My husband despises housework, so he had an employee to clean house and do laundry before we were married. Since we lived in his house after the wedding, his employee just kind of came along with the deal. What a gift! I have a hard time relaxing until all necessary chores are done. Clearly, having household help averts conflicts and resentments over housework."

Daydreaming for Future Generations

Those of us who have struggled to overcome our own Motherhood Myopia may wish to help our children avoid falling victim to it themselves. Paula (the nurse-turned-counselor) doesn't want her daughters' horizons limited because they are weighed down by housework, or even forced to overcome feelings of guilt before hiring help, as she was. One of her motivations for hiring help, besides giving herself some breathing room, was to model to her three daughters that it is permissible, even advisable, to hire needed household help and that they should include the expense in their future budgets.

It's taken a few years, but my son, Sam, has finally stopped thinking of housework as *my* job. Now, when he talks about his grown-up life, he discusses in a matter-of-fact style that one of the expenses of having a family is paying a housekeeper. Sam doesn't see housework as inconsequential or insignificant, either: When he was in second grade, he wrote an essay on the subject of "Someone I Admire" which extolled the virtues of our housekeeper and marveled at how hard she works.

The Importance of Clarity and Commitment

To make your daydreams real, two elements are key: clarity (a deep knowledge of what your dream is) and commitment (an unwavering determination to make it happen).

Adrienne Rich, a feminist poet, once wrote: "Responsibility to yourself means…that you refuse to sell your talents and aspirations short, simply to avoid conflict and confrontation.…It means that we insist on a life of meaningful work, insist that work be as meaningful as love and friendship in our lives. It means, therefore, the courage to be 'different'; not to be continuously available to others when we need time for ourselves and our work; to be able to demand of others—parents, friends, roommates, teachers, lovers, husbands, children—that they respect our sense of purpose and our integrity as persons."[4]

Although she wrote that a generation ago, many of us still face some obstacles in clarifying and committing to our dreams. We might have trouble articulating to ourselves the grown-up version of our childhood daydreams. We may lack the determination to pursue our dreams with vigor. Or we may simply feel hopeless about ever living the life that we once imagined was possible.

Sometimes we hesitate to clarify and commit to our dreams because it feels easier and safer to cast ourselves in the role of support person to our husbands' dreams.

Sometimes we fear that pursuing our dreams inconveniences others, and we value others' comfort more than our own daydreams.

And sometimes we give up our dreams because we feel overwhelmed by our responsibilities and are simply too tired to allow ourselves to want. But whatever the reason for giving up our dreams, there is a price to be paid, by ourselves and by those we love.

A Cautionary Tale

Marjorie was married to Bob, a mid-level manager in a well-known computer company. Married for 16 years, they lived a traditional lifestyle. They owned a comfortable home in the suburbs; Marjorie stayed at home to raise their three children. Bob was happy and thought Marjorie was too.

But one day, Bob woke up to discover that he was married to a suddenly rage-filled woman who wanted out of the marriage. Counseling was useless. Marjorie felt that she had silently, thanklessly, sacrificed her selfhood for years. She could barely deal with her boiling anger and emotionally left the marriage the moment she became aware of it.

Of course, the family was hurt tremendously. Everyone's standard of living was lowered considerably, due to the cost of maintaining two households in an area famous for its high cost of housing, and one of the children began exhibiting serious academic and behavioral problems.

Whether Bob's and Marjorie's marriage could have survived in the long run had she communicated her distress early on is unclear. But one thing is certain. Marjorie's long-standing, silent delay of the fulfillment of her unspoken dreams led to an explosion of bottled-up rage that damaged everything and everyone around her.

Committing To Your Dream

In Marjorie's defense, maybe she did share her dreams with Bob and he just didn't take them seriously. Or maybe he just didn't understand how sharply her household responsibilities limited her. But, as many self-help writers have asked, if she didn't believe in herself, who would?

Management expert Harold J. Leavitt addressed the importance of commitment when he wrote about "pathfinders" (corporate daydreamers): "Pathfinders must, to a certain extent, be true believers, dedicated to their own visions. Like the signers of the Declaration of Independence, they have to hold a few truths to be so self-evident, so beautiful, so worth working for, that they will steadfastly fight for them against long odds and potent enemies."[5]

Sometimes these "potent enemies" are inside ourselves. I knew I needed household help when I was pregnant with my second child. My "potent enemy" was fear of my husband's objection to spending money on a housekeeper. It took me three years to gather the strength (fueled partly by anger, partly by desperation) to overcome his imagined objections.

Debbie's "potent enemy" is her desire to make her husband suffer as she has. Debbie, a full-time court reporter and mother of a toddler, does all of the "inside" chores (grocery shopping, cooking, laundry, housecleaning) as well as all of the after-work childcare. Her husband maintains the lawn and the swimming pool.

Although they can afford a housekeeper, Debbie hesitates to hire one out of certainty that her husband would then hire a gardener and a pool service. She feels the only "fair" thing would be an imbalance in favor of her to correct past imbalances in favor of her husband. Her resentment prevents her from getting the help she needs.

Make Your Daydreams Real

Clarity and commitment are the two cornerstones in making your daydreams real. Clarity can be as simple as realizing you've misplaced your priorities by hiring a babysitter to give you time to do housework, when you should have hired a housecleaner to give you more time with your kids. Or it can be as complicated as recognizing that your expensive vacations are designed to help you escape a life you hate.

Commitment can be as simple as rejecting your mother's idea of the duties of a wife and mother. Or it can be as complicated as rejecting your husband's idea of those duties.

Commitment means taking a stand for your daydreams, making a declaration that says, "Here I am, world, and I'm worth it!" What are your daydreams worth to you? Isn't it time to make them real?

Think
Like a
Manager

I have a housecleaner, but I really hate telling her what to do. I feel like I'm being mean or bossy.

—32-year-old homemaker, mother of three

What's the point of paying somebody to do your housework if you have to spend time telling them what to do?

—31-year-old social worker, mother of one

If your professional background does not include management experience, you might feel uncomfortable with the idea of becoming someone's boss. Furthermore, you may wonder what "managing" your housekeeper means and how much time it will take.

But being a boss doesn't require you to be mean or bossy; in fact, you will be less effective if you are. Instead of thinking about you and your housekeeper as boss and subordinate, think of your relationship in terms of the classic definition of a manager: one who gets things done through others. Your housekeeper is someone who makes it possible for you to accomplish more in a given day than you could physically accomplish by yourself, thanks to some managerial magic called "leverage."

A term originating in physics, leverage refers to the process of using one's resources to produce a large amount of output with a small amount of effort. Managers create leverage by delegating, that is, by assigning a task to an employee that she can accomplish after a reasonable amount of instruction and training. Your job as a manager is to ensure your housekeeper's success in accomplishing the tasks that you delegate to her.

Too little managerial input produces insufficient or shoddy output, but too much makes the output too expensive. You want your housekeeper to do a good job, but you don't want to spend so much time managing her that it would have been easier and cheaper to do it yourself. The good news is that most of your "managerial input" comes before you've even hired your first employee. This up-front work, if done well, will keep the delegation wheels turning smoothly for years to come.

The rest of this book outlines every action you will need to take to ensure your housekeeper's success and to maximize your leverage. The remaining chapters are organized to correspond to the five functions that every manager performs, to a greater or lesser degree, and which you will, too. For a preview of coming attractions, here are those functions and how they apply to household help:

- **Planning:** Determining ahead of time the scope and requirements of the job (the focus of Chapters 5 and 6).

- **Organizing:** Structuring the systems of your home to make delegation easy (the focus of Chapter 7).

- **Staffing:** Hiring the right employee for the job, creating an appropriate compensation package, and following the law (the focus of Chapters 8, 9, and 10).

- **Directing:** Instructing your housekeeper about the duties and standards of the job, both initially and on an ongoing basis (the focus of Chapter 11).

- **Evaluating:** Providing your housekeeper with job performance feedback, both positive and negative (the focus of Chapter 12).

Create a Mutually Rewarding Business Relationship

In the mid 1980s, I worked as a sales representative for a major computer manufacturer. Many of the reps in my district, myself included, had never worked in sales before, so our district manager, Claudia, had her work cut out for her. One of the recurring themes Claudia hammered home at every district meeting was that our goal was to create "mutually rewarding business relationships." In a successful business deal, she explained, both sides benefit. Not only should we never leave a customer feeling like he or she had paid too much for too little, but we also should never "give away the store."

What does this have to do with hiring housekeepers? Well, your relationship with your housekeeper is—or should be—a mutually rewarding business relationship. But sometimes our concerns about exploitation raise an important question: How can we be sure we are creating mutual value?

Exploitation: A Shameful Part of Our Past — and Present

It is immoral to pay someone else to do that which you refuse to do yourself.
—Female sociologist who was interviewed for this book

Some say it's elitist to hire household help. I say it's snobbery to turn household labor into a moral issue. Household employment is a simple exchange: a trade of money for labor. It's to your benefit to create a pleasant working environment with well-defined job requirements, reasonable expectations, and a competitive salary. If you do, you will win loyalty from your housekeeper, who is free to look around for better opportunities. Both parties come to the negotiation voluntarily and both benefit. But we as a nation feel lingering guilt because that hasn't always been true.

Our economy is a market-driven one. In theory, differences in earning power among workers are based on the demands of the marketplace and derive from the education, talents, skill, and entrepreneurship of the worker. The free market works fairly when all workers have an opportunity to develop their marketable qualities and offer them to the marketplace. But it's a shameful part of America's history that the "market" hasn't always been "free" for many, particularly for women and people of color.

After slavery (the ultimate exploitation) ended, racial and gender job discrimination was widespread and legally sanctioned. As a result, domestic work was the only kind available to most African-American women. Without employment and educational opportunities, they were forced to work as maids, cooks, laundresses, and housecleaners, without regard to their own talents and interests.

Household workers of every ethnic background—whether African-Americans, immigrants, or uneducated farm girls—earned artificially depressed wages, often laboring long hours in inhumane working conditions. A 1938 survey of 238 domestics found that their average workweek was 84 hours long,[1] at a time when their wages were so low, some domestics' compensation consisted only of room and board.[2]

Such exploitation began to wane when wartime production demands, during both world wars, provided new employment opportunities for all women, including African-Americans. ("The war made me live better, it really did. My sister always said that Hitler was the one that got us out of the white folks' kitchen."[3]) Government intervention helped too: The Civil Rights Act of 1964 outlawed job discrimination, and fair labor laws were modified to protect domestic workers.

Today, illegal immigrants are sometimes exploited by household employers, although their exploitation has a psychological, not a legal, basis. Labor laws protect all workers, regardless of their legal status, but most illegals are afraid to complain to authorities, assuming such complaints will lead to deportation.[4] These workers are vulnerable to employers who offer illegally low wages and demand unreasonably—and illegally—long working hours.

To ensure against exploitation, follow these simple rules. Hire only a legal resident or U.S. citizen and comply with worker protection laws (Chapter 10 spells out requirements). Treat your employee with respect, as you would any co-worker or business associate (see Chapters 11 and 12 for more discussion on this topic). And win your housekeeper's loyalty not through a power play, but by making sure that the job you offer is more attractive than her other available options.

The Price of the American Dream

Sometimes the stark socioeconomic contrast between employer and employee makes it seem that exploitation is the only explanation. But if you are well educated and highly skilled, your housekeeper's wages will not approach your income. That differential is not unfairness; it's simply the reason ambitious Americans—including many household workers—make sacrifices to educate themselves, their children, and their grandchildren.

My grandmother, the daughter of Italian immigrants, worked in the garment industry as a young woman, where a machine once drove a needle through her finger. My grandfather, also first-generation Italian-American, drove a milk truck, venturing out in the middle of the night to cover his route. Eventually they were able to open a restaurant and, thanks to decades of long hours and hard work, put all six of their children through college. I'm sure you can find stories like that in your family tree.

Would they have worked that hard, made those sacrifices, without the promise of the American dream? I doubt it. The opportunities of the free market motivate innovation, education, hard work. One unfortunate side effect is the significant income disparity between rich and poor. Although many Americans agree that some degree of discrimination still lingers, most earning differences can be explained by what is valued in the marketplace: talent, training, enterprise, rarity of skill.

The neurosurgeon's income far exceeds the hospital orderly's, reflecting the doctor's many long, hard years of training and finely honed skills. The (successful) entrepreneur's net worth outshines the factory worker's, reflecting the businesswoman's innovative thinking, business acumen, at-risk capital, hard work, and, yes, luck. And sometimes wages simply reflect the size of the pool of labor—the more the available workers with a given skill, the lower the going rate.

What worries some is that the relatively low going rate for housekeepers' wages reflects continuing discrimination. But today's domestic workers' wages are not nearly as low as they were in the discriminatory pre-World War II years. And the size of the domestic worker labor pool reflects our country's high population of low-skilled workers, not job discrimination.

Domestic employment offers several advantages to a low-skilled worker, which actually make the work attractive compared to other job options. Household work affords a certain amount of autonomy. Although a number of tasks must be accomplished by the end of the workday, few employers care about how those tasks are performed or in what order. Once trust has been established, most household employers are flexible about the workday schedule when the employee has an inflexible commitment, such as a doctor's appointment or a traffic court date.

The work environment in a home is certainly more pleasant than most other employment possibilities. One of my former housekeepers found the fumes unbearable at the dry cleaner's where she worked when she first arrived in this country from Honduras. Many household workers have other obligations, such as a family of their own or a school schedule, and find it easy to dovetail part-time domestic work with the rest of their lives. So, despite the fact that domestic work is not a career to which many aspire, it holds many attractions for those with minimal job qualifications.

In our high-tech economy, the future belongs to the college-educated, especially those with technical degrees. Among those without a college degree, those who speak English fluently earn more than those who don't. The journey to a better-paid job may begin with a low-skill, low-paid day job complemented by English classes at night. Even if the college degree your housekeeper aims for is ultimately awarded to her children or grandchildren, giving people the means to better themselves—a decent job at a fair (if comparatively low) wage—supports, not oppresses, them.

If you feel uncomfortable by the "leg up" given to you by your parents and grandparents, the answer is not to deny employment to someone whose services could help make you more productive. Neither is the answer to overpay an employee out of a sense of guilt.

If you want to share the fruits of your success, you can expand opportunities for those who wish to pursue the American dream. Donate to or start a scholarship fund. Contribute to a battered women's shelter. Give to an organization that assists homeless families, not just by feeding them, but also by helping them to find jobs and housing. Best of all, give someone a job.

Go ahead and hire the assistance that you need to capitalize on the skills and talents that you've developed. Your prosperity does not cause another's poverty; your wealth was not obtained at the expense of another's. Enjoy your success; be an inspiration to others who would seek it for themselves.

■ ■ ■

There are many reasons someone chooses to work as a housekeeper. She may be a college student looking for a part-time job that dovetails well with her studies. He might be between careers, taking a breather while he plans his next move. She could be working to finance a not-so-lucrative career in the arts. As a career housekeeper, she might be satisfied with the amount of income brought in by her not-so-stressful line of work or be working in the highest-paid field for which she is qualified, using her earnings to help her children achieve something more.

But whatever the motivations of the person you choose to hire as your housekeeper, your guiding principle should be the one Claudia taught me 15 years ago: create a mutually rewarding business relationship. The rest of this book will show you how.

5 Know Where You're Headed

Yogi Berra once said, "If you don't know where you're going, you could wind up some place else." While sometimes the journey is more fun than the destination, in the case of household help, the fewer the surprises along the way, the better.

Do you want to avoid the unpleasant surprise of discovering you've hired a great person who's wrong for *your* job? Then think through what the job entails *before* you hire. Do you want to avoid hiring an employee who has glowing references but does poor work? Then decide ahead of time what the standards should be and share those with each candidate during the job interviews. Managing your housekeeper will be a lot easier, and a lot more fun, if you create a road map that both of you can follow. This chapter will show you how to create that road map.

If you haven't yet decided whether to hire help, you'll find out in this chapter how to calculate how much help you need (and in the next, how much you can afford). If you already know you are going to hire help, the groundwork you'll lay in this chapter is crucial to your success as a manager of household help.

The Best First Step

Somewhere along the way, I've developed a reputation among my friends and acquaintances as an expert on the subject of household help. (The fact that for years I was interested in talking about nothing else may have something to do with it.) Consequently, I often receive phone calls from people, some I don't even know, wanting advice about hiring help.

Frequently, the advice-seekers are confused about a very important point. Too often, their instincts are telling them that the first thing they should do is place a "help wanted" ad. But the advice I give them is this: If you want to hire an employee who is well-suited to the job *you* need done, your best first step is not to begin hiring, but to *plan*. Even if you haven't yet decided whether to hire help, planning is still the place to begin, because it will help you to quantify how much help you need and what it will cost.

Why Planning Is Important

Ginny, a 49-year-old physician's assistant, employs a five-hour-a-week housekeeper, Maria, whose duties are limited to housecleaning and ironing. After hiring Maria as a housecleaner, Ginny decided to delegate laundry as well. She discovered, too late, that she had hired the wrong employee because Maria is an incompetent laundress.

Cheryl, a 40-year-old accountant with two kids, encountered a similar problem with delegating laundry. She discovered, too late, that her housekeeper was extremely superstitious and would neither do laundry, because she thought the machines were haunted, nor dust Cheryl's daughter's art projects, because she thought they were voodoo dolls.

My first hiring mistake occurred with my first housekeeper, a Vietnamese immigrant, whom I expected to cook dinner. Although her references were enthusiastic about her cooking skills, it turned out that she only cooked Vietnamese food, which my kids refused to eat. She failed miserably at cooking most of my American recipes because she herself didn't enjoy Western food and had no instinct for its texture, temperature, or seasoning.

Don't let these stories scare you. Chapter 9 will teach you how to ask the right questions during interviews and reference checks, so you can avoid such situations. And Chapter 11 addresses cultural differences, pointing out the ones that matter and the ones that don't. Good planning is the key to short-circuiting such problems before they occur. During the planning process, you will begin to formulate your all-important interview questions.

The step-by-step planning process outlined below is designed to help you spell out exactly how much and what kind of household help you want and need. What tasks will your employee perform? Will she do laundry as well as housecleaning? What about ironing? Will she cook? If so, what about grocery shopping? Will your housekeeper also care for your children? How many hours do you need help? How will those hours fit with your family's schedules?

Once you've completed your plan, it will be easy to create a profile of your ideal employee: the skills she should have, the number of hours she should be available, the required work schedule.

We sometimes mistakenly think of household help as a "one size fits all" solution. This perception is largely due to the professional housecleaning services that are rapidly becoming big business. Charging a fixed price based on the size of your home, these companies typically send out teams of two or three and clean your house based on a set of pre-established criteria. After analyzing your needs, you may decide that this type of service is best for you. But the ways that we need help are as varied and unique as our own households. How will you get the personalized touch you need if you don't plan?

Analyzing Your Unpaid Workload

You already know you're spending more time than you'd like on housework. You also know how you'd spend that time if you could give the chores away. But to calculate how much help you need, you must first determine some specifics: what unwanted chores you're doing and exactly how much time you're spending on those chores (or how much time you *would* spend if they were done adequately).

Once you examine your unpaid workload, you'll be able to create a rough outline of the tasks to be performed by your housekeeper each week, along with an estimate of the time that each task takes.

Here is one example:

Laundry (9 loads)—20 minutes per load

Deliver/pick up dry cleaning—35 minutes per week

Ironing—75 minutes per week

Collect recycling—5 minutes per day

Unload dishwasher—10 minutes per day

Vacuum kitchen—10 minutes per day

Vacuum carpets—twice per week, 1 hour each time

Dust—twice per week, 1 hour each time

Clean bathrooms—2 hours per week

Clean kitchen—1 hour per week

Change sheets (rotating schedule)—30 minutes per week

Vacuum furniture (once a month)—average 10 minutes per week

Grocery shopping—1 hour per week

Cook dinner—3 times per week, 45 minutes each time

Bake—45 minutes per week

Miscellaneous tidying—15 minutes per day

These listed tasks total 20 hours per week. Your outline will be the basis of your housekeeper's job description.

If you already know exactly what you want done and how long it will take, congratulations! You can skip ahead to the section called "What Will It Cost to Hire Help?" But if you're like most people, to create an outline like the one above, you'll need to do a little homework first.

The Roles and Tasks Exercise

The Roles and Tasks Exercise will help you identify all of the unpaid chores you are now doing (or that need to be done) that can be effectively delegated to a paid employee. At the same time, you might discover that some chores can be eliminated and some delegated to other family members.

I'm a natural planner, and I created this exercise when I was struggling to solve my housework problem. If the thought of doing such a detailed planning exercise makes your eyes glaze over, then feel free to modify it to fit your personal style. But please keep an open mind as you read through the next few sections. As problem-solving experts know, defining a problem is the first step to solving it.

The Roles and Tasks Exercise will unfold over several days, but to begin it, give yourself some uninterrupted time in a relaxing place. You'll need several sheets of paper and a pen.

Step 1: Identify Your Roles

At the top of each piece of paper, write the name of a role that you play in your life. Some of the roles have "sub-roles." If that's the case, list each sub-role on a separate piece of paper. The table below lists some sample roles and sub-roles.

Sample Roles and Sub-Roles

Mother	**Homemaker**
Gestator/Birther/Lactator	Nutritionist
Caregiver	Cook
Disciplinarian	Housecleaner
Childrearing Philosopher	Laundress
Health Care Coordinator	Recycler
Social Director	Seamstress
Educational Liaison	Household Organizer
Homework Monitor	Interior Decorator
TV and Electronic Games Monitor	Remodeler
Personal Hygiene Supervisor	Bill Payer
Chauffeur	Consumer
Costumer	Manager of Hired Help
Storyteller	Paperwork Processor
Wife	**Daughter**
Co-Parent	**Church Member**
Financial Partner	**Family Social Secretary**
Companion/Friend	**Friend**
Sexual Partner	**Citizen**
Cheering Section	Volunteer
Roommate	Informed Voter
Professional "(Fill in the blank)"	

Continue until you have identified all of your roles and sub-roles, both professional and personal. You can include roles you hope to add in the future.

Step 2: List Specific Tasks

At this point, you should have in front of you a pile of mostly blank pages, each headed with a role or sub-role title. Now you will fill up those pages. For each of your nonprofessional roles and sub-roles, list the specific tasks that you carry out to fulfill that role or sub-role. Here is an example.

Laundress

Washing —
    once a week: lights, kids' darks, husband's darks, my darks
    twice a week: bath towels
    once every two weeks: our sheets, kids' sheets
    once every four weeks: our duvet cover, kids' duvet covers
    as needed: miscellaneous towels, whites
Folding
Putting away
Tidying drawers
Ironing —
    from weekly laundry
    duvet covers
(Note: No sorting of laundry is needed. See Chapter 7 for an explanation of how to eliminate.)

To save time, you may prefer to focus on those roles and sub-roles that are most burdensome. Don't limit yourself to exploring household-related roles, though. You've gotten your creative juices flowing in this process; you may discover new ways to handle many unwanted tasks. When I did this process, for example, I realized how simply I could get my husband to share the job of bathing the children (then preschoolers): I could change my habit of bathing them right before dinner (before he got home) and, instead, make bath-time an after-dinner activity.

Step 3: Identify Additional Roles and Tasks

Over the next few days, carry your lists around and expand on them as you remember more roles and tasks. For every chore you carry out, consider whether you've already noted it on one of your lists.

Step 4: Categorize the Tasks

As you make your lists, notice how you feel about each task. Some you enjoy; although they may be challenging and even frustrating at times, you embrace them. Others, you find less enjoyable. Put a star next to those tasks, or even entire roles, that you find less enjoyable or simply lack the time to do.

Step 5: Evaluate

Set aside a relaxed uninterrupted hour to reassess your unpaid roles and their associated tasks. (You may want to do this step or even the entire Roles and Tasks Exercise in partnership with your spouse, significant other, roommate, or older children.) For each of the starred roles and tasks, those you don't enjoy or have time for, you have four options: delegate it to another family member, keep it, eliminate it, or delegate it to a paid employee.

Delegate It to Another Family Member

When Doris, a 41-year-old real estate broker with a 5-year-old son, was feeling overwhelmed, her husband happily agreed to do the weekly grocery shopping and clean enough greens to keep the family in salad for the entire week.

Like Doris, you may find that you have taken ownership of a task better suited to someone else's interests, talents, or schedule. Rearrangement may be in order. Beware, though: If you have already established a pattern of picking up the slack when there is too much work to be done, and if you are doing the Roles and Tasks Exercise in partnership with other family members, make sure that you don't end up even more loaded down.

Keep It

When I did this exercise, I considered my role as family social secretary. Some parts of the job I like, but some I dislike, especially hiring Saturday night babysitters. I came to realize, though, that if I left it up to my husband, we'd never have a social life! I decided to keep the job. Similarly, you will choose to keep some of your roles.

Eliminate It

When Connie's twins were five, she and her husband bought them a puppy for Christmas. By the time the boys were eight, though, school and their extracurricular activities kept them away from home most of the day. They lost interest in caring for and playing with their dog, so pet care became one more item on Connie's long list of unwanted chores. After much discussion, the family decided to find a new home for the dog. Likewise, you may find you have commitments you choose to significantly reduce or eliminate.

Delegate It to a Paid Employee

Finally, there will be some tasks that can't be eliminated and which no family member wants to or has time to perform. Those you will consider delegating to a paid employee. Put a check next to each of those tasks.

When deciding which tasks to give away, don't only consider those you dislike. There may be some time-consuming chores you don't mind doing, but are easy to delegate. The free time you'd gain by delegating them would allow you to spend time on more interesting or profitable pursuits. For example, laundry is not unpleasant, but it's time consuming and easy to delegate. Bill paying, on the other hand, a less appealing activity, is best done by you or your spouse.

The Roles and Tasks Exercise

Step 1: Identify Your Roles
Step 2: List Specific Tasks
Step 3: Identify Additional Roles and Tasks
Step 4: Categorize the Tasks
Step 5: Evaluate
- **Delegate It to Another Family Member**
- **Keep It**
- **Eliminate It**
- **Delegate It to a Paid Employee**

Housekeeper, Nanny, or Housecleaning Service?

As you scan your lists of roles and tasks, an obvious pattern may appear. If most of the chores you wish to delegate involve weekly cleaning (vacuuming, dusting, bathrooms, kitchen), a housecleaning service is probably the best fit for you. If you are a mother at home with very young children, can only afford help for a few hours a week, and desperately crave some time to yourself, a babysitter may be just the thing. If you wish to delegate a sizeable volume of chores, and they all fall into the "household" category (cleaning, cooking, laundry), you probably need to hire a traditional housekeeper, either full or part time.

But if you want to delegate *some* housework and *some* childcare, you might find yourself confused about whether you need a nanny or a housekeeper. What are the differences between the two?

A nanny is a childcare professional. Whether or not she has received formal childcare training, she certainly has plenty of experience and is qualified (or ought to be) to focus on your children's developmental needs, especially if they are infants, toddlers, or preschoolers. Although few nannies enjoy doing housework and none should be expected to make it their priority (they are, after all, responsible for your precious darlings), most are able to accomplish some amount of light housekeeping—tidying up after the kids, keeping them fed, occasionally throwing in a load of laundry.

A housekeeper, on the other hand, focuses, as her job title indicates, on keeping house. Although she may be expected to supervise older children, often chauffeuring them home from school or to extracurricular activities, her attention is on the household chores. Her main interaction with the children may be simply to provide after-school snacks and to enforce previously agreed-upon house rules.

If you think a paid employee should be able to focus on both childrearing and housework simultaneously, ask yourself this: If such a job were so doable, why are you trying to get rid of it? And what wage would be high enough to compensate such a miracle-worker, if one could be found?

If you need both childcare and household help, you'll have to decide what the focus of the job should be. School-age children will probably do well with a housekeeper, especially if an enticing set of positive consequences and a foreboding set of negative ones ensure their cooperation. If you have younger children, though, you'll either need to seek out a nanny who's willing to do housework during naptime (with the understanding that the children's needs *always* take priority) and hire a weekly service for the heavy cleaning, or hire both a housekeeper and a nanny who understand that mutual cooperation is part of their job description.

Making Time Estimates

For each checked task on your list, estimate how much time it takes. Don't measure elapsed time, just the time that a human being is performing the task. For example, a load of laundry may require two hours of elapsed time from start to finish (sorting, loading the machine, running the washer, transferring the clothes to the dryer, running the dryer, folding the clothes, and putting them away), but only 30 minutes of labor. It may take two hours to cook a meal, but only 40 minutes of labor. Imagine a stopwatch that pauses every time you (or your housekeeper) walk away from the task to allow a machine to take over.

Obviously, your time estimates will be your best guess because household tasks are almost always performed in parallel with other activities, so it is not readily apparent how much time they take. I found, after hiring help, that I'd underestimated on some tasks but overestimated on others, so the magnitude of the overall job was still in the right ballpark. One way to make more accurate estimates is to break each task into sub-tasks. The figure below gives an example. This kind of micro-detail helps your employee deliver good job performance, too. I use this list of sub-tasks to help my housekeeper understand what I mean by "daily kitchen tidy-up."

By the way, if you tend to race through chores, either because you hate doing them or because you simply don't have time to do them at a more reasonable pace, be sure to scale your time estimates to take that into account. If your housekeeper has to break a sweat to keep pace with the workload, she'll burn out and soon quit the job, obviously an undesirable outcome.

Daily Kitchen Tidy-Up

2 min	Clear newspapers, breakfast dishes, etc. from table
10 min	Unload dishwasher
10 min	Vacuum kitchen floor
2 min	Carry recycling to garage
3 min	Wipe up drips in/near refrigerator
5 min	Clean fingerprints on windows, mirrors
1 min	Reload dishwasher with accumulated dirty dishes
1 min	Wipe down table and countertops
34 min	

Bertila, one of my former housekeepers, told me she appreciated the steady but reasonable pace of the workload at my house. Another employer had hired Bertila for the number of hours she could afford (instead of the number of hours it took to do the job), yet expected Bertila to finish *all* of the housework in the allotted time, or work unpaid overtime until it was completed. Although this person paid Bertila a higher hourly rate than what I was offering, Bertila quit that job out of frustration and exhaustion and was glad to take mine.

Once you've tagged each task with a time estimate, add in any new tasks that you don't have time to do yourself, but which you might have a household employee do, such as baking or extra dusting. Make time estimates for those tasks as well.

If you have hired help, it's certainly a pleasure to maintain your home at a higher standard than you are able to achieve by yourself. But adding these extra chores has an additional benefit: flexibility. Occasionally your housekeeper's workweek will be shortened due to illness or holidays. When this happens, you can eliminate the optional chores and still have your housekeeper keep up with the essential ones. If my housekeeper misses a day, she skips the weekly baking and one round of dusting and vacuuming, and we eat take-out in place of one of her meals. That way, the house stays reasonably clean, all of the laundry still gets done, and I haven't had to pick up any slack.

Fitting It All Together

Now step back and look at the tasks you'd like to delegate. Is it logistically feasible for those tasks to be performed by one employee?

For example, let's suppose you've identified 25 hours of work, including "cook breakfast" and "cook dinner." A part-time housekeeper could be in your home for one of those mealtimes, but not both. You might choose to hire a housekeeper for 20 hours per week and have her cook one meal, but not the other. Or, your housekeeper could leave pancake batter in the refrigerator before leaving at night, or chop vegetables and marinate meat before leaving in the morning.

You might find that the tasks are best done by two different employees. For example, if you wish to delegate yardwork as well as housework, perhaps a once-a-week gardener could be hired along with a part-time housekeeper.

What's the best schedule to fit with your list of chores, your family's lifestyle, and your personal preferences? I want my housekeeper to perform a number of chores that need to be done daily, so she works half days, Monday through Friday. Others prefer to minimize the number of days an outsider is in their home, so their employees' schedules involve one, two, or three long workdays each week. Some prefer their household help to work when they know they'll be home, others, when they know they won't be home.

Are all of the chores on your list easy to delegate? If a project is a one-shot deal, such as planning a birthday party, it doesn't lend itself well to delegation (except to a party-planning service). Neither should a chore be delegated if it requires decisions based on a number of factors that are difficult to quantify (shopping for school clothes, say) or, even worse, if it's a chore you don't know how to approach yourself.

When I was a teenager, I was hired one Saturday to baby-sit for a couple of school-age kids. I was dismayed when their mother instructed me, right before departing for the day, that the three of us were to reorganize the playroom. Needless to say, I failed to meet my employer's expectations on that job, although, judging from the state of the playroom, she had never tackled the job herself and didn't have a clue about how it was to be done.

The best household chores to delegate are those that are done repetitively and require a minimum of decision-making. Chapter 7 describes delegation in more detail and demonstrates ways that you can organize your household to eliminate the decision component from most household tasks.

By now, though, you should have a rough outline of the tasks you wish to delegate, along with an estimate of how much time it takes to complete them. That's a sufficient level of detail for this stage in the planning process.

Lots of Leftovers for Your Kids

If one of your concerns about hiring household help has been that your children will miss out on the responsibility and opportunity of learning to do chores, you're probably beginning to see that you hadn't fully considered what it takes to keep a household running smoothly. Even with a significant amount of household help, there will still be plenty of work left over to assign to the kids.

Suppose, for example, you've decided to hire a housekeeper to do the bulk of the housework: laundry, ironing, housecleaning, grocery shopping, cooking (dinners), and some tidying. Here are some of the leftover tasks that you could delegate to your children:

- Making beds in the morning
- Setting the table for dinner
- Cleaning the kitchen after dinner
- Putting their dirty laundry in appropriate receptacles
- Tidying bedrooms and play areas
- Helping to prepare breakfast and lunch
- Emptying backpacks and lunchboxes after school
- Carrying parcels into the house from the car
- Weeding and planting
- Doing their own laundry if desired items are not scheduled to be washed in time for targeted wearings
- Helping out in the monthly trip to the recycling center.

You can probably think of lots more.

What Will It Cost to Hire Help?

The tentative work schedule that you've outlined tells you how many hours you need help. The next step is to estimate the cost of purchasing that help.

In estimating your future employee's rate of pay, there are a number of factors to consider. First, the more hours you hire help, the lower the hourly rate you'll pay. For example, a half-time housekeeper will cost less per hour than a once-a-week cleaning service. That's because workers are usually willing to trade dollars for regularity: one employer who provides 20 hours of work each week is easier to deal with than five employers who each provide 4 hours of work. Furthermore, someone who offers a cleaning service and has many clients must spend time and money marketing her service and traveling from job to job, which is reflected in her higher hourly rate. House*cleaners* typically earn a higher hourly rate than house*keepers* for another reason as well: the work is harder. Although a housekeeper does some heavy cleaning as part of her job, that is balanced by her other, less strenuous, duties, such as cooking and laundry.

Another factor to consider is the skill level you desire. If you want someone who can speak and read English, follow recipes, understand sophisticated laundry instructions, and take initiative to perform some tasks on an "as needed" basis, you'll probably need to pay more than minimum wage. Keep in mind that minimum wage is intended for minimally trained, unskilled laborers.

Whether you intend to comply with employment and immigration laws will also affect the wage you pay. Naturally, illegal immigrants, welfare cheats, and people receiving disability or unemployment benefits will work for relatively low rates in exchange for cash-only payments. Even legal workers who are paid "under the table" (cash only) will generally accept lower wages, too. Nevertheless, I strongly recommend complying with the law (and expecting your employee to do so as well) if for no other reason than that an employee who is honest with the government is likely to be honest with you, too. Chapter 8 addresses this difficult issue in more detail.

Pay rates for household employees vary by geographic area, too. Typically, wages in urban areas are higher than in rural areas. The best way to find out the going rate in your area is to call potential employers, people like yourself, who have run ads in the "Employment Offers—Domestic" column in the classified section of your local newspaper. Introduce yourself, say why you're calling, and ask what pay rate is being offered for the job. Be sure to find out what skill level is required and whether the employer plans to pay employment taxes, so that you can determine how well the advertised position matches the one you're offering.

After researching your area's "going rate" for household help, you'll probably discover that there is not one fixed rate but, rather, a pay range for experienced housekeepers. Your challenge is to make sure you're not offering so little that you can't attract qualified candidates but, at the same time, make sure you're not paying more than you need to.

As I write this, the pay range for experienced housekeepers in my area (the San Francisco Bay Area) is $11 to $15 per hour. I've discovered that, while some job applicants may be accustomed to earning far less (and some, mostly illegals, even earn less than minimum wage), those with lower pay requirements typically don't have the housekeeping experience I need them to have.

On the other hand, I've found that those experienced housekeepers whose earnings are at the top of the pay range don't necessarily have the best housekeeping skills, just the best English skills. While those with poor English may be less employable, through superior management techniques (all taught in this book), you may be able to elicit superior job performance from one of those candidates, without having to pay top dollar.

Paying your new employee at the lower end of the pay range, to start, has other advantages, as well. Periodic pay raises, based on merit, can be highly motivating to your employee. If you start low, you have room to grow. Regular pay raises help encourage long-term loyalty, too. Wouldn't you rather stay in a job where you could count on periodic increases? Finally, starting your housekeeper at a lower pay rate, when she's still untested, is just plain smart. It's never good business to pay top dollar in the *hopes* of excellent job performance; it's always better to pay based on your employee's proven track record.

One final factor that will affect the rate you will pay for help is whether you hire through an agency. This subject is addressed in detail in Chapter 9, but, to summarize, my position is: don't. The use of an agency will significantly boost your cost of hiring help, will provide you with candidates who are no more qualified than those you can find yourself, will narrow your field of candidates in a counter-productive way, and will save you only a small amount of time in hiring.

Once you've established the hourly rate you plan to offer, to calculate your true wage expense, you should add a 10 percent allowance for the employer taxes, both state and federal, that you will be required to pay. One exception: If your worker is an independent contractor, instead of a true employee, you won't have to pay employment taxes. If you hire a cleaning service, you've probably hired an independent contractor, while a housekeeper is an employee. Chapters 8 and 10 provide more detail on the subject of employer taxes. Your tax advisor can help you decide whether you're required to pay them.

So now you've outlined the household help you need each week and estimated what it will cost. If you've already decided to hire and cost is not an obstacle, you can skip ahead to Chapter 7. If you're still grappling with the question of whether hiring help is right for you, or if you need to scrutinize your budget carefully to find a way to pay for that help, the cost-justification process described in the next chapter is the place to turn.

6 Boil It Down to Numbers

I am fascinated by differences among people. Some of us are serious, others fun loving. Some are athletic, while the rest of us happily consider ourselves couch potatoes. Some are gourmet cooks, while others specialize in making reservations. Some of us are highly analytical, while many prefer to leave the number crunching to others. Wherever *your* preferences lie, chances are that sometimes you need skills that come more naturally to other personality types.

If you're not a natural-born number cruncher, the idea of performing a cost benefit analysis for deciding whether to hire household help may be less than appealing. Nevertheless, boiling your household-help decision down to numbers will be relatively painless (I promise) and it will benefit you in several ways.

First, if it's unclear whether hiring household help is economically feasible for your family, the numbers you calculate in this chapter will make it clear. Second, if you can see that hiring help will be profitable in the long run, but your short-term budget will need to be rearranged to accommodate the cost of hiring help, this chapter will give you some ideas about how to do that. Third, if your husband is a "by the numbers" kind of guy and you need or want his agreement before you hire help, your calculations will give him the numbers he needs to feel comfortable.

The Cost-Justification Process

Your ultimate goal is to prove to yourself that hiring a housekeeper will be profitable—financially, emotionally, physically, or spiritually—for you and your family. To do so, you will assign monetary values to four categories: the benefits of hiring help (the opportunity to earn more money, for example), the cost of hiring help (your housekeeper's wages), the savings associated with hiring help (restaurant meals or other expensive services), and the costs of not hiring help (taken to an extreme, divorce). You will then plug those values into the following cost-justification formula:

> **The benefits of hiring help should be greater than**
> **the cost of hiring help**
> **minus the savings associated with hiring help**
> **minus the cost of not hiring help.**

Simply put, we hope you'll find out that what you'll gain will be more than what you'll pay.

As you read through the rest of the chapter, have a pencil, paper, and calculator handy. The following Cost Justification Worksheet suggests a format for recording your calculations, as well as listing intangible benefits and costs that don't have an associated dollar value. A completed example of that worksheet follows.

Measuring Benefits

In Chapter 3, you identified new opportunities you could pursue if you hired household help. Each opportunity potentially leads to a number of benefits, for you and for the other members of your family. Give yourself some uninterrupted time in a relaxing place and list, for every one of your new opportunities, as many benefits as you can think of. The "Opportunities and Benefits" table below might give you some ideas.

Next, assign a dollar value to each of the benefits, if possible. You will notice that some benefits are tangible (those that have a dollar value, such as income) and some are intangible (difficult to quantify, but valuable nonetheless). List the intangible benefits on the left side of your

Cost Justification Worksheet

Benefits of Hiring Help

Intangible (list)   *Tangible (list)*

Total: _____

Cost of Hiring Help

Number of hours per week _____

times hourly wage of _____ = _____

plus 10% allowance for employer taxes

Total: _____

Savings Associated with Hiring Help

(list)

Total: _____

Costs Associated with Not Hiring Help

Intangible (list)   *Tangible (list)*

Total: _____

worksheet and the tangible ones on the right. Add up the dollar value of the tangible benefits, convert to a weekly or monthly value, and record that value in the "Total" space in the Benefits section of your worksheet.

Cost Justification Worksheet (Completed)

Benefits of Hiring Help

Intangible (list)	*Tangible (list)*
I'm happier, less stressed	Start business/income potential
Marital harmony	
Less yelling at kids	
Time for exercise	
	Total: ?

Cost of Hiring Help

Number of hours per week = 20

times hourly wage of $10 = $200

plus 10% allowance for employer taxes

Total: $220/wk

Savings Associated with Hiring Help

(list)

Cleaning service	$45/week
Take-out food	$20/week
Marriage counseling	$150/month
	Total: $102.50/wk

Costs Associated with Not Hiring Help

Intangible (list)	*Tangible (list)*
Continued depression and.................Medical costs stress-related health problems	
Family conflict	
Potential divorce.............................Legal fees and cost of maintaining two households	
	Total: ?

Opportunities and Benefits

Opportunity	Benefit
Earn more income	Greater household income now
Continue education	Greater household income in future
Start a business	Greater household income in future
More time with spouse	Happier marriage, better communication, more/better sex
More time with children	Happier family life, better grades, fewer behavior problems, better communication
More time with friends, extended family	More enjoyable relationships
Exercise	Better health, fewer sick days, more energy, longer life
Hobbies	Sense of satisfaction, potential new income opportunities
Volunteer work	Contribution to community
Church activities	Sense of satisfaction, spiritual renewal
Tidier, cleaner, more comfortable home	Greater relaxation, more enjoyable entertaining
More sleep	Clearer thinking, safer driving, stronger immune system
Unstructured time to "recharge batteries"	Lower stress; clearer thinking; more energy; spiritual, physical, and emotional renewal
Role modeling	Break Motherhood Myopia cycle for sons and daughters
All of the above	More fulfillment and more fun!

The Cost of Hiring Help

In the previous chapter, you estimated your future employee's rate of pay, along with the number of hours each week that you plan to employ help. Plug those values into the calculation shown on the Cost-Justification Worksheet. Be sure to allow for employer taxes. Convert to a weekly or monthly value, to correspond to the total you calculated for "Benefits."

What Can You Save By Hiring Help?

The fact that most of us need help with household chores is clear from the proliferation of ventures that offer specialized household services. These services clean your house, walk your dog (and clean up after it), chauffeur your kids, shop for your groceries, clean your windows and carpets, and even deliver prepared meals right to your doorstep. Though badly needed, these services are expensive, because built into the fees are the costs of management and marketing. Your housekeeper can perform these functions much more economically, because no marketing expense is involved and you provide the management. As an added bonus, the services your housekeeper delivers are personalized to meet the needs and match the schedule of your family.

If you've been using any high-priced household services, you may be able to eliminate them, and save the expense, if you hire a housekeeper to perform the same functions. Note the amount you will save on your Cost-Justification Worksheet.

If your housekeeper will cook, you may also save the cost of some restaurant meals, take-out meals, and convenience foods. Of course, you will still pay for groceries, but save the huge amount that restaurants and food manufacturers charge for food preparation and service. If you know how much you spend in this category, you can easily estimate your savings. If not, you can guess or keep track of your eating expenses for a week or two to calculate what you're spending on convenience food, versus the much lower cost of groceries that your housekeeper will use to prepare home-cooked meals. As with benefits and costs, convert your savings to a weekly or monthly value.

What Does It Cost Not to Hire Help?

Besides these tangible savings, there are other, less obvious, harder to measure, but still very real costs that you bear by not hiring the help you need. In Chapter 1, we examined the health risks suffered by women who are under stress. Do you have any stress-related health problems that cost you time and money?

Are you sleep deprived? Would you function more effectively if you got enough sleep? Lack of sleep costs our country as much as $70 billion annually in lost productivity, accidents, and medical bills.[1] What do you think it costs your family? Of even more concern, if you are an inattentive driver due to drowsiness, you may be putting your own life or the lives of your children in jeopardy. Can you afford the risk?

Do you and your family eat nutritiously? The health risks of eating convenience and fast foods instead of well-balanced, nutritious meals are serious and well documented. What do you spend on medical bills for health problems that result from a poor diet? What will you spend in the future?

Many marriages are ridden with conflicts that stem from an unequal distribution of household chores. In fact, marriage counselors say that fights over housework are one of the most common, though often uncredited, causes of strife and unhappiness between couples and between parents and children.[2] In those cases, maybe money spent on marriage counseling would be better spent on a housekeeper. Taken to an extreme, a housekeeper is cheaper than a divorce.

What about the costs of frustration, dissatisfaction, even unhappiness? Do you ever find yourself spending money on indulgences designed to help you forget your problems for awhile? We all occasionally indulge in short-term "fixes" instead of solving long-term problems. What if you didn't need so many "fixes"?

What about the costs to your family members of not hiring the household help you need? How could your children benefit if you were less stressed and were able to focus more on their needs and less on household demands? What about your husband? In *The Second Shift*, Arlie Hochschild pointed out that husbands are often affected just as deeply, though indirectly, by the second shifts their wives work "through the resentment their wives feel toward them, and through their need to steel themselves against that resentment."[3] What if you no longer resented your husband and he no longer needed to steel himself against it?

What about the loss to society if, instead of making your best contribution, you are doing housework? My friend Melanie grappled with guilt over delegating housework so that she could find time to start a school for girls. "You're a talented woman, Melanie," I told her. "You should be starting schools and raising children, not folding laundry and running errands."

These costs can be difficult to quantify. But they are important to consider when deciding whether to hire help. If you can quantify at least some of the costs, list them in the "Tangible" column on your Cost-Justification Worksheet and add them up. Then list all of the other hard-to-measure costs that affect you and your family in the "Intangible" column. Your final decision will take both into account.

Cost-Justification Revisited

Remember our cost-justification formula? To refresh your memory, here it is again:

> **The benefits of hiring help should be greater than**
> **the cost of hiring help**
> **minus the savings associated with hiring help**
> **minus the cost of not hiring help.**

If your new opportunities will lead to a substantial increase in income, it may be clear that hiring a housekeeper is the right decision for you. But if intangible costs and benefits figure heavily for you, your decision may require more thought. How do you decide?

First, let's find out how much of your housekeeper's salary is unaccounted for. For example, referring to the completed Cost Justification Worksheet, suppose you calculated that a housekeeper will cost $220 per week and that you can save $102.50 per week when you hire help by eliminating other expenses.

You plan to start a business that will generate income at a future date, but none right away. And you've identified a number of costs associated with *not* hiring help, some of which would ultimately translate into large financial outlays, but are hard to plug into the cost-justification formula because they are not certainties.

The overall shape of what you see on the page, if your Cost-Justification Worksheet reads anything at all like the completed example, may indicate that hiring a housekeeper would be enormously beneficial to your family. But the short-term dollars and cents may still be a stumbling block. If that's the case, the next step is to examine your budget to see how it could be modified to accommodate the cost of a housekeeper.

Your Budgetary "Magic Number"

Before you begin to look for "wiggle room" in your family budget, make sure you're working with the right number. The dollar amount your budget must accommodate is not the cost of hiring a housekeeper, but the *residual* cost of hiring a housekeeper, that is, your housekeeper's wages with all of the other benefits and savings factored in. The formula is:

> Residual cost equals cost of hiring help
> minus savings associated with hiring help
> minus dollar cost of not hiring help
> minus dollar value of benefits of hiring help.

In our example, the residual cost is:

$220/week

minus $102.50/week

minus ?

minus ?

or $117.50 per week. Even though the question marks represent *some* dollar value, we don't know what it is. The conservative—that is, safest—approach is to assume the question marks are zero. Then when the household budget is adjusted accordingly, there is no danger of financial difficulty resulting from wishful projections that fail to pan out.

Finding Room in a Tight Budget

If you know you want to hire help, but there is no room in your budget to cover the residual cost, it's time, to borrow a term from the real estate industry, for a little creative financing. Get settled into your favorite chair and let the creative juices flow. There are only two ways to solve budget problems: increase income or decrease expenses. Here are some ideas.

Help Your Husband Increase His Income

Before I hired a housekeeper, my husband, Michael, drove the kids to school every morning. Since they attend a school several miles away, the commute time is not insignificant. Anticipating that a housekeeper would free me of several hours of chores each day, I took over the morning chauffeuring duties, freeing Michael, a consultant, to bill additional time. This arrangement turned out to be serendipitous: Michael's increased consultancy fees covered the residual cost of our housekeeper, and I discovered that, for some reason, my kids and I seem to connect best in the car. Our commutes to and from school are filled with storytelling, music, and meaningful conversations.

Can you identify any similarly painless ways to increase your household income?

Evaluate Your Other Discretionary Spending

Julia and her husband, Ted, have full-time professional careers and a six-year-old son. Until recently, they also had a marriage filled with anger and resentment. Because Ted prepares dinner every night, does all the yardwork, and spends lots of time with their son, he felt he was contributing his fair share to the household. But Julia found herself responsible for all the rest of the unpaid work, which added up to many, many hours each week. She resented not only the unequal workload, but the self-congratulatory tone that Ted used when he talked about what he did. Although their household income is substantial, their extravagant lifestyle left no room to pay for household help.

Julia and Ted evaluated their budget carefully. Avid skiers, they went to the mountains an average of 10 weekends each winter. They decided that, by skiing half as often, they could afford to pay a housekeeper, still enjoy their favorite sport, and eliminate the major source of strife in their marriage.

Examine and evaluate the money you spend on extras such as vacations, clothing, cars, entertainment, high-tech gadgets, and so on. You could even reevaluate fixed expenses, most significantly, your mortgage. Have you committed, through your chosen lifestyle, to a level of spending that emphasizes standard of living over quality of life? Maybe a major change is in order.

Get a Loan

If your new opportunities include a career change that will eventually result in a substantially higher income, but you can't make that change unless you delegate household chores, consider borrowing the money to cover the cost of hiring help. Be careful, though; borrowing against future earnings can be a risky strategy.

Set Your Sights a Little Lower

Hire only the help that you can afford, such as a weekly or twice a month cleaning service.

When Doris realized that she couldn't effectively run her real estate business unless she hired a weekly cleaning service, she called a family meeting. Doris, her husband, and their son are all avid travelers who are willing to make sacrifices to add to their vacation fund. They decided to hire a service to clean their home on alternating Mondays. On the off weeks, the three of them "blitz" the house for one hour after dinner, and Doris writes a check to the family vacation fund, in the amount she would otherwise have paid to the cleaning service.

Teri, a human resources director and mother of three kids, employs a housecleaner five hours a week. The family shares the rest of the household chores. "I fix dinner. My husband cleans up while I help the kids with homework. He puts the wash in the washer, I hang it up and put it away. The kids make their beds in the morning, take out the garbage, and keep their rooms straightened. All in all, things run fairly smoothly."

One caution: if you're only hiring a little bit of household help, make sure you haven't set your expectations too high. A cleaning service will give you some breathing room, but will probably not give you enough free time to start a business, unless there's been a major redistribution of the household workload among the other members of your family. Remember why you decided to hire help; don't simply exchange one type of overload for another.

Plan for Future Flexibility

Sometimes you really can't afford household help, and your budget offers no flexibility. If your financing options are nonexistent because you work in a low-paid field, maybe it's time to reconsider your choice, or earn the credentials that would open up more options to you. If you could be earning more in your current field, but your position is underpaid, screw up your courage and ask for the raise you deserve; if it's denied, look around for a better position. Of course, the same advice applies to your husband.

Shortsighted decisions early on, combined with high expectations, can also create a lack of flexibility. Barb, 31, has had lots of career jumps and gaps (translating into a relatively low income), because she spent her twenties prioritizing travel experiences over career progression. Her husband, Greg, who went through school on the "10-year plan," is a 30-year-old new college grad with $50,000 in school loans and an entry-level income. Although they enjoyed their twenties, now Barb and Greg are eager to catch up with their peers. They've bought a house and want to start a family right away and are financially strapped.

If this sounds like you, take a deep breath and decide whether the train you're on will take you to your desired destination. Most of us who lack flexibility have made lifestyle choices that factor in both partners' earnings, but fail to consider the cost of accomplishing household chores. Now that your eyes have been opened to this contradiction, you can adjust your plans and expectations accordingly.

Whose Budget Is It, Anyway?

One of the obstacles you may have encountered in your creative financing exercise may be "his and her" thinking. Often couples, whether consciously or unconsciously, divide financial responsibility to correspond to traditional roles. If he is the family breadwinner, his earnings fund all of the family's basic needs. She, as homemaker, earns income if she so chooses, but her income must cover the costs of her going to work (babysitters and housekeepers, as well as commute costs, a work wardrobe, and so on). Given such thinking, if her income can't cover the cost of a housekeeper, the cost can't be justified, no matter what his income looks like.

There are several fallacies in this logic. The first is that only two-career families need household help. Anyone who has spent time at home with young children knows that a full-time homemaker needs a babysitter at least for a couple of hours a week, to get regular teeth cleanings and haircuts at a minimum and, ideally, to spend a few sanity-restoring child-free hours each week.

Furthermore, to do the best job we possibly can as parents, full-time homemakers should be focusing our time on childrearing, not on housekeeping. Dr. James Dobson, a noted Christian author who hosts a radio program called *Focus on the Family*, recommends strongly that domestic help appear high on a family's list of spending priorities when there are young children at home.[4] Household help is not a luxury; it is a service that enhances the quality of family life. As such, it is a family expense, not a woman's expense.

The second fallacy built into "the wife should pay for the housekeeper" logic is the idea that money is the only way to measure value. Rita is a talented but low-paid preschool teacher who is loved by her students and widely regarded as an expert in her field. Her husband, Steve, is an equally talented but well-paid executive in the computer industry. Even though Rita's salary won't cover the expense, shouldn't they employ a housekeeper so that Rita can focus her energy where her talents lie?

Similarly, doesn't hiring a housekeeper make sense when one's best contribution can be made as a volunteer? Some of us use our wealth to contribute money to causes we believe in. Others contribute time and purchase household services to make that time available.

The third fallacy harkens back to the debate over standards. ("Her standards are higher, so the workload she generates by *caring* about housework is her responsibility.") We can easily dispense with this fallacious argument by reiterating that household chores are the result of *having* a household, thus are a household expense.

Everybody always spends *all* of his or her money. Even money saved or invested is "spent" on the intangible benefit (maybe just a feeling of comfort) of having that money tucked away. Take another look at how your household spends its income. Do your spending patterns correspond to what's most important?

Selling the Idea to Your Husband

If you do your homework and conclude that hiring a housekeeper would be profitable for your family, what loving husband wouldn't agree? Well, the best-laid plans sometimes go awry, so let's make sure your message doesn't get lost in the delivery!

The idea of a housekeeper as a time-management tool (instead of a luxury) may be shockingly new to your husband. By now, you've had a chance to clear the cobwebs from your own thinking on the subject, but he's not up to speed yet. Your job now is to help him bring his thinking to where yours is—quickly, painlessly, and effectively.

To equip yourself for this potentially life-altering task, prepare yourself well. You've already done most of the work by identifying the benefits of hiring help and analyzing its impact on the family budget. Now, all you have left to do is plan your presentation, as any good salesperson would do.

First of all, be clear in your conviction that hiring help is the right thing to do. If you still have doubts, argue the issues with yourself until you know where you stand. Then, imagine the objections your husband will offer and prepare thoughtful, clearly reasoned responses to his questions. He'll probably come up with objections you haven't thought of, but you'll have more confidence and be better equipped to think on your feet if you've anticipated most of his concerns.

You might want to rehearse ahead of time the conversation you expect to have with your husband. When I worked in computer sales, I rehearsed all of my important sales calls in my mind, as recommended by Maxwell Maltz in *Psycho-Cybernetics*. According to the research, "synthetic experience" (an experience imagined vividly and in detail) is as valuable as the real thing.[5] As a result of mental rehearsal, you will be calm and rational during your discussion, states of being that most men value.

What other advice can experts offer? Most marriage counselors tout the importance of "I-messages" (statements that describe how you feel in specific situations), rather than "you-messages" (statements that describe what the other person has done to wrong you).

Rhona Mahony, in *Kidding Ourselves: Breadwinning, Babies, and Bargaining Power*, observes that a man who loves his wife doesn't want her to be unhappy. She recommends that a woman tell her husband she is miserable, point out how much work she is doing, and appeal to his sense of fairness and partnership.[6]

John Gray's bestseller *Men Are from Mars, Women Are from Venus* contains a chapter entitled "How to Ask for Support and Get It." In that chapter, Gray advises women asking for support to choose appropriate timing, have a nondemanding attitude, be brief, be direct, and use "would you" or "will you" phrases so men don't feel nagged.[7] Here is how you would translate that advice into a real conversation.

Choose Appropriate Timing

It should come as no surprise that the middle of Monday Night Football is not the best time to bring up a potentially shocking new idea. Make an appointment with your husband, so he is prepared to give your proposal his full attention.

Have a Nondemanding Attitude

Gray points out that when women give too much, they tend to blame their partners.Take responsibility for your own anger. Assume your husband is a man of good will and that he will be willing to help if offered a workable solution.

Be Brief

Get straight to the bottom line. He may be prepared to agree right away, but become irritated if forced to listen to the details. Or he may be a victim of Motherhood Myopia too and may wish to debate the topic at length. You can encourage him to read this book, but he might want you to summarize the arguments. That's when your mental rehearsals will pay off.

Be Direct

Don't whine about how overworked you are and expect him to offer to help. Tell him simply that the housework has become a problem for you, but that you can see a workable solution.

Use "Would You"/"Will You" Phrases

According to Gray, men feel nagged when asked, "Could you?" (He thinks, "Yes, I can, but I won't.") Say, "Will you agree to reviewing our budget with me this weekend, so that we can find a way to pay for a part-time housekeeper?"

Finally, Gray reminds us that one of the key elements of assertive asking is to remain silent after you have asked for support.[8]

What if your husband feels that housework is your responsibility and that, if it's too overwhelming, you should simply reduce your other commitments? Pepper Schwartz asserts in *Peer Marriage* that many peer men (men who share domestic chores equally with their wives) are made, not born. Some peer men are veterans of failed traditional marriages who sought out peer relationships thereafter. But many simply are married to women who are good communicators and insist that their husbands share equally in the work of the home.[9] Fairness dictates that you and your husband ensure that *both* of you can fill your day with activities that are fulfilling, challenging, and enjoyable. As John Gray put it, "When she wakes up and remembers her needs, he also wakes up and wants to give her more."[10]

■ ■ ■

Before I hired a housekeeper, I tried not to notice myself doing my family's housework, since I hated it so much. When I calculated what it would actually take to replace myself in that arena, the numbers shocked me. The decision to hire a housekeeper wasn't an easy or obvious one.

Two things kept me going: the knowledge that I would not, *could* not, go on as before and my determination to find a way to resume my career while still caring for my children. Despite my strong fear that my husband would not agree to hiring a housekeeper, he assented easily because the arguments were compelling and the presentation effective. You're reading the happy ending to my story.

Hiring a housekeeper may require a leap of faith, especially if you don't know anyone else who has. But the biggest risks sometimes offer the biggest rewards.

Part 2

Managing Your Housekeeper

So, you've decided to hire a housekeeper. If you haven't already done so, you should read Chapter 5, "Know Where You're Headed," which introduces the tools that you will use to manage your employee and examines the most important step in management—planning.

The chapters in Part II focus on executing the plan that you created in Chapter 5. Corresponding to the four remaining steps in the management process, the following chapters discuss, in turn, organizing, staffing (Chapters 8, 9, and 10), directing, and evaluating. Together, these chapters will equip you for success with your new employee.

7 Solve Each Problem Only Once

"I need a wife!" That's the secret, or not-so-secret, fantasy of almost every busy woman I know. Are we saying that, literally, we want a third, same-sex marriage partner? Of course not. What we want is someone else to take care of the thousands of mind-numbing household details that exhaust us and keep us from all the activities that we really love.

A lucky few of us can afford to hire the equivalent of a wife—someone who has not only the know-how, but also the judgment to successfully run a family household. But judgment, or the ability to make good decisions, is an expensive quality in an employee, and few of us can afford the salary requirements of someone who is, effectively, a clone of ourselves.

Starkey International is a Colorado firm that trains and places professional staff for very large households and estates—the kinds of homes that typically require an entire team of household employees. Although its clients may employ one or more domestic workers, Starkey knows that such employers also need a professional household manager—someone to do household planning, make decisions, and keep the rest of the staff on track. Starkey says that entry-level household managers earn between $35,000 and $60,000 annually, plus housing.[1] An Ohio placement agency, Professional Domestic Services, quotes annual salary rates from $35,000 to $100,000 or more for such positions.[2]

Don't despair if you can't afford to hire a wife-equivalent household manager. When high-paying Starkey clients hire household help, they are delegating both components of housework: the mental and the physical. Because it is easiest and cheapest to hire help with the physical component, that's the part you can delegate. The purpose of this chapter is to teach you how to separate the physical and mental components of household tasks, then minimize the mental work that you will still be doing yourself.

How can you minimize housework's mental component? Conduct a search-and-destroy mission on redundant mental tasks. Management experts know it costs time and money to make the same decisions over and over again. Yet sometimes it seems as if housework is defined by its repeated decision-making: Do I have enough laundry for a full washload of darks? What shall we have for dinner? Where can I put these project piles so I have room to cook? Read on to find out how to eliminate or minimize those decisions.

Getting Organized: How Much Is Enough?

The magnitude of housework's mental component varies from task to task. Cleaning, for example, involves very little decision-making. It is a routine task that primarily involves physical labor. Laundry, on the other hand, is a bit more sophisticated. Ranging from color sorting to selecting machine settings to knowing what belongs to whom (for putting clothes away), the number of decisions involved are potentially much greater. Cooking is the most sophisticated task of all, requiring knowledge of nutrition, appealing recipes, family food preferences, grocery purchasing, and so on.

Because of those differences, cleaning is easiest to delegate. You might even find you can successfully employ a housecleaner without following any of the advice in this chapter, especially if your household is already fairly well organized. But if you need more sophisticated help than that, you may need to restructure the tasks of your household.

I faced a dilemma when writing this chapter. I didn't want to overwhelm you, the reader, with unnecessary organizing advice. On the other hand, I didn't want to withhold useful advice, in case you wish to delegate sophisticated household tasks.

Be selective when reading this chapter. Read it through at least once. If some of the suggestions seem appropriate for your household, go ahead and implement them. If others seem like overkill or just not your style, ignore them.

Paula, for example, whom we met in Chapter 3, successfully employs a team of housekeepers for 5 hours each week (10 person-hours) and provides absolutely no written instructions, counter to the advice in this book. At the other end of the spectrum, you may want to implement some of the suggestions even if you don't hire any help. The best way to share housework with your husband or to delegate it to your kids is to first make sure that the number of household decisions that need to be made are few.

If the task of organizing your household seems overwhelming, you can even hire help with that. The Resources section of this book contains suggestions for hiring a professional organizer. Just make sure that the consultant you hire reads this chapter first!

Are You a "Systems" Person?

Even if you've never thought about it, your household routine consists of a set of systems. For example, every household typically has a system for laundry, one for meal planning and preparation, one for housecleaning, one for yardwork, and so on. A household system is simply a set of methods and routines for accomplishing a specific task. It has two dimensions: space (where things go and how they get there) and time (when the household chores are done and by whom).

But how well those systems work—how much decision-making they require—depends on how consciously they were designed. Consciously designed systems work well because they anticipate needs and create actions to meet those needs, like my weekly meal-planning ritual, which is described later in this chapter. At the other end of the spectrum, needs are met through on-the-spot actions created in response to urgent demands, like a fast-food drive-up meal purchased when the children are hungry, the hour is late, or the cupboard is bare.

To illustrate the benefits of a well-designed household system, let's imagine how laundry gets handled in two hypothetical households.

The Smiths

In the Smith house, dirty laundry is supposed to go into a hamper kept in the hall bathroom. In reality, though, most dirty clothes never make it there, for several reasons. For one thing, the hamper is simply not large enough to hold all of the dirty clothes for the family of five and is often filled to overflowing. For another thing, with two teenage girls in the family, the bathroom is often occupied, so access to the hamper is limited. Even when well-intentioned family members do carry an armload of dirty clothes into the bathroom, their efforts are often made more difficult by a stack of books and magazines weighing down the hamper lid.

As a result, the children usually allow their dirty laundry to accumulate on their bedroom floors until a crisis is reached—they have no clean clothes to wear or their mother, Sharon, explodes in frustration over the unkempt appearance of their bedrooms.

Laundry is mostly done on an "as-needed" basis, usually late at night or early in the morning. Because there is no set routine for sorting through the accumulation of dirty clothes, those at the bottom of the hamper often mildew. And since, most of the time, clothes are laundered because something is needed immediately, there is no time to fold or hang the remainder of the freshly laundered clothes, causing garments to wrinkle as they sit, untended, in the dryer. Without a better system, Sharon finds herself forced to live in a household that seems to be in a perpetual state of "laundry emergency."

The Joneses

In the Jones house, things work differently. Instead of a communal hamper in the bathroom, each family member has a large basket for dirty laundry in his or her bedroom. Monday is designated laundry day, so on Sunday evenings, those who want to avoid washing their own clothes that week are expected to sort their laundry and leave it in neat piles outside their bedroom doors. Alternate Mondays are "sheets day," and anyone who wants clean sheets is responsible for stripping his or her bed and leaving a pile of sheets next to the sorted dirty laundry.

By Monday evening, stacks of clean, folded laundry are returned to the appropriate bedrooms, and family members put away their clean clothes. The system is enforced by daily room checks; not only must clean laundry be put away on Mondays, but dirty laundry also must be put into personal hampers by bedtime every night. The children learned this system at a very young age and willingly comply.

Before she hired household help, Judy Jones, who works part-time in a home-based business, devoted her Mondays to laundry. It took the better part of the day, but then she was finished for the week, and everyone had enough clean clothes to last until the next laundry day. When she decided to hire help, delegating the laundry task was easy, because the system was already in place. She hired a team of two housekeepers to work for five hours every Monday, cleaning house and making beds while simultaneously washing, drying, folding, and distributing eight loads of laundry.

The only complication arose because five hours was enough time to wash, but not to dry, eight loads of laundry. Judy could have hired one housekeeper to come to her house twice a week for five hours each time, which would have solved the problem. But she wanted to continue the family tradition of Monday as laundry day. Plus, she liked knowing that she would have peace and quiet to concentrate on her business for the rest of the week. Judy invested in a second clothes dryer so that the team could complete their work in five hours on Mondays.

Ground Rules for Effective Household Systems

Is your laundry system more like the Smiths or the Joneses? If the answer is "Smiths," chances are that other household systems are out of control, too. For example, are you a "clutter shuffler"? Do you find yourself shifting "stuff" (newspapers, magazines, unprocessed mail, shoes, jackets, backpacks, project piles) from one place to another because it doesn't really have a home?

Now imagine a household employee trying to deal with all that stuff. Just think: you'll be paying someone to shuffle clutter and, odds are, wherever she decides to put it, that's not the place you would have thought of, and you won't be able to find it later when your housekeeper has gone home.

Although you might not favor the Jones family's laundry system (a variety of other systems work equally well), it's effective because it adheres to seven important ground rules, which are characteristic of all well-designed households. If you modify your household systems to adhere to these ground rules, chores will be easy to delegate to a housekeeper, and your family life as a whole will run smoother, too.

A Place for Everything

Maria Montessori, an Italian physician famous for her innovative educational philosophy, popularized the now-familiar concept, "A place for everything, and everything in its place." Children, she noticed, are comforted by an atmosphere of calm and order. An environment in which everything has a place is an extension of the routine and consistency that children love.[3]

Effective Household System Ground Rules

1. A place for everything
2. A place that makes sense
3. Everything in its place
4. A routine
5. Clearly defined responsibilities
6. No entropy generators
7. The tools to do the job

Whether or not you find comfort in routine and consistency, the resulting atmosphere of calm and order is what we're aiming for here. Any clutter that you find yourself shuffling is wearing an invisible sign that's screaming, "I need a home!"

One hint: If you have trouble finding a place for everything, maybe you have too much "stuff." You might want to consider giving away, selling, throwing away, or storing the excess.

A Place That Makes Sense

It's not enough, however, simply to make sure that every item has a home; it must be a place that makes sense. If certain belongings never seem to get put away properly, maybe they should be stored closer to where they are used.

In the Smith family, dirty laundry did have a place (in the hamper in the hall bathroom), but that place didn't make sense because it was too small and too inaccessible. In the Jones family, the place for dirty laundry (baskets in each bedroom) made sense.

In my house, the coat closet is in the bedroom hallway, far from the front door. My clue that I needed to rethink our "system" for coat storage was the constant accumulation of coats and jackets in the living room, draped over the backs of chairs. By placing a coat tree near the front door, I created a place that made sense. Now, most of our coats hang in the hall closet, while the current favorites hang on the coat tree.

Everything in Its Place

Like a library book that is incorrectly shelved and thus lost unless discovered by accident, belongings that are stored other than in their intended home can't be reliably retrieved when needed. Children's board games are unusable when playing pieces are scooped up and thrown into a catch-all toy box, instead of being carefully matched to their respective games. Important bills can become delinquent when they are mixed with junk mail and school papers and shoved into a drawer. Car keys that are not consistently placed in an established location near the door can trigger hide-and-seek sessions that can make you late for appointments.

Once you've established a storage place—one that makes sense—for every item in your household, educate your family on the new system. (This will be easier if they helped create the system or at least provided input.) Furthermore, you should help everyone develop the discipline to put things away "where they go." You could use a system of rewards and punishments to ensure your children's cooperation or simply expect it by virtue of their participation in the family. In any event, one thing you will need for sure: a routine.

A Routine

Avoid repeated decision-making: that's the primary message of this chapter. Nothing necessitates burdensome, excessive, and repetitive decisions like the lack of a household routine. I learned this lesson when I was a full-time mother and homemaker.

The part of my life I hated the most, back then, was making decisions about laundry. Every morning, I would survey the laundry baskets and our remaining supply of clean clothes, and calculate whether I needed to do laundry that day. Inevitably, I came to one of two conclusions: either the levels of dirty laundry looked so low, it seemed that it would have been a waste of water to run the machine, or we had accumulated—seemingly overnight—so much dirty laundry that I was suddenly faced with having to wash four or five loads.

I feared the latter situation so much that, every morning when I began my laundry assessment, an enormous knot formed in my stomach. I even began to dread getting out of bed in anticipation of what I might find. Finally, sick of how laundry determined my emotional state, I decided a reorganization was in order.

First, I established a schedule that laid out the specific loads of wash that would routinely be done each day of the week. For example, on Mondays I would wash my whites and the kids' whites. Tuesdays were for bath towels and my husband's darks, and so on. Then I resolved to adhere to this schedule no matter what, which freed me from the daily laundry calculation chore. Of course, I have made minor adjustments in the routine over the years since.

Though I was still expending physical energy on doing my family's laundry, the amount of mental and emotional energy I saved by eliminating repeated decision-making was substantial. Furthermore, by applying the concept to the other systems of my household, I began to see how easily I could delegate the housework. My newly defined household routine was, in fact, the skeletal structure of my future housekeeper's schedule.

Like me, you should examine every aspect of your household to see where you can establish routines that eliminate or reduce decision-making. Many specific suggestions appear later in this chapter. As you create or refine your household routines, think about which parts you could delegate to a housekeeper.

Clearly Defined Responsibilities

One of the useful aspects of a routine is that it allows you to define who is responsible for what tasks and then hold those individuals accountable.

For example, let's suppose that recyclables are stored (until collection day) in a bin in the garage. Obviously, it's unrealistic to expect family members to make a trip to the garage every time they empty one bottle or can. But what if you establish a staging area for recyclables—on the kitchen counter beside the sink, say—and ask your housekeeper to carry all the bottles and cans to the garage once a day? Then, teach family members that it is their responsibility to rinse any bottles or cans that they have used and place them in the staging area.

Battles with children over chores and with husbands over "standards" often result from a lack of routine and defined responsibilities. In the case of recyclables, for example, when would the recycling get carried to the garage if there were no routine? When someone could no longer stand to look at the accumulation? When there was no room to cook? When would the bottles and cans get rinsed? Immediately after use? Prior to being carried to the garage? When ants invaded? Who would do the rinsing? The person who was about to carry the recyclables out? The person who cared about ants in the kitchen? A household routine answers all of those questions ahead of time, reducing the chances for potentially stressful daily negotiations.

Clearly defined responsibilities also help your employee feel more like a paid professional and less like an indentured servant. She will be a key member of the highly tuned team that is your household, instead of some kind of menial drudge. Not only does a defined routine ensure that your housekeeper will do what you need her to do, but it also gives her the satisfaction of knowing that she's met your expectations.

No Entropy Generators

A physics term, "entropy" refers to the natural tendency of the universe to become increasingly disorganized over time. This concept can easily be applied to households. I've coined the term "entropy generators" to describe household habits that are likely to promote chaos.

Have you ever noticed how wire clothes hangers tend to proliferate over time? My theory is that they mate and reproduce in the middle of the night. (That's why you so often find them tangled up—that's their mating position.) Wire hangers are a sure-fire way to generate entropy in your closet. I've banned them from my house. All of our clothes hang on plastic hangers, the kind that can be purchased ten for a dollar from the drugstore. When clothing comes home from the cleaners, each item gets transferred from its wire hanger to a plastic hanger before being hung in the closet, and the wire hangers go back to the dry cleaners for recycling.

Most households contain many other entropy generators besides wire hangers. Newspapers and magazines can easily take over a living room.

To solve this problem, my family keeps a newspaper rack in our utility room that serves as both a storage bin and a recycling staging area. Shoes on closet floors never stay lined up the way they are supposed to. I like to place cardboard shoe organizers on upper closet shelves and use the floor space for laundry baskets. Plastic tubs for storing leftovers, like wire hangers, seem to propagate in the middle of the night. Just keep what you will use and recycle the rest. The worst offenders, though, are "miscellaneous" files and junk drawers. Just say no.

If a particular area of your household is difficult to keep organized, you might ask yourself whether it contains an entropy generator.

The Tools to Do the Job

I recently took an upholstery class because I wanted to learn how to salvage some well-loved furniture. I had done some minor reupholstering in the past, so I knew what a pain it was going to be to remove the hundreds of staples that were holding the worn-out fabric in place. I assumed that I would be using a screwdriver, hammer, and pliers to coax each staple out of the wood. To my pleasant surprise, the first day of class, I was told to buy a "staple remover"—a handy tool that cost $15 and allowed me to remove staples quickly and easily.

Similarly, there are dozens of tools that make household chores easier and quicker. For the sake of every member of your household team, especially your housekeeper, invest in the necessary tools and keep them in good repair. These include not only big-ticket items like vacuum cleaners (both the corded and cordless kinds) but handy gadgets like dusters on telescoping handles (for reaching cobwebs in high places), plastic caddies (for carrying cleaning supplies around the house), and rubber gloves, as well as a variety of cleaning agents.

When you hire your housekeeper, show her the tools that you own, ask her if she prefers something that you don't yet have, and explain how she can keep you informed when cleaning supplies are low or a tool needs to be repaired or replaced. Then, make an effort to replenish supplies and make repairs promptly. Trying to cut corners on household tools signals to your housekeeper that you place little value on the work that she does.

Conversely, small investments can pay big dividends. I own (and have worn out and replaced several times) a cordless upright vacuum cleaner that is convenient for "sweeping" my large kitchen floor. Without exception, every housekeeper I have interviewed has exclaimed in delight when shown that vacuum cleaner, commenting that such a handy tool makes a tedious chore easy.

How to Prepare for Your Housekeeper

Now that you've streamlined your household systems, the next step is to add some "housekeeper-friendly" finishing touches.

An Instruction Manual

You'll save yourself hours of explanation if you write a generic instruction manual for your housekeeper. Does the thought of developing one seem intimidating? Never fear—you've been developing the contents as you've read this book. In Chapter 5, you identified the specific tasks you plan to delegate to a housekeeper. Earlier in this chapter, you created a routine to accomplish those tasks. Now, you just need to write it all down and add explanations where necessary.

Appendix A reproduces the instruction manual that I use. The first page lists the tasks that should be done every day and those that should be done on an as-needed basis. The rest of the manual outlines the tasks that should be done on specific days of the week. Note that there are four different Thursday schedules. That's because the bedsheets are changed on a rotating schedule, over a cycle of four weeks.

Besides the list of daily tasks, some detailed instructions are included as well (most notably, laundry settings), providing crucial information in a handy location. When you write your instruction manual, be sure to include the details that you think are important. But save the file (if you write the manual on a computer) because you might want to add details later.

Storage Spaces

Now is the time to get to the closet cleaning that you've been meaning to do for years. Your new housekeeper will do a much better job at keeping these spaces organized if they start out that way.

Start with your pantry. Be ruthless. Get rid of any food items that you know won't be consumed in the next few months. Donate the edible ones to a homeless shelter; toss the rest. Then, arrange the contents of the pantry so that like is with like: soups with soups, spices together, baking supplies together, and so on. Be sure to leave spaces next to each grouping to allow for expansion. And don't forget to place the most frequently used items at eye level.

Now, move on to your kitchen cabinets. Again, be ruthless. Start by weeding out never-used items and donate or discard them. (If you can't bear to part with old wedding gifts, then at least banish them to a box on a high shelf in the garage.) Next, rearrange the cabinets so that rarely used items are on the highest and lowest shelves and the most frequently used ones are easiest to reach. Place the glasses nearest the sink, the dishes nearest the table. Make sure you haven't inconveniently combined items. For example, if you stack the salad plates on top of the dinner plates, you'll have to lift the whole stack of salad plates every time you need a dinner plate. They should be in two separate stacks.

Next, take a look at your linen closets. Once again, weed out as much as you can. Rather than just storing things randomly, you may want to designate one shelf for sheets, one for bath towels, one for beach towels, and one for old towels for car and dog washing.

If you don't already have one, you need to develop a system for paper management. Your housekeeper won't be handling your papers, but if your current "system" consists of piles of paper on your kitchen counters, you won't be leaving her enough room to work. If you don't know how to create a paper management system, one of the books listed in the Resources section can give you guidance.

Finally, if you are very ambitious, you may want to move on to your closets and the kids' bedrooms. To keep the kids' bedrooms tidy, our family periodically weeds out old toys, books, clothing, and collections. Without aggressive weeding, dusting in the kids' rooms is a near-impossible task. If your housekeeper will be maintaining your wardrobe, her job will be more manageable if your closet is not bursting at the seams. Besides eliminating outdated clothing, I like to hang my clothes in categories—pants together, blouses together, blazers together, and so on. My housekeeper maintains the categories when putting clean clothes away.

Cleaning Supplies

One final storage space that is particularly important to your housekeeper is the one for cleaning supplies. It's best if the supplies are kept in one location. If you have children, the supplies should be kept either in an overhead cabinet or in one with childproof latches.

Make sure that on your housekeeper's first day, the cleaning supply cabinet is tidy and well stocked. Below is a checklist of suggested cleaning tools and supplies.

Household Tools and Supplies

Glass cleaner

Plastic cleaner (if you have any Plexiglas)

Basin/tub/tile cleaner

Mildew stain remover

Toilet bowl cleaner

Floor cleaner

General-purpose cleaner

Furniture polish

Metal polish

Laundry detergent

Bleach—with and without chlorine

Fabric softener

Sponges—with and without scrubber attached

Toilet bowl brush

Toothbrushes and/or grout brush

Rubber gloves

Plastic carrying caddy

Soft cloths for dusting

Old towels and washcloths

Paper towels

Fine-gauge steel wool

Vacuum cleaner and replacement bags and filters

Cordless vacuum cleaners—handheld and upright

Mop and bucket

Broom and dustpan

Duster on telescoping wand

Iron and ironing board

Stepladder

You should also establish a mechanism for replenishing supplies when they get low and tell your housekeeper what it is. Every week, I stick a large, fresh Post-It® note on the side of one kitchen cabinet. (The cabinet so designated happens to be positioned at a rarely seen angle.) When any household items are needed, whether cleaning supplies or food, the name of the item is added to this note. Once a week, when I make the shopping list, I consult the note.

A "Space" for Your Housekeeper

Although housekeeping is not a desk job, your housekeeper will need a place where she can store and use written materials. For example, if you provide an instruction manual like the one in Appendix A, she will need a place to keep it. You may be providing daily or weekly notes that clarify or expand on the generic instructions. If your housekeeper will cook, you will provide a weekly menu plan and the relevant recipes. And you'll probably leave an envelope containing cash to be used for grocery shopping and other errands.

Set aside a drawer or other small space for these materials. A small pad of paper and a pencil or a pen stored there will come in handy for your housekeeper, too.

Clothing Identification

Unless your children have significant age differences or very distinctive (and contrasting) clothing styles, your housekeeper may have difficulty determining what belongs to whom, especially if your kids wear school uniforms. You can make her laundry task easier, and save yourself the chore of repeatedly answering the same questions, by identifying the questionable items of clothing.

Mark the child's name on the clothing tag using a laundry marker, or pick different thread colors for each child and sew a loop of thread to the inside of each collar or waistband. If your child needs to have his or her clothing labeled for school or camp, order sew-in or iron-on labels customized with your child's name.

By the way, this is a task that you can easily delegate to your housekeeper once she's on board. Just make sure, during hiring, that she can sew with a needle and thread.

You may think of other preparations that you want to make before you hire a housekeeper. As a guideline, imagine someone unfamiliar with your household trying to accomplish your household chores. What questions will she have? What decisions will she need to make? The best preparations answer as many questions and eliminate as many decisions as possible.

Some Example Household Systems

The way that you design your household systems is going to be unique to your lifestyle, the layout of your home, the needs of your family, and your preferences. Some household systems, however, are more complex than others. The balance of this chapter outlines some specific approaches that might work well for you and your family.

Laundry

Along with my weekly laundry routine, I've also created a scheme that completely eliminates the need to sort laundry.

On the floor of his or her closet, each member of my family has two or three laundry baskets. Each basket corresponds to a particular category of laundry. Some of the baskets are personal and some are communal. For example, we each have one basket for lights in our closet and one for darks. The dry cleaning goes into a basket in my husband's closet and the drip-dry clothes go into a basket in mine. In addition, the skirted sink in our powder room (off the kitchen) hides a basket for towels and cleaning rags.

When an item of clothing becomes dirty, its owner places it into the appropriate laundry basket. It's been easy to teach my husband and kids this system. Even a two-year-old can tell the difference between light and dark clothing.

Whether the housekeeper washes a load of laundry or one of my family members does, the procedure is the same: carry the appropriate laundry basket to the utility room (for some loads the contents of two or three baskets are combined), load the washer, and follow the instructions in the housekeeper's manual for that particular category of laundry. Voila! Clean laundry, no thinking, no decision-making required.

Food Management

When many people share a refrigerator and pantry, organized spaces make for better kitchen mates. Besides cleaning and organizing your pantry as suggested earlier in this chapter, you may want to give some thought to the layout of your refrigerator.

Rather than just putting food into the refrigerator wherever it will fit, you can establish some conventions. For example, the two bottom bins in my refrigerator always contain fruit (prewashed by my housekeeper). Bottled water, fruit juice, and milk go on the top shelf. Vegetables are stored in large rectangular plastic storage containers that stack together neatly and efficiently: one for lettuce, one for "long vegetables" (carrots, celery, green onions), one for all the rest.

Meal Planning

To minimize the number of trips to the grocery store, decide in advance what the upcoming meals will be. I plan meals weekly. Some families have a preset cycle of meals that they rotate through (a four-week cycle is typical), which is excellent because it removes decision-making from meal planning.

My weekly meal planning session takes place on Sunday evenings. I start out by consulting the calendar for the upcoming week. Usually, we plan to sit down to a hot meal at 6 p.m., which our housekeeper cooks before she leaves for the day. But if something will interfere with our family dinner hour—a school play in the late afternoon, for example— I note that the housekeeper should make a meal-sized salad that day and leave it in the refrigerator for us.

Next, I choose meals for the rest of the week. I try to vary the meals, including pasta dishes, soups, chicken, and so forth. Often I allow the children each to plan one meal. I outline the meal plan for the housekeeper on a small piece of paper, like the example shown below.

Once the plan is made, I collect the recipes that will be needed that week. (I keep each recipe in a clear vinyl sheet protector and stored in a three-ring binder, organized by category.) The recipes in my family repertoire have all been rewritten in a housekeeper-friendly form that includes both ingredients and cooking instructions. Appendix B contains several examples. The notations next to the ingredient lists are used in making my grocery shopping list, as explained below.

Weekly Meal Plan

Monday:
  Chocolate chip cookies*

Tuesday:
  Spaghetti, spaghetti sauce, green salad, garlic bread

Wednesday:
  Tacos

Thursday:
  Chicken fricassee

Friday:
  Great American bean salad

* No, we won't be eating chocolate chip cookies for dinner. In the time allotted for cooking this day, the housekeeper will bake, so we will eat take-out for dinner.

Grocery Shopping

I have found grocery shopping to be the single most difficult task to delegate to a housekeeper, especially if she comes from another country or culture. The problem is that the choices available in a typical American supermarket are so overwhelming that it takes a highly educated consumer to successfully navigate its aisles.

I've even noticed the impact of the proliferation of new products during the course of my 16-year marriage. In our newlywed days, I made the shopping list and Michael (successfully) did the shopping. If something I requested wasn't available, Michael was always able to make an intelligent substitution.

But lately, my husband feels increasingly overwhelmed by the choices. Only with the help of a cell phone for emergency consultations does he feel confident about "bringing home the bacon."

If you want your housekeeper to buy groceries, you will need to do two things: be as specific as possible when you make the shopping list, and give her rules to follow when substitutions are needed. Here are some ideas.

Make a Master Shopping List

You can make a master list of your most frequently purchased food items, arranging them according to the food category or supermarket aisle where they're located, even indicating brand names and size if you wish. An example follows. Make several copies of your list. Then, using a fresh copy each week, make a shopping list for your housekeeper by simply highlighting the items you need. You can write the quantity right next to the item. For one-time purchases, you can just write them in by hand at the bottom of the page. With this method, you are giving specific, helpful instructions to your housekeeper, without having to write out a detailed list from scratch each week.

The major disadvantage of this system is that making the master list can be a huge undertaking. You can make the process go more smoothly if you have a home computer. For your housekeeper's first week on the job, simply make a shopping list on your computer and save the file. The next week, add the new purchases to the list, and so on. You'll be adding a few new purchases each week, until eventually you'll have a full-size master list.

By the way, your favorite grocery store most likely can provide you with a store layout, showing the types of food located on each aisle. Once, when I asked the store manager for one, he replied that they didn't have a current one, but that he would request one from company headquarters. A fresh-off-the-press store layout was available within a couple of weeks.

If you have "housekeeper-friendly" recipes like the examples in Appendix B, you can have your housekeeper prepare the shopping list from the week's recipes. (In this case, you might want to indicate aisle number next to each ingredient in the recipe.) No doubt you will need your housekeeper to purchase grocery items besides the recipe ingredients. Write those down on the shopping list, or make an "always buy" list for your housekeeper. When I make my shopping list each week, I finish by consulting the sticky note that we've been adding to all week (see *Cleaning Supplies*, above). I also review a reminder list that I've made for myself, which lists the snacks and staples that our family likes to have on hand, to see if any of those need to be replenished. (See the example.)

Master Shopping List

Aisle 1

Philadelphia brand Neufchatel cheese, 8 oz size
Kraft aged swiss cheese slices, deli-thin, 8 oz package
NY sharp cheese, brick, extra sharp if available
Kraft Singles, cheddar cheese, 24 slice package
Sliced ham, Oscar Meyer, honey ham flavor
Sliced turkey breast, Oscar Meyer
Sliced bologna, Oscar Meyer
Chicken franks (hot dogs), package of 10
Harvest Crisps, 5-grain crackers
Triscuits, Low Salt, biggest box available
Wheat Thins, Low Salt, biggest box available
Pepperidge Farms goldfish crackers, cheddar cheese flavor, 9 ½ oz box
Ritz Bits, plain, peanut butter sandwiches, or cheese sandwiches
Oreos

Aisle 2

Thomas' English muffins, sourdough, 6- or 12-pack
Garlic bread, Toscana or Romano bread
Bread, Whole wheat, Country Hearth or Hearth Farms
Stella Doro breadsticks, plain
Sourdough bread, large round loaf, sour flavor

Aisle 3

Good Seasons Italian salad dressing, box of 4 packets
Italian Kitchen red wine vinegar
Tuna, chunk light, packed in water, 6 ¼ or 3 ½ oz sizes
Crab meat, 6 ½ oz can
Progresso or Contadina tomato sauce, 28 oz can
Progresso or Contadina tomato paste, 12 oz can
DaVinci pastas:
    Thin spaghetti, Linguine, Fettuccini, Cappellini, Rigatoni,
    Fusilli, Elbow macaroni, Large shells, Small shells, Ziti
Brown rice, Farmer's Select, short grain

White rice, long grain
MJB Farmhouse Long grain and wild rice, herb and butter flavor
Ketchup, squeeze bottle, Heinz, 28 oz size
Mustard, Gulden's
Mustard, Grey Poupon
Del Monte sweet pickle relish, 12 oz size
Best Foods Light reduced calorie mayonnaise, 32 oz size

Aisle 4

Edge shaving gel, unscented, gray can
O.B. tampons, regular or super absorbency, box of 27
Vidal Sassoon shampoo, type D for dry or coarse hair
Head and Shoulders shampoo for normal to dry hair, large size
Contact lens care:
    Clerz II
    Ultrazyme, largest quantity available
    Unisol 4

Aisle 5

Quaker 100% natural cereal with raisins
Quaker 100% natural cereal without raisins
Product 19
Cheerios, small box
Froot Loops, small box
Mott's juice boxes, fruit punch, 100% juice, package of 3
Frookies, chocolate and vanilla sandwich cookies
Frookies, vanilla sandwich cookies
Frookies, lemon sandwich cookies
Nutrigrain bars: apple, blueberry, peach, strawberry, raspberry
Progresso or Contadina crushed tomatoes, 28 oz can
Progresso or Contadina crushed tomatoes, 16 oz can
S&W garbanzo beans, low salt, 15 oz can
S&W kidney beans, low salt, 15 oz can

Master Shopping List, (continued)

Aisle 6

Log Cabin pancake syrup, large squeeze bottle
Jiffy Baking Mix
C&H white sugar, 5 lb box
C&H brown sugar, 2 lb box
Tollhouse semi-sweet chocolate morsels
Vanilla extract
Star olive oil, extra virgin
Star olive oil, virgin
Saffola cooking oil
Spices

Aisle 7

Pampers Ultra Dry Thins, girls, size L (large),
  package of 26
Huggies PullUps, girls, size 2, large package
Baby Fresh wipes, large box
Johnson's baby shampoo
Johnson's baby bath
Napkins, white, 100% recycled
Toilet paper, Northern Quilted, package of 12 or 18
Paper towels, select-a-size, any brand
Kleenex, Classic Foil
Glad pleated sandwich bags, box of 150
ZipLoc bags, quart size, box of 50
Wax paper
Batteries, alkaline
Light bulbs

Aisle 8

Dial soap, any color, 12 bars
Ivory soap, 12 bars
Camay soap, any color, 12 bars
Softsoap antibacterial hand soap, with lemon juice
Tide Free, 42 load size

Clorox bleach, 64 oz size
Cascade dishwasher detergent, 65 oz size
409 refill
Windex refill
Tilex
Tuffy scrubbers

Aisle 9

Planters Honey Roasted Peanuts, jar
Ripples Choice potato chips, 13 oz bag
Quaker rice cakes, lightly salted, 4 ½ oz bag
Bavarian pretzels, large box

Aisle 10

Diet Pepsi, with caffeine, 6 pack
Pepsi, caffeine free, 6 pack

Aisle 11

Miller Genuine Draft beer, 12 pack, in bottles

Dairy

Eggs, extra large, grade AA, 1 doz
Milk, LactAid, nonfat, 1 quart
Butter, Land O Lakes, 1 lb

Produce

Large Washington Red Delicious apples
Granny Smith apples
Fuji apples
Large naval oranges
Cantaloupe
Green seedless grapes
Red seedless grapes
Bartlett pears
Nectarines
Tangerines

Cherries
Plums
Strawberries
Blueberries
Raspberries
Bananas
Pineapple
Watermelon
Celery
Green onions
Red leaf lettuce
Parsley
Avocado
Tomatoes, large
Tomatoes, romano
Artichokes
Asparagus
Brussels sprouts
Red onions
Yellow onions
Potatoes, baking
Broccoli
Cauliflower
Green cabbage
Green beans
Green peppers
Red peppers
Cucumbers
Zucchini
Carrots
Basil
Jalapeno peppers
Mushrooms
Garlic

Reminder List

Milk (at least one full quart)
Juice Squeeze (at least one 4-pack of each flavor)
Calistoga water (at least two bottles, variety of flavors)
Eggs
String cheese
Sandwich meat (turkey, bologna, ham)
Sharp cheese
Pepsi (caffeine-free)
Diet Pepsi (with caffeine)
Eggos
Popcorn

Apples—10 plus (Red Delicious), 2 (Granny Smith), 2 (Fuji)
Bananas—10 plus (mixture of green and yellow)
Avocado
Kiwis
Cantaloupe
Oranges
Pineapple
Grapes
Strawberries
Pears
Nectarines
Cherries

Use a Shopping Service

With the rapid growth of the Internet and the proliferation of home computers, computer-based grocery-shopping services are fast becoming big business. With my first housekeeper, I used the method described above, but have since switched to an on-line grocery-shopping service. This approach allows me to control purchases, but still keeps me out of the grocery store.

After doing the weekly meal planning, I use my home computer to order the week's groceries. The groceries are delivered during my housekeeper's work hours; she signs for the groceries (which are paid for by credit card), tips the driver, and puts them away.

Do the Shopping Yourself

If you enjoy grocery shopping, or are unwilling or unable to delegate such a complex task, you can still make good use of your housekeeper by shopping during her work hours. Once you've arrived home with your purchases, she can unload the car, wash the produce, and put the groceries away.

Some Combination of the Above

Because I don't like the produce offered through my on-line grocery-shopping service, my housekeeper makes a weekly shopping trip to a specialty store that sells wonderful produce. Produce items are much simpler to describe than most grocery store items, so this approach works well.

Before my housekeeper heads out to buy the produce (during her workday on Monday), she consults the week's menu plan and checks the recipes' ingredients to compile a list of needed produce. Along with the menu plan, I've left her a note listing the additional produce that we need (primarily fruits and vegetables for snacking). My notes plus the produce needed for the week's meals become my housekeeper's shopping list. When she returns from her shopping trip, she washes all the produce and puts it away.

By combining approaches, I've achieved the best of both worlds—control over purchase decisions that can be complex and confusing and access to the highest quality products available—while minimizing the investment of my time.

Incidentally, one additional task is part of my weekly meal planning/grocery shopping routine. At this time, I also reconcile the previous week's cash. I add up the purchase receipts and the remaining cash to ensure that it roughly equals the amount available at the beginning of the week. (I've *never* had a problem in this regard.) Then I replenish the cash envelope, including a nontaxable reimbursement for my housekeeper's car expense.

The "Clean Shower" Approach

A new cleaning product is storming the market, as I write this. Based on the number of radio ads I've heard, the manufacturer must have a huge advertising budget. The idea is this: once you get your shower completely clean using conventional cleaning methods, you can maintain its pristine state just by spritzing the product once a day. If you follow this procedure, the ads promise, you'll never have to scrub your shower again.

While I can't vouch for the product (I've never tried it), I can vouch for the process. If organizing your household is like the unpleasant cleaning job that you'll only have to do once, a consciously designed household routine is the daily "spritz" that will keep everything running smoothly.

It's not necessary to implement every suggestion in this chapter. But the more that you can define your household routine—and the more household decisions you can eliminate—the more predictable the results that you'll achieve with your soon-to-be-hired housekeeper. One added bonus: your well-run household will attract the highest-caliber employees. Now let's talk about hiring.

8 Decide on Benefits

Do you remember *The Brady Bunch*? I was fascinated with that television show when I was in my early teens. I'm not sure what the appeal was then (Greg, maybe?), but now, as I watch the cable TV reruns with my kids, I'm struck by Carol Brady's incredible luck. Where did she ever find her terrific housekeeper, Alice?

The house was always spotless, Alice cooked three delicious meals a day, and she still had plenty of time to dispense pearls of wisdom to the Brady kids. She seemed like one of the family, and maybe she was—as far as we viewers could tell, she was never paid!

Here in the real world, there aren't many "Alices" offering their services, and they are available only at the highest salaries through the priciest agencies. But I'll bet that you can find a real-world version of "Alice" who is well qualified to take care of your household. By mapping out a hiring strategy, you'll increase your chances of finding your own personal "Alice."

If you've followed this book's advice, you've avoided the most common household help pitfall: beginning the hiring process too soon. So far, you've defined your future housekeeper's job including duties, number of hours, and work schedule (Chapters 5 and 7). You've figured out the wage that you'll offer by researching the going rate (Chapter 5).

Benefits You Can Offer	To a Housekeeper	To a Cleaning Service
A job description and instruction manual	Yes	Yes
Training	Yes	Yes
Defined work hours	Yes	Defined job duties
Prompt payment	Yes	Yes
Reimbursement of car expenses	Yes	No
Full pay, year round	Yes	No
Paid time off	Yes	No
Bonuses	Yes	Holiday bonus
Periodic reviews and raises	Yes	Usually initiated by service
Legally mandated benefits	Yes	Maybe

Before you begin searching for candidates, you need to iron out one final detail: the benefits you'll offer.

The Benefit of Benefits

When most of us hear the term "benefits," we think immediately of the insurance package that corporations typically provide to their employees. Most household employers don't provide insurance coverage (the Resources section lists some companies that sell individual policies at group rates, if you decide to offer this), but you can offer your housekeeper a number of attractive benefits that will cost you relatively little.

Once you decide which benefits you'll offer, be prepared to discuss them with the job candidates you interview. In the competition for good housekeepers, you will win if you can show job seekers that the salary you are offering, combined with the noncash benefits, put you way ahead of the field.

A Job Description and Instruction Manual

You've worked hard to identify exactly what your housekeeper's duties will be and devised an appropriate schedule. Having a well-defined job description is as advantageous to your future housekeeper as it is to you, so it's a benefit that you should emphasize to job seekers. Because household priorities are so personal, and because the work of the home is never done, without specific instructions, your employee can never really be sure if she's met your expectations. That can be demoralizing. On the contrary, when she is certain of what you expect, she can feel satisfaction in the job that she does for you.

During hiring, I always mention to job seekers that I have written a detailed instruction manual, and most people respond with delight. One of my former housekeepers, Yelena, told me how much she appreciated having everything written down. "Because you already made the schedule, I know what to do. I want to do a good job, and this helps me do it."

Training

While you won't be teaching your employee how to do housework (experience is a *must*), it is a major plus if you can spend some time initially helping her get up to speed. At a minimum, you should plan to walk your housekeeper through the work schedule at least once, be available for questions the first couple of weeks, and provide a mechanism for ongoing communication. (Chapter 11 covers training in more detail.)

Can you imagine the frustration of working for a boss who is never around and never gives you any feedback? Like well-written instructions, a promise to provide training gives a job candidate confidence that she'll have the information she needs to do the job you want her to do. Both training and written instructions are especially important if you plan to ask your employee to perform a variety of tasks beyond simple housecleaning.

Defined Work Hours

Along with the dozens of household employers I talked to while researching this book, I interviewed many nannies and housekeepers. Almost universally, disgruntled employees complained about unreasonable working hours.

Some complained about hours that were simply too long. One live-in nanny, for example, had to wake the children at 6 a.m., yet couldn't go to bed until after midnight because she slept on a hide-a-bed in the den, where her male employer liked to watch late-night TV.

Others complained about hours that were too short for the amount of work to be done. One housekeeper I know was paid for five hours of work daily, while being given up to seven hours of work to do. She was expected to work unpaid overtime until the work was complete. (See Chapter 10 for a discussion of fair labor practices.)

Still others complained about new duties being added with no adjustments made to the workload. After one family's teenage boy broke his leg, their cook was asked to drive him to daily physical therapy sessions, with no compensatory reduction in her cooking responsibilities.

If you pay your housekeeper by the hour, give her a list of expected tasks that can be reasonably accomplished during her normal working hours. To make sure your housekeeper stays busy, you can certainly give her a too-long list of tasks. Just be sure to arrange them in priority order and make it clear that you don't require her to complete everything on the list.

If you pay your housekeeper by the job (as is often done with weekly cleaning services), then expect to renegotiate the fee if you add tasks. Most housecleaners will perform an extra task on occasion without charge, but it's not fair to add tasks on a regular basis and expect them to be done for free.

If you can promise a set job description, with adjustments when priorities change, job candidates will feel assured of a predictable schedule, a reasonable workload, and payment for the hours they actually work.

Prompt Payment

Although legally you may be entitled to pay your housekeeper as infrequently as twice a month, with payments lagging the end of the pay period by as much as 10 days (labor laws vary by state), this much delay would be a financial hardship for most housekeepers. Why not promise your housekeeper a weekly paycheck, with payment covering all hours worked that week? Then, be scrupulous about writing paychecks on time.

I write my housekeeper a paycheck every Friday. To keeps things simple—to avoid recomputing paycheck deductions every week—and to provide my housekeeper with a predictable wage, we handle small amounts of time off informally. For example, if my housekeeper misses an hour of work one week because of a doctor's appointment, she might come to work 30 minutes earlier two days the following week.

Reimbursement of Car Expenses

If your housekeeper will be using her own car to run errands, reimburse her mileage costs. Although covering expenses that your employee has incurred on your behalf seems like an obvious business courtesy, it's rarely done: job candidates always act surprised and pleased when I tell them I plan to do so.

You can ask your housekeeper to log the miles she drives, and pay her an amount based on miles driven, for example, 30¢ per mile. A simpler approach, and the one I use, is to pay a flat amount each week, which is a generous approximation of what a per-mile amount would have been. This can be paid in cash, since the payment, as an expense reimbursement, is not subject to taxes. (In most cases, it will fall under the "deminimus fringe benefit" exclusion, spelled out in the IRS Code Section 132.)

Full Pay, Year Round

Once a housekeeper accepts a job with you, she has taken herself off the job market. If, like some employers, you ask her not to report to work when her services are not needed (for example, when you are on vacation), you force her into temporary unemployment, which is a great hardship. She experiences a loss of income, but is not free to look for a new job because she must be available to resume work when you return.

I recommend that you promise your housekeeper a steady income, both because it is fair and because your housekeeper will see it as a job benefit. And the wages that you pay during down times won't necessarily be lost. You can ask your housekeeper to do special projects, like spring cleaning, when you will be away. Of course, you also can ask her not to report, while still paying her for the hours missed.

If you hire a once-a-week cleaning service rather than a part-time or full-time housekeeper, it would be more reasonable to pay only for the weeks you actually receive service. For one thing, as an ongoing business, the person or company providing the housecleaning service is in a better position to fill in with another client when a timeslot opens up. For another, someone providing housecleaning services has presumably set her rates high enough to account for the occasional cancellation. (For the same reason, you would not offer to a cleaning service some of the other benefits mentioned in this section.)

If you are hiring a cleaning service, be sure to negotiate up front the circumstances under which cancellations are acceptable (vacation, for example, provided you give sufficient notice) and which are not (you had an urge to clean the house yourself that week).

Paid Time Off

There are three categories of paid time off you may wish to offer: holidays, vacation, and sick leave. I think it's best to follow the example of corporations that combine vacation and sick leave into one category, flexible time off. With that approach, any personal days off come out of one "bank," no matter what the reason. You avoid the problem of a healthy employee calling in sick just to use time to which she feels entitled, and you also avoid punishing a healthy, honest employee who never gets to enjoy her sick leave benefit.

Because household workers are notoriously short-term employees (83 percent of nannies last less than two years with a family,[1] and the statistics are probably comparable for housekeepers), you may wish to tie paid time off to your housekeeper's longevity in the job. For example, during her first year of employment, you can offer her a small number of paid holidays (five, for example) and a small amount of flexible time off (maybe two or three days). You can then promise to increase both of these numbers after one year.

During interviews, discuss with each job candidate whether she plans to take additional, unpaid, days off. If she travels to her native country to visit her family for six weeks each winter, for example, you want to find that out *before* you hire her!

If you will require your housekeeper to work on holidays, you should discuss that during interviews as well. You'll find that some job candidates are happy to work holidays, while others prefer to spend those days with their families. Of course, employees who work holidays should be paid a premium for that time. If your housekeeper won't work on holidays, you can plan in advance to make sure the most important tasks are accomplished by temporarily modifying that week's work schedule.

See Chapter 12 for a discussion of how to handle extended absences by your housekeeper.

Bonuses

As a simple "thank-you," you'll probably want to pay your housekeeper a modest annual holiday bonus. If the unemployment rate is very low and good job candidates are hard to attract, you may also want to offer a retention bonus, which is a lump sum paid at the end of six months or a year on the job.

Periodic Reviews and Raises

As your housekeeper becomes more attuned to your household, she will be more valuable to you. If you like her work, it is in your best interest to periodically increase her wages, both to acknowledge her value to you and to make sure your now-indispensable employee doesn't look around for a better position. At the time of hiring, you can tell your new housekeeper how frequently her wages will be reevaluated, typically every six months or a year. Chapter 12 discusses in detail the best ways to give employee feedback, both positive and negative.

Legally Mandated Benefits

Some types of insurance are so important that the government has created special programs and passed laws to require employers and employees to participate in those programs. The best known of these is Social Security. Participants in the Social Security program are entitled to retirement benefits, as well as payments if they or their dependents experience certain types of disability. Participants in the Medicare program are entitled to healthcare after age 65, or after experiencing certain categories of disability. Although not uniform nationwide, most states have created mandatory unemployment and disability insurance programs. Chapter 10 explains specifically how you are required to provide these benefits.

Participation in these programs is very important for your employee. When people of means experience health or job disruptions, their financial reserves can see them through rough times. But those with the fewest resources—and your housekeeper most likely fits into that category—are ill equipped to roll with life's most disastrous punches. Government insurance programs can be a lifeline in those circumstances.

The "Nanny Tax" Controversy

In 1993, President Bill Clinton nominated Zoe Baird for the position of attorney general. A great controversy erupted when it was discovered she had failed to pay the legally required employment taxes for her nanny. She withdrew her name for consideration. Since then, the topic of "nanny taxes" (mandatory participation in government insurance programs on behalf of household workers) has remained in the news.

We household employers are required to pay employment taxes for our nannies, housekeepers, cooks, maids, laundresses, and other domestic employees. Yet few of us pay the taxes, or are even fully aware of our obligations to do so. The reason? A handful of myths, misperceptions, and unfortunate realities.

"Nanny Tax" Myths, Misperceptions, and Realities

- The myth of the independent contractor
- The perception that the paperwork is too hard
- The perception that Social Security is a rip-off
- Lack of enforcement
- Demands of the marketplace

The Myth of the Independent Contractor

Most of us believe the mistaken notion that part-time employees can optionally choose to work as "independent contractors." This myth is reinforced by agencies that assure potential clients, "All of our workers are independents, so you don't have to worry about the taxes."

The fact is that IRS rules, not the worker or employer, determine who is an employee and who is an independent contractor. Here is what the IRS says on the topic:

"A household worker is your employee if you can control not only what work is done, but how it is done. If the worker is your employee, it does not matter whether the work is full time or part time, or that you hired the worker through an agency or from a list provided by an agency or association. It also does not matter whether you pay the worker on an hourly, daily, or weekly basis, or by the job.

"If only the worker can control how the work is done, the worker is not your employee but is self-employed. A self-employed worker usually provides his or her own tools and offers services to the general public in an independent business. If an agency provides the worker and controls what work is done and how it is done, the worker is not your employee.

"*Example 1.* You pay Betty Shore to babysit your child and do light housework 4 days a week in your home. Betty follows your specific instructions about household and child care duties. You provide the household equipment and supplies that Betty needs to do her work. Betty is your household employee.

"*Example 2.* You pay John Peters to care for your lawn. John also offers lawn care services to other homeowners in your neighborhood. He provides his own tools and supplies, and he hires and pays any helpers he needs. Neither John nor his helpers are your household employees."[2]

Weekly housecleaners exist in a murky gray area. Are they employees or independent contractors? Some cleaners run a business through which they offer a fairly standard service. During an initial visit to your home, after viewing its size and condition, they make a bid on the cost to clean your home. If they also supply all tools and cleaning products, as is typical of this type of service, it would be reasonable to treat them as independent contractors.

On the other hand, suppose you hire an individual to come to your home once a week for four hours. This person's duties primarily include cleaning, with needed supplies provided by you, but you have the option of asking her to spend some of her time doing laundry or cooking. (Cleaning services like those described in the preceding paragraph don't perform noncleaning tasks.) Your housecleaner is most likely an employee.

If you aren't sure whether the person you'll hire is an employee or independent contractor, you can read a more thorough explanation in IRS Publication 15-A, *Employer's Supplemental Tax Guide*. You can call 1 800-TAX-FORM to order a copy or read it on-line at *www.irs.ustreas.gov*. Or check with your tax advisor.

The Perception That the Paperwork Is Too Hard

It is certainly true that, in the past, the paperwork burden on household employers was unreasonable, because the government treated household employers the same as business employers. But the IRS has recently modified the tax rules to make the process much simpler, and most states have followed suit. The paperwork requirements are outlined in Chapter 10. Personally, I find them quite manageable, and Chapter 10 offers some suggestions for further streamlining the process. There are also services that will perform the necessary paperwork for you, for a fee. The Resources section lists a few of them.

The Perception That Social Security Is a Rip-Off

The benefits of participation in the Social Security system can seem tenuous to both you and your housekeeper come payday. Your employee's share of Social Security and Medicare combined is 7.65 percent of her gross pay. (You pay an equal amount.) That's more than $15 to be deducted from a $200 paycheck, a significant amount for someone whose finances are very tight.

But keep in mind the purpose of these programs: to provide a financial safety net for elderly Americans who may not have been able to build their own during their working years. Although the tax rate seems steep, low-income workers benefit disproportionally from these programs. Besides, Congress recognizes the unreasonable bite that taxes can take out of low-income workers' paychecks. That's why it has established the Earned Income Credit, which reduces the tax obligations of the working poor. (Chapter 10 explains the EIC further.)

Social Security payments were never intended to provide a comfortable retirement pension, simply a safety net. But those workers most in need of it can't benefit if they and their employers ignore payroll tax laws.

Lack of Enforcement

It is an unfortunate fact that the "nanny tax" laws are simply not enforced. The IRS has not made it a priority to crack down on this category of tax scofflaw (terminology that is harsh but accurate). As a result, these laws are widely ignored.

This oversight is distressing for three reasons. First, the U.S. Treasury misses out on an estimated $1.2 billion in revenue each year.[3] Second, domestic workers—members of society who are ill equipped to speak out for themselves—are cheated out of benefits to which they are legally entitled. And third, the few honest citizens who do comply are made to feel like chumps.

I've spoken to a few household employers who justify their lack of compliance as a form of civil disobedience. While I'm not convinced their motives are pure—their stance seems based more on convenience than on any moral conviction—I'm especially concerned because their tax dodge harms the weak.

Lack of enforcement and the resulting lack of compliance do not invalidate the "nanny tax" laws. As our mothers used to say, "Just because everybody else is doing something doesn't make it right."

Demands of the Marketplace

One of the consequences of "everybody else is doing it" is that those who do comply with the laws may be at a disadvantage when hiring. If you offer a candidate $10 per hour "on the books" while another employer is offering $10 per hour "off the books," the simple fact may be that she can't afford to take your job, because of her lower net earnings.

During hiring (which Chapter 9 discusses in depth), you'll try to decide whether you want to *buy* a candidate's housekeeping services and also try to *sell* her on the idea of coming to work for you. That's why it's essential to be able to identify and explain all of the job benefits you are offering, including the importance of participating in government insurance programs.

Once you've convinced a candidate that it's in her best interest to work "on the books," she will probably be willing to split the wage differential with you—accepting lower net pay than she was expecting, if you agree to increase the gross pay slightly to at least partially offset her payroll deductions. In our $10 per hour example, the candidate might be willing to accept $11 per hour instead, to partially offset deductions for Social Security, Medicare, and state disability insurance, as well as income tax withholding.

Why It Pays to Pay the "Nanny Tax"

The negative image of the "nanny tax" laws notwithstanding, compliance with them will benefit both you and your housekeeper in many ways. Let's look at those benefits.

You Are Protected

Despite the widespread flouting of the "nanny tax" laws, taxpayers are still held responsible for paying them, with potentially disastrous consequences if they don't. Because household employment tax paperwork is now incorporated into the personal tax return, and you sign your tax return under penalty of perjury, if caught cheating, you'd owe penalties and interest, as well as back taxes. Complying with the tax laws ensures that you'll never be vulnerable to the whims of a disgruntled ex-employee who decides to turn you in to the IRS.

Compliance with the "nanny tax" laws may protect you from other legal problems, too. If, at some point in the future, a former employee tries to collect government benefits, you could be liable to pay the benefits if the required taxes were not paid. In his book *Employing Household Help: How to Avoid Tax and Legal Problems*, Chad R. Turner tells the story of a family who employed an older man to provide companionship care for their aging mother, off the books, for 15 years. When he retired and tried unsuccessfully to collect Social Security benefits, he sued his former employers to fund his retirement and pay his attorney fees. The predicament ended up costing them far more than if they had complied with the laws in the first place.[4]

On a more positive note, a job candidate's willingness to be paid "on the books" tells you something about who she is. You know that she is not an illegal immigrant or a welfare or disability cheat and, furthermore, sees herself as a responsible, honest participant in society. Because it's so easy to cheat the system, it speaks volumes when someone chooses not to.

Your Employee Is Protected

Besides enjoying the benefits of participating in government insurance programs, as discussed above, your housekeeper will reap many other rewards if she legally documents her earnings. By cooperating with her employer in following the tax laws and by submitting annual tax returns, a newcomer to this country can begin to establish a financial identity.

After a year of working for me, one of my former housekeepers was finally able to prove to the Immigration and Naturalization Service (INS) that she had the financial means to support an additional child. After she submitted copies of her tax return, the INS granted immigration permission to her young son, who still resided with his grandmother in their native country.

Another former housekeeper recently contacted me for a copy of her three-year-old W-2. She was applying for a loan and needed to document her income history. Because she had been working "on the books," beginning with her year of employment with me, she was able to do so.

Even some of your housekeeper's family members may benefit from her full participation in the American tax system. If her immigration was "sponsored," someone accepted legal and financial responsibility for her, most likely a relative. Their responsibility only ends when she becomes a citizen or has paid taxes for 10 years.[5]

Just as a job candidate's willingness to be paid "on the books" tells *you* something about *her*, it tells *her* something about *herself*, too. Some rungs on the ladder of success are largely symbolic. Why not encourage your housekeeper to take the step that symbolizes her participation in mainstream society?

■ ■ ■

So now you know exactly what you need your housekeeper to do, and what you can offer her. Next, let's talk about how to find great job candidates.

9 Hire the Right Person

Finally—after all your preparation, it's time to start the search for your new employee. If you're like most people, all along you've been wondering, "But where do I find a good housekeeper?" You will rely heavily on your own instincts throughout the hiring process. But following the steps laid out in this chapter will provide you with the best opportunities to use that good sense.

If you've skipped ahead to this chapter because you think this is where all the "good stuff" is, be careful about plunging into hiring prematurely. Yes, this chapter offers some crucial hiring advice. But if you want to hire someone who is right for your household, be sure to first spend some time thinking about exactly what you're looking for.

Finding Job Candidates

Shortly after I finished college with a degree in computer science, I went to work for a large computer manufacturer as an engineer in its research and development department. One of my most interesting duties was to help interview new college graduates who were being considered for entry-level positions with the company.

Every spring, our department interviewed dozens of candidates, typically hiring only three or four of the batch. Although each candidate had a strong resume, only a few were the right fit for our work environment and corporate culture.

Housekeepers aren't computer engineers, and I don't apply the same standards when interviewing them. However, I find that, as with engineers, it pays to have several job candidates vying for one position. The bigger the pool of candidates you can consider, the better the odds that you'll find a housekeeper who's the right fit for your household.

There are several ways to find job candidates: agencies; referrals (word of mouth); job boards at colleges, churches, and resource centers; "growing" your own; and classified newspaper ads. The likely success or failure of each of those options depends on the type of help you want to hire (cleaning service vs. housekeeper, for example), the resources available in your area, and luck. Let's look at each of the options.

Agencies

Contacting an agency strikes most people as the easiest way to find a good housekeeper. Occasionally, an agency *is* the easiest solution to the hiring problem, if the agency is a good one and you don't mind paying the fee. The difficulty is that it can be harder to find a good agency than it is to find good job candidates.

It's important to distinguish among agencies that are actually placement services, those that provide temporary workers, and those that furnish housecleaning services. The first type, placement services, work like most nanny agencies do. They supply a few well-screened job candidates, whom you can then interview. If you decide to hire one of the candidates, you pay the agency a fee, typically the equivalent of your housekeeper's first two months' salary. There may be an up-front fee, as well. Not only are these fees hefty, but the job candidates who are sufficiently qualified to approach placement-service agencies also command a fairly high salary. If cost doesn't matter, using this type of agency can be the right approach for you.

The second type of agency, one that provides temporary workers, is more questionable. It makes money by charging you one hourly rate and paying the workers a different, substantially lower, rate. (As an example, I paid one agency $13 per hour, which in turn paid the housekeeper $6 per hour.) In my experience, workers employed by these agencies are not well screened, typically have limited experience, and can be unreliable. After all, why would well-qualified individuals work for such low rates?

The fact that you pay the agency and the agency pays the worker complicates your ability to comply with the "nanny tax" laws. Despite what the agency may claim, a worker from such an agency is your employee. One agency assured me during my initial phone inquiry that it took care of the workers' taxes, then sent a form for me to sign indicating that I understood that *I* was responsible!

Advantages and Disadvantages of Recruiting Methods

Agencies

Advantages: Easy if good agency, good way to hire cleaning service

Disadvantages: Poor quality help if bad agency, expensive

Referrals

Advantages: Can be easy, person comes with recommendation

Disadvantages: Offend friend if don't hire referral, few candidates to choose from, can be hard to find available housekeepers

Tips: Ask housekeepers of your friends, not just friends; best for hiring housecleaner

Job Boards

Advantage: Candidates usually have low pay expectations

Disadvantages: Response can be slow, candidates not always experienced

Growing Your Own

Advantage: Employee is a known quantity

Disadvantage: Opportunity is rare

Newspaper Ads

Advantage: Lots of candidates to choose from

Disadvantages: Disruptive if large response, can be expensive

---

Although you might want to use such an agency in a pinch, it's probably best not to use it to hire a long-term employee. These agencies charge a steep premium, but provide very little service in return.

The third type of agency supplies housecleaning services and employs the workers who do the cleaning. The many national maid service chains fit into this category. If you are only looking for a weekly cleaning service, such an agency may be the best bet for you. You'll pay a premium, compared to hiring the worker directly. But you might find the extra expense worthwhile, given the relatively few hours of service, because it allows you to avoid the "nanny tax" paperwork. Be sure to confirm with the agency, in writing, that it is the workers' employer and has complied with all the relevant employment laws.

You can find agencies listed in the Yellow Pages under "House Cleaning" or in ads in local family publications.

Referrals

Wouldn't it be great if you could just ask around a bit to find the perfect housekeeper? Sometimes you can. If you're looking for someone to clean once a week, talk to everyone you know. Chances are you'll soon find a cleaner who is both qualified and has a suitable timeslot available for you.

But if you're looking for a housekeeper for many hours each week, or for someone who has special skills such as cooking, direct referrals won't be as fruitful. After all, what are the chances that someone with the skills you need who is available during the hours you need help is coincidentally employed during *different* hours by someone you know? Instead, the indirect method might be a better bet: ask your friends' housekeepers if they have any housekeeper friends who are looking for work. Using this method, my friend Alison found a terrific nanny/housekeeper in one phone call.

Job Boards

Many churches and community colleges host "job boards" where you can post a help-wanted notice. In addition, some communities have resource centers serving the needy and maintain job listings for their clients who are seeking work.

While good matches are often made through job boards, there are a few disadvantages. First, there can be a delay between the time you contact the organization and when your job opening is actually posted, which can slow your search. Second, because job openings are read by all job seekers, not just experienced housekeepers, you must screen candidates carefully to be sure they have relevant experience. Third, a candidate who looks for work through such a job board may well be in a transitional phase in her life and could be less than reliable; again, careful screening is required.

Nevertheless, the price is right; the use of such job boards is typically free. And resource centers may permit you to peruse its listing of job seekers, allowing you to contact only those candidates who appear on paper to be most qualified. To find such centers, look in the Yellow Pages under "Social Service Organizations."

Growing Your Own

Occasionally, you may hire a worker for one task and like her so well that you expand her responsibilities and working hours, effectively "growing your own" housekeeper. Sandra hired Ruth to clean her house once a week. At first, Sandra and her young daughter, Amy, made plans to leave the house when Ruth was there. But Amy was fascinated with Ruth and began to ask to stay home during Ruth's cleaning hours, and the two developed a mutual fondness.

When Sandra's second child was born, it became clear that she would need more help. So she asked Ruth to come a few days a week instead of only one half-day. Not only did Ruth take over most of the laundry and cleaning chores, but she began babysitting as well so that Sandra, an at-home mom, could have a few child-free hours each week.

Not all housecleaners are qualified to do every household task, and not all housecleaners want to do other tasks, but if you already employ someone you like, growing your own housekeeper may be an option for you.

Newspaper Ads

I have had the best success finding good job candidates through classified newspaper ads. Advertising is the second most expensive way to find potential employees, after agencies, but it's the best way to give yourself a good selection of well-qualified candidates from which to choose.

If you live in a small- to medium-sized city, you may have only one local newspaper to use, but if you live in a large metropolitan area, there may be a couple of options. First, there is probably a metropolitan newspaper with a wide geographic distribution, including the areas where job seekers are most likely to live. Ads are likely to be pricey, but will generate a large response.

Second, there may be several local weekly papers, each serving a small community within the larger area. Ads in these weeklies are usually very reasonably priced and will generate a small but high-quality response. Experienced housekeepers know that the best household jobs are offered in wealthy communities, so they check the classifieds in those communities' newspapers. If you don't live in a community that's known for its wealth, advertise in the newspaper of the wealthy community that's nearest to where you live.

Because you pay by the line, choose the wording for your ad carefully. To save yourself unnecessary phone conversations, include information that candidates can use to disqualify themselves where appropriate. Mention nonnegotiable items in your ad—for example, the working hours and the fact that experience and references are required. *Never* mention the wage being offered. If you do, you will be deluged with phone calls from unqualified job seekers who are currently being paid a lower wage. I have used the three-line ad in the sample below to find experienced housekeepers who are available during the hours I need help, and who are prepared, when they call, to supply me with the names of references. As you can see, abbreviations can save you space.

Because ad rates are lower in a community newspaper, you can afford to be wordier there. Use the extra space to describe your household. Job candidates may have preferences regarding the presence of children, the formality of the household, and so on. The four-line ad below gives an example of this type of ad.

Most classified departments offer the best value on ads placed for a two-week minimum; cancellation and a partial refund are typically available once the position is filled. I recommend allowing your ad to run for a full two weeks, to give you time to gather a good sampling of the available candidates. Even if you do hire someone before the two weeks end, allow the ad to run and continue to collect names and phone numbers. If the person you hire does not work out for some reason, you won't have to start over again at square one.

Three-Line Ad Sample

HOUSEKEEPER/Cook M-F,
2-6pm, exper'd., refs. own
car, Engl. Call 321 555-1234

Four-Line Ad Sample

HOUSEKEEPER/Cook needed 20 hrs per
week 2-6pm weekdays. Family of 4, well
organized household. Must have exp,
refs, own car, English. Call 321 555-1234

Screening

Once you've found yourself a pool of job candidates, you'll decide which one is best for your job. How will you know? Four steps of screening—phone screening, reference checking, background checking, and interviewing—will give you the answer. Think of each of these steps as a filter. As you progress through screening, you'll "filter out" candidates who are unsuited for your job, leaving you, at the end, with one or more gold nuggets.

To help yourself recognize the gold nuggets, start by making a checklist of all the qualities you want a candidate to have. For example, what special skills should she have (ironing, cooking)? Will she need a car to run errands? What hours will she need to work? Should she be available to work holidays? Does she need to be able to read and write in English?

Throughout the screening process, not only will you be asking these key questions, but you will also seek information that tells you about the job candidate's character and how well-suited she is, temperamentally, to working for you.

You will want to find out:

- *Why did she leave her last job?*

  Was the termination of her last job a normal transition (she just moved into the area, the children in the family she worked for grew up and left home) or was there some difficulty?

- *Why is she looking for work?*

  A job candidate should be hungry, but not starving, for work. If a candidate depends on your paycheck for her next meal, she won't have the resources to deal with life's minor challenges—for example, her car breaking down. On the other extreme, if a candidate is being supported by her wealthy uncle and is looking for a job to make a show of being responsible, she'll quit working for you (or simply not show up at work for a day or two) whenever an interesting opportunity arises.

- *How stable is her life? Will she be reliable?*

  What is the big picture of her life? No matter how well-intentioned she is, a candidate who goes to school full time, has a young child with chronic ear infections (translation: lots of trips to the doctor), and is in the middle of a bitter custody battle with her ex-husband (translation: lots of time in court or her lawyer's office) will not show up at work often. Believe me, I've been there. (See "Fair Hiring Practices" in Chapter 10 for more information.)

- *Does she enjoy/want to do housework?*

  Is the candidate looking for just any job or specifically a housekeeper job? Just as some people love sales and others love accounting, housework holds a certain appeal for only some people. Make sure the person you hire is one of them. And listen to her words carefully: being *willing* to do housework is different from enjoying it.

- *Does she have relevant experience?*

  My biggest hiring mistakes were "crossovers"—people who worked in related fields who convinced me that they could easily and happily do housework. Eldercare, even though it includes light housekeeping, is primarily a nursing career. The emphasis is on caretaking, not on housework. And the household chores in a family household are substantially greater than those in a household with one elderly, bed-ridden adult. I made the mistake—twice!—of hiring someone whose only experience was in eldercare. They were caring and compassionate people, but did lousy housework.

  By the same token, nannies who have done light housekeeping as part of their job duties are typically not prepared for an all-housework workload. The work is more physically demanding than they're used to and it lacks the nurturing component they probably crave. Learn from my mistakes: hire only an experienced housekeeper.

- *Does she have references?*

  Never hire anyone without talking to her references. And don't waste time talking to a candidate if she can't supply you with at least one, preferably two. Because you can't tell which excuses are phony, don't make exceptions if a candidate tells you, "My former employer will be traveling for the next three months."

- *Is she available long term?*

  Household workers are not known for their job longevity, but why create a problem for yourself? Is the job candidate a student who has only one year left before she graduates? Is she working to save money to move to Arizona and only has $500 to go? Or is she looking for a long-term situation?

- *Does she have the legal right to work? Is she willing to work on the books?*

Ask these questions early to avoid wasting time. I once spent several hours talking to a candidate on the phone, checking her references, and interviewing her in person. I loved her. I offered her the job and she accepted. We shook hands on the deal as I mentioned that I would be paying her on the books. Startled, she informed me that she had to be paid in cash, since she was on welfare.

This was no struggling uneducated mom, trying to pull herself off the welfare rolls. It turns out she was a chemical engineer who had calculated that she could earn just as much by being on welfare, collecting medical benefits, and working "under the table," as she could by working in her chosen profession. And she found housework far less stressful than chemical engineering. I'm glad I didn't inadvertently contribute to her illicit lifestyle.

- *Do you like her? Does she fit into the mood and environment of your household?*

What kinds of people do you get along with best? Will a very quiet person make you uncomfortable because you'll have trouble interpreting her silences? Will you find a chatty person annoying, simply one more emotional demand on you? Would you prefer an employee who remains unobtrusively in the background or helps create an upbeat mood in your house? Chances are you'd be comfortable with a wide range of personality types, but if you find one extreme or another particularly difficult, you should take that into consideration when hiring.

If you have pets, make sure that they are a match with your housekeeper. Even if you have only one small cat who is sure to hide whenever a stranger is around, check to make sure your housekeeper doesn't have a cat allergy. Dogs are more problematic. Not only should you check for allergies, but you should also have a plan for relocating an inside dog while an employee is there. If the dog is kept outside, can your housekeeper get to all necessary work areas without having to confront the dog? Some candidates might feel an aversion to working around more exotic pets, like snakes or tarantulas, even if they are safely caged. Save yourself time by checking for pet compatibility early in the screening process.

The Phone Screen

Before you meet any job candidate in person, you will speak with her on the phone. This is true whether you've found her through an agency, a job board, a referral, or a newspaper ad. The phone screen allows you to weed out obviously unsuitable candidates, before you've spent too much time with them.

If you've listed yourself with a job board or run a newspaper ad, be prepared to respond to a fairly high volume of phone calls. You will want to quickly determine two things: whether the caller is interested in the job *you* are offering and whether the caller meets the basic job requirements.

To accomplish the first objective, you can give each caller a 30-second spiel that expands on your newspaper ad. For example, I would tell callers responding to the ads shown above, "I am looking for a housekeeper-cook to come to my home every day, Monday through Friday, from 2 to 6 p.m. You would be doing housecleaning, laundry, ironing, a small amount of grocery shopping and errands, cooking dinners four nights a week, baking once a week, and doing daily tidy-up like emptying the dishwasher and watering plants. I live in Pleasantville."

Some callers will say something like, "It sounds great, but I can't work on Wednesdays," or "I can do all of that except cook." Tell them you're sorry, but those are the requirements of the job, and move on. A few will cut the conversation short because they live too far away. Other callers will say, "That's just what I'm looking for." Continue talking to them, to determine whether they meet the basic job requirements.

So that I don't forget anything important, I like to use a phone screen worksheet that lists all of the important requirements, in checklist form, and prompts me to ask other important questions. An example follows.

You can ask candidates about each requirement one by one, or converse more informally. I like to start by asking an open-ended question such as, "Tell me about yourself and your work history." In most cases, you'll find out most of what you need to know by her response; you can ask specific questions to fill in any blanks. If the caller seems shy or can't guess what she should tell you, you can get her started talking by asking something more specific, such as, "Where are you working now and why are you looking for a new position?"

Phone Screen

Name _____

Address _____

Telephone(s) _____

Current situation _____

_____

Why seeking job _____

Current pay/pay requirements _____

Job requirements:

Legal status _____

OK to pay on books _____

Has reliable car _____

Can cook _____

Likes housework _____

Has references _____

Experienced _____

Available PMs _____

Can read English _____

Available long term _____

Notes (personality, enthusiasm, communication skills) _____

_____

_____

_____

_____

_____

_____

_____

_____

_____

_____

_____

_____

_____

A give-and-take conversation puts callers at ease. As you are learning about the candidate, you can also tell her more about your household. For example, I always mention that I will provide written daily instructions, that I have two school-age children, that I work at home, and that our meals tend to be fairly simple, prepared mostly with fresh ingredients. By the end of the conversation, you and the caller will both know whether you should proceed further.

Be sure to find out the caller's current pay rate or salary expectations. You shouldn't commit to a pay rate yet, but you want to find out whether her pay expectations are out of reach. If the caller presses you, you can say something like, "I was planning to offer something in your current pay range," assuming that you are.

If you are looking for a housekeeper with good English skills, you shouldn't necessarily feel dissuaded by a caller with a heavy accent. An accent does not imply an ignorance of language, and telephone communication is more difficult than that done face to face. However, if a caller is phoning on behalf of someone else (because of poor language skills), you should insist that the candidate phone personally.

Before you hang up, assuming you wish to proceed, the candidate should give you the name of a reference or two and should describe the job she did for those references. If possible, the reference jobs should be very similar to the job you are offering. For example, if your housekeeper will cook, you should talk to at least one family for whom she has cooked. Housecleaning references alone will not tell you enough about the candidate's ability to do general housekeeping tasks. Again, you can use a worksheet, like the one below, to record this information.

If the caller says that she has references, but that she doesn't have their phone numbers, politely invite her to find the numbers and call you back. Then don't be surprised if you never hear from her again. If the caller says that she has a written reference, thank her, but tell her that you'll also need to speak to the person who wrote the letter. Then stick to your guns. If the reference-giver is unavailable for phone calls, there is probably a good reason for that. Employers who fire their housekeepers sometimes give them a positive reference letter to ease the departure, but would be reluctant to repeat such praise over the phone.

I was secretly amused by one caller who claimed that her credentials were impeccable, because she was formerly employed by several

---

Reference Check

Candidate name _____

- -

Reference name _____

Telephone(s) _____

Term of employment _____

Job responsibilities (per candidate) _____

_____

Job responsibilities (per reference) _____

_____

Comments _____

_____

_____

_____

_____

_____

_____

_____

_____

- -

Reference name _____

Telephone(s) _____

Term of employment _____

Job responsibilities (per candidate) _____

_____

Job responsibilities (per reference) _____

_____

Comments _____

_____

_____

_____

_____

_____

_____

---

celebrities. Yet, over the course of several phone conversations, she wasn't able to produce a single phone number! She tried to distract me by calling me "honey," telling me how nice I sounded, and expressing her strong desire to work for me, but I wasn't fooled—I noticed at the end of each exchange, I still didn't have a way to verify her claims.

Another candidate also claimed to have worked for a celebrity, but was unwilling to give me his phone number, professing concern for his privacy. I believed that she had worked for him, but because she wasn't even willing to have *him* call *me* (thus avoiding the need to give me his private phone number), I concluded she had some ambivalence about working for me. I was proven right when she decided to go to work in her husband's security business.

Reference Checking

Although most candidates will request an interview at this point, it is too early to invite anyone to your home. The next step in screening is to check the references of all the candidates who pass the phone screen, which may be a small percentage of the job seekers who contact you. The purpose of reference checking is to verify the candidate's claims about her work history, find out about her reliability and the quality of her work, and identify any potential red flags.

When you contact each reference, introduce yourself, say that you are calling because so-and-so had given his or her name as a job reference, and ask if he or she has a few minutes to chat. No references have ever refused to speak with me, and some have gone out of their way to talk to me, even returning calls long distance while traveling on business.

To break the ice, you might simply ask the reference to describe the candidate's job duties and how long she worked there. Be sure to find out why the job ended, too. I recommend that you ask explicitly whether the reference feels the candidate is trustworthy and reliable.

You should try to find out how well the candidate performed the types of tasks that you will be asking her to do. Ask specific questions related to your job requirements. If English is not the candidate's first language, you can ask the reference how well she understands written and spoken instructions. If your housekeeper will cook, ask the reference specifically whether she is able to follow written recipes.

Expect positive comments, since the candidate wouldn't have given this reference if she expected otherwise. You will have to "listen between the lines" to uncover any potential problems. Other than explicitly negative comments, things to listen for include:

Very careful or specific wording.

If the reference says, "The quality of the work that she *did* do was very high," you should question him or her further. Is the reference trying to say that the candidate works very slowly? Is unreliable? Refuses to do certain tasks?

Faint praise.

If a reference tells you, "The work that she did was okay," inquire further. Every candidate will have her strengths and weaknesses. You want to identify the weaknesses of the candidates you are considering and decide which ones you can live with. Maybe the reference was delighted with the housework the candidate did for her, but not some of the childcare. If your job doesn't require childcare, this won't matter. However, if the reference says that the candidate requires strong direction and needs to be prodded to complete her work, you'll probably want to steer clear.

An overemphasis on one quality.

If the reference talks only about the candidate's reliability, is he or she trying to avoid saying something bad about her work, or is the candidate simply so reliable that it's hard for the reference to think of anything else to say? It never hurts to ask clarifying questions. Sometimes he or she wants to avoid saying anything negative. Sometimes ambiguous comments are simply the reference's communication style.

Comments that just don't add up.

I once talked at length with a reference who had nothing but glowing comments about the candidate. Several times the reference told me, "We love her like a daughter. We just hated to see her go." I didn't understand why the reference (who said she still needed a housekeeper) would allow such a gem to quit, so I finally asked her about that. She explained that the candidate had a violent ex-boyfriend who was stalking her. Because he even followed her to work, the reference was worried about the safety of her family and had to fire the candidate. But she really wanted me to hire her because she hated the thought of the young woman being out of a job!

If you can't speak to a candidate's references, because they are out of town, for example, or don't return your phone calls, do not proceed to the next step. Without speaking to a candidate's references, you lack important information about her. You can ask the candidate to help you contact the reference or give you alternative names. In the meantime, continue to screen other candidates.

One more comment about references: if you found your potential housekeeper through a referral, you may wish to ask for a second reference, in addition to the friend who gave you the referral. Because your friend might see herself in more of a matchmaker role and not strictly as a job reference, she might oversell the candidate. You might also feel uncomfortable asking probing questions of your friend if you get the sense that she is feeling protective toward the housekeeper. A second reference will solve this dilemma.

Background Checking

By the time a candidate has passed the phone screen and you have spoken with her references, you have a pretty good idea of who that person is. You may not need to run a formal background check. Frankly, I have never done so and have never regretted my decision. However, if the housekeeper will be also caring for your children, you probably want to err on the side of caution. (Never use a background check to find out whether bad "vibes" about the candidate have foundation. If you have concerns that you just can't put your finger on, simply don't hire that person and keep looking.)

Background checks can answer three main questions: whether the candidate has credit problems that might make her especially vulnerable to temptation, whether the candidate has a good driving record (important if she will be chauffeuring your kids), and whether the candidate has a criminal record.

The candidate herself can do the research if you only want driving and credit information. She can request a copy of her driving record at the local motor vehicles department. She can get a copy of her own credit report by calling one of the large credit reporting agencies; the Resources section lists phone numbers.

If you want to research the candidate's criminal background, however, you will need help. A number of services, listed in the Resources section, will check the background of potential childcare providers, for a fee. You can also hire a private investigator to do the checks for you; look in the Yellow Pages under "Investigators." You will need the candidate's agreement to investigate her background. Contact a service early so that you are ready with the necessary permission forms when you meet a candidate you like.

There are some actions that you can take to minimize your risk against theft. If you give a key to your housekeeper, tell her not to label it with your address and never to give it away. You can install a second lock on each door, one that doesn't work with the house key, so that when you are at home, you can lock out intruders who may have a key.

Always lock up large amounts of cash or valuable jewelry. Be especially cautious if you have not personally screened and interviewed the cleaner—for example, if you've used a temporary agency for short-term help, if a substitute for your regular, trusted, cleaner has been sent, or if you've hired someone through a word-of-mouth referral and have not done a thorough screening. In these cases, you might want to stay home during the cleaning and observe the cleaner as much as possible.

Make sure your homeowner's or renter's insurance policy is up to date. If you are a victim of a theft, even if you aren't sure who the perpetrator is, your insurance company will compensate you for your loss once you have filed a police report. In contrast, housecleaning agencies that offer "bonding" or theft insurance may be giving a false sense of security. In most cases, these policies only pay out once the housecleaner has been convicted of the theft, which may prove difficult if there are no witnesses. There are often dollar limits associated with these policies, as well.

If you own valuable collectibles, you may also be concerned about breakage. Accidents do happen, and it is unreasonable to expect a low-income employee to be held financially accountable in such cases. Besides, it may even be illegal in your state to require a household employee to pay for accidental breakage, as it is in California. Regular homeowner's and renter's policies don't normally cover breakage, so why not insure your valuables under a personal articles policy? You can also ask your housekeeper not to handle or dust your valuables if you are unduly concerned.

Interviewing

You will interview only those candidates who have successfully "passed" the phone screen and reference check. You may wish to postpone background checking until after the interview because it can be expensive and will require the candidate's consent.

As was mentioned in Chapter 8, during the hiring process you'll be making a "buy" decision (whether to hire the candidate) while also attempting to "sell" the candidate on the idea of working for you. Because your previous steps have given you most of the information you will need to make your "buy" decision, the interview will be heavily weighted toward "sell" mode.

To facilitate the "sales" process, plan to present your household at its best. Although you're hiring a housekeeper because you need help, you don't want to create the impression that she will have to fight through mountains of overripe laundry, moldy dishes, and tumbleweed-sized dustballs her first day on the job. Hire a cleaning service from the Yellow Pages for an emergency clean-up, if you need to, and reduce clutter to a minimum.

Depending on whether your housekeeper will also care for your children, you may or may not wish to have them present. Because normally well-behaved children have the capacity for ill-timed "meltdowns," and the presence of children can make adult conversation disjointed even in the best of circumstances, I recommend keeping children out of the picture at first. If the housekeeper will care for your children, you will undoubtedly want to have them meet, but you can schedule a second interview, after you have approved her based on all of the job criteria not related to childcare.

First Impressions

The beginning of the interview will tell you most of what you need to know to finalize your "buy" decision. The candidate demonstrates her reliability and professionalism by how she arrives. Is she prompt? (I am impressed by a candidate who arrives early and waits in her car until the appointed time.) Is her personal grooming acceptable? Does she have a pleasant demeanor?

You will also need to assess whether the candidate is up to the physical challenges of housework. You are not subject to the Americans with Disabilities Act (see Chapter 10), but even if you were, you would not be obligated to hire an employee who is physically incapable of fulfilling the requirements of the job.

Dana hired an obese housekeeper/nanny, Monique, who was supposed to do housework while the kids napped or watched their daily video ration. Instead, the housework did not get done because Monique needed to rest during the kids' down time, and the kids ended up watching an inordinate amount of TV because she rarely had the energy to take them outside to play. Dana had formerly employed an overweight nanny whom she loved, so she was eager to overlook Monique's limitations. In retrospect, Dana admitted, Monique's difficulty getting out of an armchair during the interview was a red flag that she should have heeded.

Out of a desire to avoid age discrimination, I also mistakenly hired a housekeeper who couldn't do the work. She had volunteered over the phone that she was in her early sixties, but I didn't become concerned until the interview, when she could barely keep up with me as I showed her around the house. She quit after six weeks, having rarely been able to complete what I considered to be a minimal workload.

The Nitty-Gritty

Once you've invited the candidate inside and made her comfortable, you should give her a concrete idea of what her work day will be like. If you have written an instruction manual, you can show it to her at this point, as well as any recipes that you will ask her to follow.

If you have doubts about the candidate's comfort with the English language, you can watch her reaction to this written material. Although you won't take the time right then to have her read the instructions through in detail, it's a good sign if she seems comfortable skimming them and asks one or two intelligent questions about them. You might be surprised by some heavily accented candidates' comfort with written English—the language is easier to read than to speak. On the other hand, if the candidate appears to have no interest in reading the instructions, you can ask her to read part of them aloud to you, as a way to test her abilities.

Next, give her a tour of your house, commenting on particular areas as you go. For example, when I am interviewing a housekeeper and we get to the children's bedrooms, I always point out that the children are responsible for putting away their own toys and dirty clothes and that she will be responsible for doing their laundry, changing their sheets, and dusting and vacuuming their rooms.

If you have pets, introduce them to the candidate. Make sure she is comfortable with the animals (and vice versa) and understands and agrees to any special arrangements you've made for the pets. One housecleaner didn't take seriously instructions never to start work early and ended up cornered by a very protective 140-pound Newfoundland whose owners had not yet removed him from the house!

During your house tour, the candidate will probably ask questions or make comments that give you a sense of how positively or negatively she is reacting to your household. If not, you can ask leading questions like, "Does this seem like the type of household you like to work in?" By the time you finish your house tour, you should have a good sense of whether there is a fit between you and this candidate. You may even be ready to make a hiring decision.

Concluding the Visit

If you know that you won't be hiring the candidate, you can end the interview gracefully by saying that you have a few more people to interview and that you will call her with your decision in a few days. Then do so, saying simply that you found someone else whom you felt was better qualified.

If you still have questions or definitely like the candidate, invite her to sit down with you for a chat. Then, ask any remaining questions you have, and invite her to ask questions, too. If you haven't already presented the list of benefits that you plan to offer (which you identified in Chapter 8), now is the time to do so.

If you have more candidates to interview, you can cordially end the visit with a promise to call her in a few days. In that case, you can make the offer over the phone. If you want to schedule a second interview so your housekeeper can meet your children, now would be the time to do so. Of course, you will only involve your children if you definitely like the candidate.

If you are ready to hire the candidate, you can make an offer on the spot. If you wish to formally check her background, you can make an offer contingent on satisfactory results and have her fill out the necessary paperwork at the conclusion of the interview.

The moment that you make a job offer and your future housekeeper accepts is probably the most exciting one in your relationship. All of your preparations have resulted in finding someone who is right for your household. Your new housekeeper can tell that yours is a well-managed household and is looking forward to working in it.

To capitalize on these good feelings, and to show your housekeeper that you intend to keep your promises and expect her to follow through on hers, you can give her an employment letter within her first week on the job. This letter confirms the terms of her employment (wage, hours, duties, and so on) and reiterates the benefits that you promised to provide. A sample appears below.

Sample Employment Letter

<your name>
<your address>

<date>
<housekeeper's name>
<housekeeper's address>

Dear <housekeeper's name>:

The following is a letter of understanding describing the terms of your employment.

1. You will work 20 hours per week at my home, from 2:00 p.m. until 6:00 p.m. each day, Monday through Friday.

2. Your duties will include grocery shopping, cooking, baking, laundry, ironing, bed making, cleaning, tidying, and running errands.

3. General daily instructions have been provided to you. In addition, each Monday you will be given a shopping list, the menu plan for the week, and a list of special projects, if any. I will leave cash, which you will use for the dry cleaning and grocery shopping. Please bring the receipts back to me.

4. I welcome your questions. I plan to spend time training you during the initial employment period.

5. You will be paid $11.00 per hour.

6. Payday will be each Friday and will cover the hours worked the preceding week. Along with a check for the net amount owed to you, I will give you a statement showing hours worked, gross wages, deductions taken, and net wages.

7. You will receive $5.00 cash per week for gas. This will not be taxed.

8. You will be paid for five holidays during the year. You can let me know later which holidays you would like to take. The major holidays this year are as follows:

    Memorial Day—Monday, May 25

    Independence Day—Wednesday, July 4

    Labor Day—Monday, September 7

    Thanksgiving Day—Thursday, November 26

    Christmas Day—Friday, December 25

    New Year's Day—Friday, January 1

9. When we are on vacation, you will be paid your full salary, even though your duties will be reduced during that time.

10. You have been given a key to our house. Although you may label it in some way (to identify it to yourself), please do not put our address on it, in case it is lost or stolen.

In one year, this agreement will be revised if you decide to continue employment with us.

I look forward to working with you.

Sincerely,

<your name>

I recommend that you don't ask your employee to sign a formal employment contract. Such a formal document may intimidate your new housekeeper, and the employment letter is a sufficiently effective way to set expectations. Furthermore, any additional terms that you might include in a contract, such as length of employment or termination notice period, are likely to be unenforceable.

Some Hiring Tips

As you gain experience in hiring and managing household help, you will develop your own storehouse of insider information. To give you a head start, let me share with you a few tips that I've garnered in almost 20 years of hiring and managing household help.

No quick decisions.

The worst mistakes are likely to be made if you feel pressure to hire someone quickly. If you are drowning in housework and have finally decided to hire help, you may be so eager to get started that you use bad judgment in hiring the first job candidate who comes along. To avoid this problem, find a way to temporarily reduce your workload, so that you have the luxury of considering candidates carefully. Stop cooking for a week or two, and eat take-out or serve your family frozen dinners. Take your laundry to a laundromat that has a wash-and-fold service. Hire a franchised maid service to do the cleaning. Avoid the panic that will cloud your perspective when judging job candidates.

Hire in summer.

While chances are good that you will find a suitable housekeeper most times of the year, the largest pool of candidates will be available in the summertime. That's because families typically make changes when the school year ends. Experienced housekeepers often find themselves without a job when their employers move, or when children graduate and leave home, which significantly lightens the household workload. Ads placed during the summer will typically generate a large response. The worst time to hire is during the end-of-the-year holidays.

Take compassion out of the hiring equation.

One implication of creating a mutually rewarding business relationship is that you should only hire employees who can do the job that you need done. To refuse to hire a housekeeper who can't perform reliably does not demonstrate a lack of compassion, even if her need is great. Keep your charitable acts separate from your business relationships. Hire employees who can do the job.

If it sounds too good to be true, it probably is.

If "Alice" from *The Brady Bunch* shows up on your doorstep, you should assume that it's Halloween. Unless you're offering top dollar, it is unlikely that you will be able to attract dream candidates.

When a job candidate seems like a dream come true, pinch yourself awake. You may be sorely tempted, whenever you're contacted by a seemingly overqualified job seeker (a gourmet cook, a professional butler), to ignore the hiring fundamentals. If you do, however, you may be brought back to reality with a thud. Maybe the gourmet cook will prepare restaurant-quality meals, but spend three hours doing so and ignore the laundry and cleaning. Maybe the butler is really qualified to manage a large estate but can't find a position right now; he'll quit your job as soon as something better opens up.

Don't turn away a great candidate. Just be suspicious if you feel like you've won the lottery.

Every rule has an exception.

Just as you shouldn't turn away great candidates, you shouldn't necessarily reject a candidate who doesn't perfectly meet the job qualifications. Unless there are no limits to the wage you can offer, there is an inevitable tension between the qualifications you desire in a candidate and the wage you're willing to pay. As a result, you may have to make compromises in your hiring decisions, and that might mean breaking a rule or two.

Maybe you've found a great housecleaner who has no professional cooking experience. If she cooks for her family and gives as a reference a neighbor who can vouch for her cooking, she might be worth a shot. Maybe you've found a former nanny whose favorite time of her workday was naptime because then she got to do housework. (Anything's possible!) If her references agree that her aptitude lies in housekeeping, not childcare, go for it.

Your thorough preparations have clarified exactly what you need in a housekeeper. The pool of candidates you've considered has showed you exactly what kind of help is available. In the end, your instincts will guide you as you make your choice. Trust them.

■ ■ ■

Congratulations! Now that you have an employee, you are a boss. Chapters 11 and 12 will teach you how to be a good one. But first, Chapter 10 will explain what Uncle Sam requires of you.

10 Fulfill Your Legal Obligations

When I decided to start paying employment taxes in 1993, never in my wildest imaginings did I anticipate the difficulties I would encounter. Because I had finally decided to come around to the "right" side of the law, I thought that the government would make it easy for me to participate. Boy, was I wrong.

I spent hours navigating phone trees and waiting on hold, only to discover I had reached the wrong agency. Even when I reached the right one, many of the clerks I talked to weren't sure what to do with me. There was no single source for information, so it took months, even years, before I fully understood all of my obligations. The mounds of paperwork I was required to complete made the task confusing and burdensome. Even my tax advisor had little understanding of the requirements.

Luckily, times have changed. The "nanny tax" scandal (described in Chapter 8) made it apparent how badly the IRS was mistreating well-meaning employers who simply wanted to comply with the law. As a result, the IRS has streamlined the process. Because of these improvements, combined with the explanations in this chapter, your experience should be much more positive than mine.

Even so, the requirements can seem overwhelming. Keep in mind that most of the work comes at the beginning—establishing yourself as an employer and your housekeeper as an employee—and that many of the forms mentioned in this chapter apply to exceptional cases and won't normally be necessary. The checklist below summarizes and organizes the process.

The explanations in this chapter assume that you will do your own tax and payroll paperwork. If you'd rather pay someone to do this, contact your tax provider, look in the Yellow Pages under "Bookkeeping Services," or use one of the "nanny tax" services mentioned in the Resources section in this book. You can get help at several levels: creating an employer-tax "infrastructure" (then you would do the ongoing paperwork), filling out the year-end tax paperwork, or calculating and writing the weekly paychecks.

Even if you delegate this paperwork chore, try to understand as much of the process as you can because not all tax preparers fully understand the "nanny tax" laws. Use the checklist to make sure they're covering all the bases.

This chapter presents a general picture of your legal obligations and reproduces key information contained in relevant government publications. However, because the laws relating to household employment can change frequently, it is impossible to guarantee accuracy. Please contact each of the government agencies mentioned to obtain up-to-date information.

Your legal obligations as a household employer fit into two main categories: tax requirements and fair labor practices. Let's look at tax requirements first.

Taxes: Not Such a Taxing Problem

The most important change the IRS has made to help new household employers is to offer Publication 926, *Household Employer's Tax Guide*, which makes getting started very easy. This document, which is brief and clearly written, summarizes your obligations and directs you to every other government entity with which you will need to interact. If you order this document before you hire your first employee, you'll have plenty of time to make sure you have all the required forms and understand when

Employment Tax Checklist

Before hiring:
- [ ] Order recommended forms.
- [ ] File SS-4 to obtain Federal Employer Identification Number.
- [ ] Obtain employer identification number from your state department of labor.

With new employee:
- [ ] Fill out I-9.
- [ ] Record employee's Social Security number and name as it appears on the card.
- [ ] Report new employee to your state.
- [ ] Obtain W-4 from employee, if you will be withholding income tax.
- [ ] Create blank pay stub.
- [ ] Calculate paycheck adjustments for typical workweek.

Each pay period:
- [ ] Fill out pay stub. Keep a copy.
- [ ] Set aside amount withheld from paycheck, along with your share of employment taxes.

Quarterly:
- [ ] Submit employment taxes to the IRS (optional).
- [ ] Submit quarterly report to your state department of labor, if required.

Yearly:
- [ ] Make sure you've received your *Instructions for Household Employers*.
- [ ] Fill out W-2(s). Hand or mail to employee(s).
- [ ] Fill out W-3. Mail that plus copies of W-2(s) to Social Security Administration.
- [ ] Submit 1040 Schedule H with your personal tax return.
- [ ] Make end-of-year tax payment to your state department of labor.

For five to six years:
- [ ] Keep records.

and how to use them. (Ordering information appears below in the figure titled "Which Forms to Request from Which Agencies.")

This document will help you determine whether your household worker is an employee or an independent contractor, how to prove your employee is legally allowed to work in the United States, and whether you need to pay employment taxes. It also explains which taxes you need to pay and how to pay them, whether you need to withhold federal income tax, and which forms you must file and when. Because your state may have additional requirements, the phone numbers of each state's department of labor are listed in an appendix in the back of the document.

Which Forms to Request from Which Agencies

Internal Revenue Service
Phone: 1-800-TAX-FORM (1-800-829-3676)
Website: www.irs.ustreas.gov

Form/Publication	Purpose
* Publication 926 *Household Employer's Tax Guide*	To get started
Form W-7 *Application for IRS Individual Taxpayer Identification Number*	For the employee to apply for an ITIN if she is an illegal immigrant
* Form SS-4 *Application for Employer Identification Number*	If you are a new employer and don't yet have an EIN
* Form W-4 *Employee's Withholding Allowance Certificate*	If you will withhold federal income tax
Form W-5 *Earned Income Credit Advance Payment Certificate*	For employee to fill out if she is eligible
Publication 15 *Circular E, Employer's Tax Guide*	To find out how much to withhold
* 1040-ES *Estimated Tax for Individuals*	To make quarterly payments of employment tax
Publication 503 *Child and Dependent Care Expenses*	To determine whether you are eligible for the child and dependent care expense tax credit
Form 2441 *Child and Dependent Care Expenses*	To attach to your 1040 to claim the child and dependent care expense tax credit

* Recommended

Which Forms to Request . . . (continued)

Social Security Administration
Phone: 1-800-772-1213
Website: www.ssa.gov

Form/Publication	Purpose
SS-5 *Application for a Social Security Card*	For your employee to apply for a Social Security number

Immigration and Naturalization Service
Phone: 1-800-755-0777
Website: www.ins.usdoj.gov

Form/Publication	Purpose
* I-9 *Employment Eligibility Verification*	To determine whether your employee has the legal right to work
Handbook for Employers	Explanation of rules, contains I-9

State Department of Labor

* Request all materials needed for household employers, including application for employer identification number, form for reporting new employee, formulas for calculating employment taxes and income tax withholding, and forms for reporting wages and paying taxes.

* *Recommended*

Deciding Whether You Must Pay Employment Taxes

If you pay your housekeeper more than a certain amount annually (currently $1,200), you are obligated to pay employment taxes, with a few exceptions.

If she is an independent contractor, rather than an employee, you are exempt from employment taxes. Publication 926 describes the difference between the two, and most of that information is excerpted in Chapter 8.

If you hire your spouse, your child under age 21, your parent (with some exceptions explained in Publication 926), or an employee under 18 for whom household work is not her principal occupation, you are exempt as well.

Hiring Your Employee

Before you hire your first employee, you should obtain, at a minimum, Publication 926 and an I-9. In addition, you should contact your state department of labor.

The I-9 is a requirement of the Department of Justice's Immigration and Naturalization Service. You'll fill out this form with your new employee to verify that she is legally eligible for employment. Then keep it on file. You must complete this form within your employee's first three days of work. This form is required for all new employees, even native-born Americans.

Other Informative Government Publications

Internal Revenue Service
Phone: 1-800-TAX-FORM (1-800-829-3676)
Website: www.irs.ustreas.gov

Form/Publication	Purpose
Publication 15-A Employer's Supplemental Tax Guide	For explanation of difference between employee and independent contractor

Social Security Administration
Phone: 1-800-772-1213
Website: www.ssa.gov

Publication 05-10021 *Household Workers*	For a discussion of Social Security and household workers

U.S. Department of Labor
Phone: 1-202-693-0067
Website: www.dol.gov

Employment Standards Administration, Wage and Hour Division, *Handy Reference Guide*	For a discussion of the Fair Labor Standards Act and how it applies to household workers

U.S. Equal Employment Opportunity Commission
Phone: 1-800-669-4000
Website: www.eeoc.gov

Ask for written materials on fair hiring laws

On her first day of work, be sure to note your employee's Social Security number and her name exactly as it appears on the card; it will be required on the forms you submit to federal and state tax agencies. If she doesn't have one, she can apply for it by submitting SSA form SS-5 to the Social Security Administration. If your housekeeper is an illegal immigrant, she will not be able to obtain a Social Security number. However, she can submit tax returns to the IRS without jeopardy because the IRS does not share information with the INS. In this case, she should use IRS form W-7 to apply for an Individual Taxpayer Identification Number.

A federal law requires that employers report certain information about all new employees within 20 calendar days of the start of work, to help reduce welfare fraud and increase child support collections. The specific reporting mechanism, however, is implemented by each state, so contact your state department of labor to get the necessary form.

If the IRS does not know that you are a household employer, obtain an Employer Identification Number. You can accomplish this by completing and submitting IRS form SS-4. The IRS gives you until February 1 of the next calendar year to do this, although you should do it sooner because you will need the number before then. Your state probably has a similar requirement.

Agreeing on Paycheck Adjustments with Your Employee

There are three types of adjustments that you may be making to your employee's paycheck. First, you will deduct employment taxes. Second, you might withhold income taxes. Third, you might give your employee an advance on earned income credit.

Employment taxes are mandatory payments made to insurance programs including Social Security, Medicare, and any state programs such as disability. Social Security and Medicare together are referred to as FICA (Federal Insurance Contributions Act). The law dictates that, for FICA taxes, you pay half and your employee pays half. You do have the option of paying these taxes on behalf of your employee. In that case, you would not need to take deductions for them. (However, your employee's share of the FICA tax would then be considered taxable income to her.) Otherwise, you would deduct her half from her paycheck.

Paycheck deductions for income tax withholding, on the other hand, are optional. You are required to withhold income tax (both state and federal) only if you and your housekeeper agree that you should do so.

If this is your housekeeper's first "on the books" job, she may not understand what income tax withholding really means. Although you are not obliged to do so, you may want to explain its benefits. You can tell her that, at the end of the year, she will be liable to pay a certain amount in taxes. Tax withholding is a payment toward this liability because you will be sending the amount withheld to the IRS. Then, at the end of the year, she will file a tax return, calculate the exact amount of tax she should have paid, and discover either that she owes the IRS a balance or that the IRS owes her a refund. Income tax withholding helps her avoid the unpleasant discovery that she owes a large amount to the IRS.

Assuming that she decides she wants you to withhold income tax, whether or not your explanation is needed, give her a W-4 form to fill out and return to you, which supplies the information you need to compute her deductions. Then, keep the W-4 form on file.

Your housekeeper may be eligible for the Earned Income Credit. This is a federal assistance program for the working poor, which reduces their tax obligation and sometimes even supplements their income. If your housekeeper qualifies for this credit, it is applied first to her income tax, then to her FICA taxes. If more credit remains, she is eligible for a cash payment.

Rather than waiting to receive the Earned Income Credit (which probably would result in a tax refund) until after filing her yearly tax return, your EIC-eligible employee may wish to receive advance payments with each paycheck. If so, she should fill out a W-5 form and give it to you. Then, along with the deductions you take from her paycheck, you will add a specified amount, which will increase her net pay. You will be reimbursed for these payments through your personal year-end tax return, using the 1040 Schedule H. Caution: your housekeeper's financial circumstances can change significantly from year to year. For her protection, be sure to get a new W-5 every year.

Calculating and Documenting Withholding Amounts

If you will be withholding federal income tax from your housekeeper's paycheck, you will need a copy of IRS Publication 15, *Circular E, Employer's Tax Guide*. This document contains tax tables that tell you how much to withhold from each paycheck, depending on the number of withholding allowances your employee has claimed on her W-4. A similar publication is available from your state department of labor.

If you will provide room and board to your employee, you may be required to consider its "fair value" as part of her wages. If such services are provided at *your* convenience—in other words, if you require your housekeeper to "live in"—the value of room and board is not taxable. If, however, the services are provided at *her* convenience—for example, if she needs a place to live and you offer to provide it—the value of the room and board is taxable.

If you are providing taxable room and board, its "fair value" (noncash wages) is added to cash wages. Total wages are used when computing income tax withholding. However, employment taxes (FICA, FUTA, state disability, and so on) are based only on cash wages. Contact your state department of labor for the amounts that are considered "fair value" for meals and lodging in your state.

Publication 926 contains the formula for calculating FICA taxes. (As of this writing, you should deduct 7.65 percent of your employee's wages for these taxes.) Formulas for required state deductions will be included in publications you obtain from your state department of labor.

To compute the advance earned income credit, if your housekeeper is eligible, refer to the tables in the back of Publication 15.

Along with every paycheck, you should give your housekeeper a document—a pay stub—that records the date, the amount of gross (pretax) wages, federal and state employment tax deductions, federal and state income tax withholding, and advance earned income credit payments. To avoid having to recalculate these amounts each pay period, you can plan your housekeeper's hours so that they remain as consistent as possible.

You can create a generic pay stub for your employee, like the example shown below, and make copies of it. Then, each pay period, you can fill in the blanks on two pay stubs, giving one to your housekeeper along with her paycheck and keeping one for your own records.

You are obligated to keep all employment records for at least four years. The four-year clock doesn't start until you've paid the taxes and submitted your tax return for a given year, so plan on keeping the records for five to six years past the date when the work was done.

Calculating Your Own Tax Liability

Besides the employment taxes that are deducted from your housekeeper's paycheck, you will be paying a share as well. First, you will owe FICA taxes, in an amount (currently 7.65 percent) equal to what your employee pays. As mentioned above, you have the option of paying both your and your employee's share of FICA (for a total, currently, of 15.3 percent).

Although you are obligated to pay FICA if you pay *annual* wages that exceed a certain level (currently $1,200), you must pay FUTA, (Federal Unemployment Tax Act), only if the wages you pay exceed a certain *quarterly* amount (currently $1,000). This tax is paid by you only and is not deducted from your housekeeper's paycheck; part of it is paid to your state and part to the IRS. The total amount you will pay, as of this writing, is a maximum of 6.2 percent of your employee's wages. In most cases, you will

---

Sample Pay Stub

Employer:
Emily Employer
123 Any Street
Pleasantville, My State 98765

Employee:
Wanda Worker
456 Main Street
Anytown, My State 98321
SS# 123-45-6789

Paycheck Date _____
Period Covering _____
Number of Hours _____
Hourly Rate _____

Gross Wages: _____

Deductions:
State Disability Insurance _____
State Income Tax _____
FICA (Soc Sec & Medicare) _____
Federal Income Tax _____

Total Deductions: _____

Advances:
Earned Income Credit _____

Net Paycheck: _____

pay much less, typically 0.8 percent to the IRS plus a larger amount to your state. Wages over $7,000 per year are not subject to FUTA.

There is a tricky distinction between the minimum thresholds for FICA and FUTA wages, besides the fact that one is an annual figure and one is a quarterly figure. For FICA, the $1,200 figure refers to wages paid to any *one* employee. For FUTA, the $1,000 figure refers to *all* wages paid to household employees in any one calendar quarter of the past two years. Even if wages fall below this threshold in a particular quarter, you still must pay FUTA if you've paid above the threshold at least once, because you've established yourself as a FUTA employer by doing so.

Your state department of labor may levy some additional, most likely small, employment taxes. Whether you are obligated to pay them may depend on the amount of wages you pay per year or quarter. As with FUTA, there could be maximum thresholds as well.

It would be very wise to hold in reserve all amounts deducted from your housekeeper's wages, employment taxes plus income tax withholding minus advance earned income credit, because you will later pass those payments on to the IRS and your state tax authority. In addition, if you set aside your own share of the employment taxes as you accrue them, you won't be surprised by a big tax bill at the end of the year.

Filing Forms and Making Tax Payments

If the IRS knows that you are a household employer, at the end of the calendar year you will receive a stapled packet called *Instructions for Household Employers*. It contains all of the required federal reporting forms (W-2, W-3, 1040 Schedule H), as well as instructions on how and when to complete them. If you have not received this packet by mid-January, contact the IRS and request that it be mailed to you.

Before the end of January, you'll fill out a W-2 form for each household worker you employed during the previous year. The W-2 summarizes the wages you paid to each employee and itemizes and totals all amounts that you withheld from her paychecks. You can either hand or mail the W-2(s) to your employee(s).

Before the end of February, you will fill out a W-3 form, which summarizes the information contained in the W-2s, and mail that plus a copy of each W-2 to the Social Security Administration.

When you file your personal tax return, include Schedule H with your 1040. Schedule H allows you to spell out all of the employment taxes due, plus federal income tax you have withheld from your housekeepers' wages, along with any advance earned income credit payments you have made. The net total amount due to the IRS is then added to your personal tax liability.

Here is a caution: the IRS expects that your personal withholding (if you are employed) or your estimated tax payments (if you are self-employed) are large enough to cover this additional tax liability. If not, you could be assessed a penalty. To avoid this risk, you can increase the amount of federal income tax that is currently being withheld from your paycheck by filing a new W-4 with your employer, or pay your employment taxes quarterly, using IRS Form 1040-ES.

Most states have streamlined their household employment laws to be compatible with the new IRS rules. Check with your state department of labor to be sure you understand how to report your employees' wages and how to make state tax payments.

All's Not Fair in Hiring

As Chapter 4 acknowledged, the relationship between this country's household employers and their employees has not always been fair. To remedy that situation, the Fair Labor Standards Act (FLSA), a federal law, now covers household workers. The Department of Labor's *Handy Reference Guide* describes this law and how it applies to you.

FLSA Requirements

If the FLSA covers your housekeeper, she is entitled to a minimum hourly wage of $5.15, effective September 1, 1997. For all hours worked beyond 40 hours per week, your housekeeper should be paid at least one and one-half times her regular rate.

If you provide room and board to your employee (see *Calculating and Documenting Withholding Amounts*, above), you can possibly consider its "fair value" to be part of her wages, allowing you to pay less in cash than the minimum wage would otherwise require. However, you are only entitled to do so if the room and board is considered taxable (noncash wages), as previously explained. To recap, if you require your employee to "live in," the value of her meals and lodging is not taxable, and you cannot use it to justify paying less than minimum wage.

If you hire a child under age 16, other than your own, the child labor provisions of the FLSA dictate the number of hours that can be worked each week, the time of day that work must end, and so on. For details, consult the *Handy Reference Guide*.

Finally, the FLSA requires that you maintain records of wages, hours, paycheck deductions, and so forth—in short, the same information that the IRS requires you to maintain.

Who Is Covered

Your household employee is protected by the FLSA if you meet the IRS test for paying employment taxes (currently, if you pay her more than $1,200 annually). Even if you don't meet the IRS test, she's covered if she works more than eight hours per week, total, for all her employers. Therefore, it's a pretty safe bet that the FLSA covers your housekeeper and that you must comply with its requirements.

Some household workers are exempt from the minimum wage and overtime provisions, even if covered by the FLSA. These include casual babysitters (those who babysit less than 20 hours per week and for whom babysitting is not their primary profession) and those who provide companionship to the disabled or the elderly. These employees could be paid less than minimum wage and are not entitled to time-and-a-half for overtime.

Finally, live-in household workers, while covered by the FLSA, are exempt from its overtime provisions. They are not entitled to time-and-a-half for hours worked beyond 40 hours per week, although you certainly could provide it. None of the FLSA provisions is intended to limit the wages or benefits that you can offer your employee.

State Requirements

Most likely, your state has enacted some additional labor laws. Your state department of labor can tell you what they are.

The minimum wage in your state may be higher than the federal minimum, and overtime restrictions may be more stringent. It is likely that your state establishes a maximum pay period length and sets rules about how quickly payday must follow the end of the pay period. There may be rules about periodic (unpaid) meal breaks, days off, and short paid breaks during the workday. None of these rules is likely to be difficult to follow. Chances are that you are already in full compliance with them.

Please note, though, that you may be required to provide worker's compensation insurance for your household employee to cover work-related injuries and illnesses. If so, your homeowner's or renter's insurance policy most likely provides this coverage, or it may be available directly from the state. Be sure to check on this. If your housekeeper is injured on the job and you have failed to provide required insurance coverage, you could be held responsible for her medical bills.

If your state does not require you to provide worker's compensation insurance, it would be wise to check with your insurance provider to make sure that the liability limits and no-fault medical coverage on your homeowner's or renter's policy are sufficient to protect you from potential lawsuits.

Fair Hiring Practices

If you have hired employees in a corporate environment, you know that fair hiring laws can make hiring a legal minefield. Fortunately, as a household employer, you are exempt from the specific requirements of the federal antidiscrimination laws.

For example, Title VII of the Civil Rights Act of 1964, which prohibits employers from refusing to hire, or from firing, employees based on their race, color, religion, sex, or national origin, applies only to employers with 15 or more employees. The Age Discrimination in Employment Act of 1967, which extends this protection to individuals who are 40 years of age or older, applies to the same size employers. The Americans with Disabilities Act of 1990, which extends the protection to those with physical or mental disabilities, applies only to those with 20 or more employees. And the Equal Pay Act of 1963, which prohibits wage discrimination between men and women, applies to employers of all sizes, but only those engaged in commerce.

Some states have extended antidiscrimination laws to cover smaller employers than those covered by the federal laws, but you are still likely to be exempt. California laws, for example, apply to employers with three or more employees. (One exception: sexual harassment laws protect California workers in *all* work environments.) You can check with your state department of fair employment to learn if your state has fair hiring laws that apply to you.

Careful definitions of the term "employer" have been incorporated into the laws because lawmakers understand how burdensome such stringent regulations can be to small employers. Employers who are subject to these laws need extensive—and expensive—legal advice to interpret the laws and understand how they can hire well-qualified individuals without discriminating (or even appearing to).

While you certainly should avoid discriminatory hiring practices, you can feel comfortable asking the questions that will help you determine whether a job candidate is both qualified and capable of doing the job that you want her (or him!) to do.

By the way, the fair hiring laws recognize that some job requirements, even if they appear to have a discriminatory effect, are genuine. For example, if a job candidate is an experienced cook who can only prepare Asian food, she cannot fulfill the requirement for an employee who can prepare American food. Similarly, if a candidate's English is so poor that she cannot read your written instructions or carry on a conversation, she cannot fill the bona fide job requirement for moderate skill in English. It is not discriminatory to consider how cultural or language differences affect a candidate's ability to do the job.

Now, A Law That Benefits You

The IRS recognizes that, in two-income families (or in one-income, single-parent families), the cost of delegating the work of the home is a legitimate expense. Under certain circumstances, you can take a tax credit for a portion of this expense. IRS Publication 503, *Child and Dependent Care Expenses*, explains how to determine whether you are eligible for this credit and how to figure and claim it.

If you found the employment tax rules confusing, the rules for the child and dependent care expense credit can make you downright bleary eyed. You may want to leave the calculations to your tax preparer. In general, the rules are as follows. First, you must have a "qualifying" dependent, which means a child under age 13 or a spouse or other dependent who is unable to care for himself.

Second, the care expenses that you incur must be so that you can work, look for work, or attend school full time. "Care expenses" are those that provide for the qualifying person's well-being and protection, including both childcare and household services. You are allowed to include expenses for household services even if they only partially benefit the qualifying person, for example, the expense for a housekeeper who cooks family meals, does laundry for the entire family, or cleans the whole house.

Third, both you and your spouse must have earned income during the year, unless one of you was disabled or a full-time student. Fourth, you must keep up a home, whether rented or owned. Fifth, payments for these expenses must not be made to your child or dependent. And finally, you must know the care provider's name, address, and Social Security number or make a reasonable effort to find out.

If you meet these tests, you can attach Form 2441 to your personal income tax return to claim the credit. Please be aware that the credit is likely to be small. The credit you can claim is only a percentage of your care expense; the allowed percentage is based on your adjusted gross income. Under current law, the allowed credit for adjusted gross income greater than $28,000 is 20 percent of the care expense.

Furthermore, the maximum care expense you can claim is $2,400 per dependent, and other factors can reduce this dollar amount. For example, the expense amount used in the calculations cannot exceed the smaller of your and your spouse's income. Nevertheless, the tax credit for child and dependent care expenses is one you should take, if you are so entitled.

You also may be able to reduce your housekeeper expense if you work for a company that offers a dependent care assistance program. Under such a program, your employer pays you a nontaxable amount, up to $5,000, that you can use to pay your care expenses, whether childcare or household services. If your employer does provide this benefit, you may still be eligible for the child and dependent care expense tax credit, but the amount of expense that you can consider for the credit is reduced by the expense assistance your employer furnishes.[1] Contact your company's benefits administrator to find out if your employer offers such a program.

Your state may offer a similar dependent care credit. Contact your state tax board or your tax preparer for details.

■　■　■

So those are your legal obligations. While they may seem overwhelming at first, you'll soon be able to take them in stride.

Next, let's move on to the point of this book—putting your new housekeeper to work.

11 Share the Road Map

When my husband and I were considering our first real estate purchase, our agent helped us make an important distinction. As we drove through middle-class neighborhoods, most properties seemed to be in good condition. A few looked run-down; those, our agent pointed out, were occupied by renters and owned by absentee landlords.

But an equal few existed at the opposite end of the maintenance spectrum. These exceptional properties were clearly cared for by loving hands. The lawns were so well manicured, it seemed as though embroidery scissors were used to do the edging. Windows sparkled, and window coverings hung crisp and straight. Paint was fresh and bright, plants were healthy and vibrant, and ornamental touches, such as stone frogs or country-style wreaths, were frequently visible.

"What you are seeing," said our agent, "is 'pride of ownership.' The people who live there are proud of what they have acquired. Their careful maintenance tells us how they feel about their home."

One of the biggest complaints that household employers make of their housekeepers and housecleaners is that "she doesn't do as good a job as I do." In other words, she lacks "pride of ownership." How can you instill this sense in your employee?

Obviously, your housekeeper will never become the literal owner of your home. You can't give her part ownership, the way start-up companies often offer stock or stock options to their employees. But you can give her a "sense of ownership" in your home. Consider the following two contrasting situations.

My first job after college was with an aerospace company in Silicon Valley. Because the company needed to formally investigate my background before assigning me to my permanent work group, I spent four months "on ice," associated temporarily with a group of computer programmers.

Because I was soon to be moving on, I was given no serious duties. I did my best to help "debug" the programs of those in my temporary group, but it was difficult to do so because I was never given an orientation explaining that group's mission.

Over time, I became less and less enthusiastic about showing up at work, and after the first few weeks, I must confess, found myself spending at least a couple of hours a day reading the newspaper and chatting with co-workers. By the time I was cleared to work on my regular assignment, I had lost enthusiasm for the company and left within a year.

Next, I joined a Silicon Valley computer manufacturer and received a welcome that contrasted markedly with my earlier experience. Not only was I assigned a cubicle that was tidy and well-stocked with office supplies, but I also was introduced individually to everyone in the department and given a thorough briefing on the project to which I was assigned.

I was included in a two-day orientation for all new hires that covered the history and organization of the company, business philosophy, available career growth paths, and tours of some nearby manufacturing facilities. Many of the company's "top brass" spoke to the group and repeatedly reminded us of how much the company valued our talents. I stayed at that company for six years, even though my temperament is ill suited to large organizations. Why? I was told that my contribution made a difference and given the tools to make that difference.

Although you will not be giving your housekeeper a two-day orientation, the direction that you give your new employee will set the tone for your working relationship, demonstrate that you value her contribution, and clarify what you expect that contribution to be. The time that you spend "orienting" your new employee will pay big dividends down the road in terms of both professionalism and loyalty on the part of your housekeeper. Best of all, it will help her to gain a sense of ownership toward your household.

The Initial Training Period

Assuming that you have prepared the instruction manual that is described in Chapters 5 and 7 (and included by example in Appendix A), you have already done the bulk of your housekeeper training. You may wish to give this manual to your new housekeeper before her first day on the job, so that she has a chance to familiarize herself with it.

Spend some time on her first workday walking her through her duties. (Depending on the complexity of what you will be delegating to your housekeeper, you will need to spend, initially, from 30 minutes to two hours with her.) If your housekeeper will normally work when you are not home, you can arrange a special training session that will allow you to explain her job duties face to face.

You can communicate quality standards and priorities as you explain the work schedule. For example, "Here is how my husband likes his T-shirts to be folded." Or, "I'd like the kids to be able to work on their homework uninterrupted. So I'd appreciate it if you'd finish in their bedrooms before they get home from school." Or, "Please wipe up any detergent that drips on the top or sides of the washing machine." Or, "I've allowed two hours a week for dusting, but that's the lowest priority. I don't expect you to keep everything perfectly dusted all the time. If you're short on time, just be sure to check for fingerprints on the entry hall mirror."

After you've completed the one-on-one walkthrough with your housekeeper and she sets to work, she'll probably discover that she has further questions. You'll get the best results if you can make yourself available for questions, personally or by phone, especially in the beginning. It may take several weeks for your housekeeper to get fully up to speed. Don't hover, though. Your housekeeper won't enjoy feeling like you're looking over her shoulder. Allow her to develop her own work style.

Be sure to invite your housekeeper to feel at home as she works. You should let her know that she is welcome to help herself to food or drinks, unless there is something specific that you want to place off limits. It's unlikely that she will abuse this privilege, and by extending such an invitation, you'll increase the chances that she'll develop a sense of ownership about your household. If she'll be working for several hours, you should encourage her to take a break of 10 or 15 minutes if she needs it or a lunch break if she'll work all day. (She may, in fact, be legally entitled to a break; see Chapter 10.)

If your housekeeper will cook using your recipes, it will take a little longer to complete her training. To avoid overwhelming a new housekeeper, in the first couple of weeks I typically limit the number of recipes that I expect her to learn. During that time, I allow her to cook her own recipes, defrost freezer meals (I usually have some soups and casseroles saved for emergencies), and learn one new recipe each week.

As with the initial one-on-one walkthroughs, I find that meal preparations in the early weeks are much more successful if I am at home to answer questions. Once my housekeeper is comfortable with the household and has learned the organization of my kitchen, I accelerate the pace with which she learns new recipes. Once familiar with my cooking style, she can learn new recipes without my personal supervision, after a brief discussion about them.

Ongoing Communication

Depending on the complexity of the tasks that you've delegated to your housekeeper, you will need to have regular, ongoing communication with her. For example, if she will cook, you'll probably leave a written weekly menu plan for her along with the recipes she will use. You may be leaving grocery shopping lists or lists of errands to be run. If the schedule will change for some reason (holidays, vacation), modify your instructions. If you don't provide a set work schedule, leave a list of priorities. If you do have a set schedule, you may leave a list of extra projects to be worked on if she finishes her normal workload early. (Be sure to adjust the schedule and provide needed training if you assign new tasks.)

You can do all of this in writing, but you should check in, by phone or in person, at least weekly. Ongoing personal contact with you, even just to exchange pleasantries, will help your housekeeper feel valued, which is important if she is to have a sense of ownership about your household. If you prefer to have your housekeeper perform the bulk of her work when you are not home, you can schedule your return to coincide with the last half-hour of her workday, or you can leave home shortly after she's arrived and settled in.

As will be addressed later, personal contact is a highly effective way to nip problems in the bud. It's human nature to wait until problems become major irritants before addressing them in writing. But casual requests delivered in a relaxed tone will leave neither of you feeling stressed. The next chapter addresses giving feedback, both positive and negative, in detail.

Differences in Language, Culture, and Personality

Have you ever noticed that people are different? It's a silly question, but it addresses a fact that seems almost against human nature to accept. My husband and I spend so much time trying to help our children understand it that the phrase "different people like different things" has become a mantra in our house.

The profile of the typical housekeeper varies in different parts of this country, based on a couple of factors. Near the borders—the East and West Coasts and the Southwest—there is a high concentration of immigrants, so the household labor pool draws heavily from that population. In the Midwest, housekeepers are more typically native-born Americans. In the South, immigration is higher than in the Midwest, but welfare allowances are low, so the household labor pool is varied.[1] If you have hired an immigrant, your most immediate challenge may be that you don't—literally—speak the same language.

Language Differences

Unless you are fluent in the foreign language spoken by your immigrant housekeeper, you'll need to hire someone who has at least a rudimentary grasp of the English language. But the way that you'll communicate with her will depend on how she learned the language.

English is a difficult language to learn, particularly because of its inconsistent pronunciation rules. As a result, some immigrants can read far more English than they speak, especially if they learned English in a formal classroom setting in their native countries. If this is the case for your housekeeper, you can rely heavily on written communication. If you

- Speak slowly and clearly.
- Use conventional, grammatically correct English.
- Avoid slang and idioms.
- Write down or spell words if necessary.
- Speak face to face.
- Demonstrate your meaning if possible.
- Be specific.
- Use words your housekeeper already knows.
- Repeat and rephrase words and ideas to confirm understanding.

have time, you can help her improve her English by verbally reviewing your written instructions with her.

On the other hand, immigrants with little formal education who learned English only after they arrived in this country may have a poor grasp of written English and may speak better English than they read. If this describes your housekeeper, you can leave written instructions for her, but review them verbally to make sure that they're understood.

Wherever your housekeeper's English strengths and weaknesses lie, a few guidelines will help you make yourself understood.[2] First, speak slowly and clearly. Rather than tossing instructions over your shoulder while you're running out the door, you'll get better results if you speak face-to-face with your housekeeper. That way, she won't miss anything and can use your facial expressions to help gauge your meaning. Even better, demonstrate what you mean whenever possible.

Second, avoid using slang or idiomatic expressions. If you ask your immigrant housekeeper to "whip this place into shape," chances are you won't get what you want. Instead, give specific instructions using conventional English.

Third, follow your housekeeper's lead in word choice. Those of us who have spoken English all our lives are sometimes unaware of how many synonyms we can use to express similar concepts. Yet each synonym is another new word for your housekeeper to learn. (I've frustrated a couple of housekeepers by using the terms "skillet" and "frying pan" interchangeably.) Take note of the words that your housekeeper already understands, then make a habit of using those words when instructing her.

Fourth, avoid using Pidgin English. Your housekeeper may speak that way, but she'll understand clear, simple, grammatically correct English. And such interactions with you will help her improve her language skills.

Fifth, write down or spell words (when communication is going either way) if your housekeeper's spoken English is very poor.

Finally, repeat your housekeeper's words to confirm that you've understood her, and ask her to do the same. You might also ask her to rephrase your instructions to make sure she's not simply parroting you.

Cultural Differences

As Deborah Tannen documented so well in her book *That's Not What I Meant!*, communication styles even among different regions of this country are incompatible enough to cause frustration. For example, in the South, people are comfortable expressing themselves indirectly, while New Yorkers tend to "tell it like it is." A relationship between a Southerner and a New Yorker can be fraught with difficulties, the Southerner taking offense at the New Yorker's brusque, forthright style and the New Yorker frustrated at the Southerner's perceived unwillingness to say what she means.[3]

With such communication style variation within our own borders, imagine the obstacles we face when trying to communicate with people from other countries and other cultures. You will most likely face a few such challenges if you've hired an immigrant housekeeper.

The most common cultural conflict between housekeepers and their employers is in how they address problems. Of course, you'd like your housekeeper to let you know if she doesn't understand an instruction, so that you can clear things up. But your housekeeper may come from a culture that values avoiding confrontation (typically, Hispanic cultures) or saving face (most likely, Asian cultures).[4]

In the movie *El Norte*, set in Los Angeles, two Guatemalan housekeepers are looking for work. The more experienced one tells the other, "Whatever they say, just smile and say yes."[5] If you sense that your housekeeper might be signifying agreement without really understanding what you're saying, ask her to explain to you what she thinks you've told her. If you're correct that she's agreeing without really understanding, emphasize how important it is that she understands your instructions. Make it clear that you expect her to ask questions and to tell you when she doesn't understand something.

If your housekeeper never asks questions and never takes the initiative to work on something unless you've specifically instructed her to, she may be concerned about saving face, both hers and yours. She might be afraid that asking questions would be an insult to you (because you had given inadequate instructions) or embarrassing to her (because she was unable to understand them). If this sounds like your housekeeper, explain to her that asking questions is part of her job and that she will not be penalized for doing so. Furthermore, you expect her to notice if something extra needs to be done and either mention it to you or take the initiative to do it.

You might also need to tell such an employee that you expect her to tell you when a household item must be repaired or replaced. Otherwise, she might fear that you would interpret pointing out such problems as a criticism or that she would be blamed for any damage.

You may occasionally want to roll up your sleeves and work alongside your housekeeper. This might make your housekeeper uncomfortable. Although such an egalitarian approach may seem like simple teamwork to you, in some cultures such action could be taken as an insult, an implication that the employee's work is lacking.[6] If you are working on an "extra" project that is possible because your housekeeper has taken most of the workload off your shoulders, you can explain this to her, expressing your gratitude that her hard work gives you this extra time. But if you are pitching in because you feel guilty about the work that she's doing, stop it! Chances are you are only getting in the way.

If your most comfortable communication style is indirect speaking, you'll have more success with your housekeeper if you can set that aside momentarily when giving instructions. It's asking far too much of a newcomer to this country to learn both the language *and* subtle social conventions. Give clear and direct instructions.

On the other hand, take care when delivering corrections. First of all, make sure that all reprimands are delivered in private. Second, think about how your message will be perceived. If you have a direct style, facing-saving methods of communication, "I" messages, for example, will soften your message's effect. If you have an indirect style, make sure that you have made yourself clear. Chapter 12 discusses correction in more detail.

In some cultures, and for some personality types, friendly chats always precede getting down to work. If you can tell that your housekeeper wants to socialize with you, spend a few minutes if you can. Then excuse yourself in a way that won't make her feel personally rejected. For example, you can say, "I'd love to chat more, but I'm up against a deadline and I've really got to get back to work," or, "I'd love to chat more, but I've been promising all day to play a board game with my daughter."

Several excellent books cited in the Resources section address cultural differences in more detail.

Personality Differences

Even before diversity consciousness came into vogue, enlightened corporations helped their employees understand that human beings have personality style differences that can affect working relationships. But you don't have to be an expert in personality differences to learn to get along with your housekeeper. You can learn a lot just by asking.

I once had a housekeeper who would breeze right in and buckle down to work with barely a "hello." I was concerned that her unsmiling face meant that she was unhappy with her job and asked her directly how I should interpret her body language. Surprised, she assured me that she loved her job and was simply so eager to get started each day that it didn't occur to her to "waste time" on pleasantries!

When in doubt, check it out.

On-the-Job Friendships

The development of a pseudo-friendship is a common dilemma faced by employers of household help, especially if the employee comes from a culture or has a personality style that values socializing on the job. Because your housekeeper spends so much time in your "personal space" taking care of intimate details of your life and sees you at home where you have taken your emotional armor off, your relationship with her can begin to feel like a friendship.

However, this can never be a relationship between equals. You are, after all, employer and employee. As we are learning in the workplace with respect to sexual harassment, we must step lightly when developing friendships that would be significantly less complicated when begun outside the employment context.

The problem, unfortunately, is much more easily avoided than solved. If you already feel like your housekeeper is taking emotional "liberties," it's time to put the brakes on. If you don't have a problem yet, but can sense your relationship with your housekeeper is headed in the wrong (too-familiar) direction, take steps now to get your relationship back on track. Here are some guidelines.

Don't Volunteer Personal Information

Although it can seem tempting to pour your heart out to a handy, sympathetic listener, especially if you feel isolated as an at-home mom or a home-based entrepreneur, your housekeeper is a poor choice. Once you've shared your problems with her, you've provided an implicit invitation for her to do the same. Are you sure you want to pay someone while you listen to her problems?

Although you will periodically engage in friendly chit-chat, as discussed above, keep it fairly impersonal, just as you would in an office setting. You know which topics have emotional power for you; avoid discussing them with your housekeeper.

Avoid Live-In Situations

Unless you really need live-in help, live-out help might be best because having your housekeeper live with you can significantly blur professional boundaries. The situation can be further complicated when your employee is young—a college student, for example—and begins to play "rebellious teenager" to your "mom" persona the minute she's unpacked her bags.

Juliana has decided, based on two painful experiences, never to hire live-in help again: "In both cases, the duties included both housecleaning and childcare. It was the housecleaning that suffered the most and the quickest. As soon as they moved in (in both cases), they either wanted to renegotiate the cleaning out or just didn't do it or didn't do it well enough. When someone is living with the family, it's harder to delineate the boss/worker line. They become part of the family to some degree, especially because of the childcare aspect. When a person moves into the home, you get more than domestic help. You get all the baggage of their lives as well. Whether it's school problems, love problems, health problems, or even their own insecurities, it all becomes a part of your life to some extent. So for me, it was like adopting another child."

If you do decide to hire live-in help, you can minimize the undesirable patterns by creating as much emotional space as possible. Provide your housekeeper a separate entrance to her living quarters, if you can. Don't ask her to account for her off-hours. Don't ask her to work when she's off-duty. Provide a TV for her room, so she won't need to join the family in the evening. Above all, be aware of the potentially difficult dynamics and be on guard against them.

Remember Your Relationship's Mutual Benefit

If you were taught gracious hospitality as a girl, as most of us were, the presence of another adult in your home may trigger an automatic "hostess" response that competes with the employer/employee relationship that you have with your housekeeper.

Do you feel uncomfortable knowing that your housekeeper is grabbing a quick bite in the kitchen while you and your dinner guests enjoy a meal in the formal dining room? Do you feel guilty settling into your favorite overstuffed chair with the latest bestseller while your housekeeper scurries to put the laundry away?

It is fine, in fact admirable, to treat your employee with caring compassion. But remember that you've hired her to do a job, and you're paying her a fair wage and providing an attractive work environment. Feel free to enjoy the activities of your choice while she does that job.

This advice might seem to contradict the "sense of ownership" that you aim to instill in your housekeeper. But she can feel responsible for and proud of meeting the physical needs of your family without getting intimately involved in your emotional lives.

If your housekeeper repeatedly indicates that she expects to be included in family activities, you have failed to establish appropriate boundaries with her. You can try having a heart-to-heart talk with her, but more extreme action might be necessary. I once fired a housecleaner (a friend whom I'd hired when she lost her job) because she continually interrupted me in my home office in an attempt to engage me in conversation.

If establishing boundaries is an area of personal difficulty for you, see the Resources section for more help on this subject.

■ ■ ■

Next, we'll look at the best ways to give your housekeeper feedback, both positive and negative.

12 "How Am I Doing, Boss?"

I was very young when I was offered my first management position—too young, probably, because I lacked the experience that would have taught me how best to relate to my staff. Luckily for me, one of the engineers on my team was an enthusiastic, ambitious, direct, and highly competent young man named Jim who would quiz me, at least weekly, "How am I doing, boss?"

Don't we all love praise? A pat on the back feels best, but as Jim taught me, most people also want to know if they're not meeting expectations so they can take corrective action. The benefits of regular feedback are clear: acknowledgment and appreciation for good job performance encourages more of the same; expedient correction of small problems prevents them from growing into large ones.

Don't Forget the Praise

There's an old joke about an undemonstrative elderly man who's been married for 50 years to his affection-starved wife. Finally deciding to ask for the affection that she needs, the wife screws up her courage to query her husband, "Do you still love me?" Surprised, he sternly replies, "I told you when I married you that I loved you. I'll let you know if anything changes."

Unfortunately, bosses are notorious for treating their employees the same way. The only comments they share are negative ones, and they take the unspoken stance with their employees that "if I keep paying you, you can assume that I like what you're doing." Saving yourself effort with this kind of treatment is false economy, since studies show that workplace praise is a powerful motivator, and lack of praise is an equally powerful de-motivator.[1, 2]

When praising your housekeeper, you can make general comments like, "You're doing a great job," but specific compliments will have the best effect. "Dinner last night was delicious!" or "The bathroom is absolutely sparkling!" It's especially important to notice and comment on any "extra" efforts she makes. You can also help your housekeeper feel needed by telling her how her work makes you more effective. "Thanks for being so dependable. I was able to meet my big deadline because I didn't have to stop to think about dinner."

You can create an environment of appreciation and respect for your housekeeper by making sure your children are privy to the praise you give her. Be sure to teach them to speak to her politely and to keep up with their household chores so that she can do hers. "Would you clean up your Legos now, please, so Judith can vacuum your room?"

You might wish to check in with your housekeeper periodically to find out if the job is meeting her expectations, too. She could have some useful suggestions, for example, using different cleaning products or rearranging closets. Be aware of the kind of input you are seeking though—remember that it's not your housekeeper's role to give you approval or relieve your guilt.

In professional work environments, one way that employers reward and acknowledge employees for good work is by offering career growth opportunities. But unless you have an estate-sized household with numerous staff positions, including managerial ones, you won't be able to offer career growth in the usual sense.

Depending on the capabilities of the housekeeper you hire, you can delegate increasing levels of responsibility. If your housekeeper wants to take over some of the managerial tasks like planning meals or organizing closets, allowing her to do so might be the best way to keep her feeling challenged and fulfilled. For other housekeepers, career growth is not a priority. For them, a steady source of income is their greatest need, and they might be more comfortable leaving all the managerial decisions in your hands. You'll quickly recognize which category your housekeeper fits into.

The best kind of praise replaces the "p" with a dollar sign: a raise. Plan to give your housekeeper a periodic increase, perhaps yearly. If she has far exceeded your expectations and has taken on substantial new responsibilities, you may want to give her a significant increase. Otherwise, a modest increase to reflect the cost of living and to say, "We appreciate your work," will be sufficient. You may also want to periodically increase the noncash benefits you offer, for example, the number of paid days off.

When Correction Is in Order

There are many benign reasons that your new housekeeper might perform certain tasks in ways that are not to your liking or fail to perform them at all. Overwhelmed with the newness of your household, she may simply have forgotten your instructions. She may have misunderstood what you told her. Or she may have her own method for performing a specific task and not understand why you prefer your method. In these cases, the correction that you give your housekeeper is simply a training update.

Mistakes Are Learning Opportunities

As enlightened managers recognize, most people don't start their workdays with a desire to fail. It is the manager's job to help her employee succeed.

The most basic way to ensure your employee's success is to make sure that she understands your instructions. If your housekeeper is not performing a task properly, have you communicated your expectations clearly? Richard Carlson, author of *Don't Sweat the Small Stuff with Your Family*, tells of a favorite babysitter who consistently left their kitchen looking as though a bomb had struck, despite his and his wife's instructions that she should "clean up after herself." After they took the time to explain (and demonstrate) exactly what "clean up" meant to them, their sitter unfailingly cleaned the kitchen just the way they like it.[3]

Most tasks can be performed a number of different ways. But if you want a particular task to be done in a particular way, you'll need to tell your housekeeper.

I have an exceptionally tidy underwear drawer (is this far more information than you ever wanted to know about me?), and I expect my housekeeper to place the underwear "just so" when putting my clean laundry away. When my new housekeeper failed to follow my layout method, I explained the reason for my supposed fastidiousness: I am the first one out of bed in the morning, so I get dressed in the dark; if my underwear is not where I expect it to be, I have to turn a light on, disturbing my husband's sleep. After I explained the reason for my "pickiness," my housekeeper was diligent in keeping my drawer in order.

By the way, "just because I want it that way" is a valid reason, but be judicious in how many times you use it, and always say it with a smile on your face. Remember, if you want your housekeeper to feel like an important member of the team, it helps her to understand and agree to the rules of the game.

How to Deliver Your Message

As marriage counselors will attest, the tone of the communication often determines its success or failure. "I" messages are always easier to hear than more accusatory "you" messages.

"I" messages take the form, "When <event> occurs, I feel <emotion> because <consequence>." It's not always a good idea to share your emotional state with your housekeeper, so you can shorten the form to "When <event> occurs, then <consequence>." Less effective "you" messages are unedited statements from the speaker of what the listener has done to wrong her.

In my underwear drawer example, here is how I approached my housekeeper. "Bertila, I need to speak with you about my underwear drawer." (Then I walked with her to the bedroom, so I could demonstrate.) "Since I am the first one awake in the morning, I get dressed in the dark. I need to be able to find my underwear by feeling it. When the bras are lined up on the left, like this, and the underpants on lined up on the right, like this, I can find everything. But when they are mixed together, I can't find what I need and I have to turn on the light. That wakes up Michael."

Imagine if I had spoken in the tone often used by warring spouses. "Bertila! Why did you mix up my underwear like this? Don't you know I like it organized? You must not care about what I ask you to do! You don't listen!"

Even in a gentler tone, "you" messages are still harder to hear than "I" messages. "Bertila, you arranged my underwear drawer all wrong. You're supposed to put the underpants on the right and the bras on the left. Could you fix it, please?"

As you can see, "I" messages emphasize the effect that a specific action has on the speaker, while "you" messages often simply attack the listener. "I" messages work because it's left to the listener to draw conclusions about how she could improve the situation, thus allowing her to save face.

If you've already addressed the problem with your housekeeper and it recurs, it's possible that she forgot your instruction or ran out of time. You can let her know that a correction is needed while maintaining a light tone by leaving a written note titled "Needs Attention," simply listing the items without explanation. Or, you could give her a verbal reminder by saying something simple like, "Bertila, would you please check my underwear drawer?" If the problem remains uncorrected, you might double-check to make sure she understood your instruction.

What If the Problem Is More Serious?

What if you are having problems that require something more serious than a training update? For example, what if you've asked your housekeeper to make the same correction repeatedly, with no result? What if your housekeeper refuses outright to perform certain tasks? What if significant new problems crop up routinely, to the point that you dread arriving home because you are afraid to face the next new disaster? What if your housekeeper is cutting her work hours short or taking unpaid days off too frequently? What if you suspect your housekeeper has stolen something from you?

If the relationship has so deteriorated that you are determined to start fresh immediately, or if your housekeeper's infraction or mistake is so egregious that you know you'll never be able to trust her again, then dismissal is warranted. The section "Firing Your Housekeeper" later in this chapter discusses this task.

But if you'd like to try to salvage the situation, determine whether the problem is one of attitude or capability. The resolution of an attitude problem will be strictly in your housekeeper's hands. If your housekeeper's ability is in question, you may be able to help her improve, she may be able to improve on her own, or her lack of ability might be a problem that neither of you can solve. A talk with your housekeeper will help you identify the type of problem you are dealing with.

Once again, use "I" messages, but you may want to add the statement of emotion, described above in "How to Deliver Your Message," if you're having trouble getting your housekeeper to take your concerns seriously. If you discuss your concerns directly and emphatically, your housekeeper will probably give you important information.

At the beginning of one summer, I employed a young college student, Kim, who initially did a great job and was exceptionally reliable. But by late fall, she began leaving work earlier and earlier each day.

Several conversations about the problem produced little result. "When I realized that you'd left work one hour early, I felt angry, because I don't like paying for work that isn't done." "My son's jeans were wet when he pulled them out of the drawer the next morning, and my daughter's T-shirt was wrinkled, because it wasn't completely dry when it was put in her drawer. That meant that I had to spend extra time helping the kids dress for school. In your rush to leave, did you take the clothes out of the dryer when they were still damp?" Kim's responses were typically limited to a terse "OK" and a promise to do better, with little change resulting.

Finally, after a stern warning that her job required being at my home for the prescribed hours, Kim revealed something about her personal life. Because her parents were deceased, she lived with her sister and brother-in-law. As an immigrant from a very traditional family, she was subject to the authority of her brother-in-law, who insisted that she be home before dark every day. (He did not know about her job, because he would never have given permission, and did not support her educational goals.) This rule had presented no difficulty during the long days of summer, but she couldn't fit both school and work into the short daylight hours of winter.

Once I understood the situation, I tried to be as flexible as I could, but the fact remained that Kim was simply unavailable to work the hours I needed her. After a few months, it became apparent to Kim that a better living situation was called for, and she moved out of town, giving me several weeks' notice.

Although we weren't able to resolve this problem in a way that kept Kim on the job, it was enormously beneficial to identify the problem as one of capability, rather than attitude. When I thought that Kim was cutting her work hours short because of a bad attitude (she didn't care about the job, she was trying to steal time from me, this was her way of thumbing her nose at me), I was very angry about the situation. There was no action I could think of short of firing Kim, and I knew that taking such an action would only create more anger and bitterness.

But once I realized that Kim just *couldn't* work the required hours because of cultural restrictions placed on her, the situation became much more tolerable. Even though the ultimate result was that Kim left the job, our parting was amicable, and I felt compassion toward her instead of anger. If she had managed to stay, our relationship would have remained intact, undamaged by lingering anger. The experience taught me that it's best to check in when problems arise, before jumping to conclusions. As a rule, good employees don't develop attitude problems out of the blue.

The situation with Kim illustrates an unfortunate reality: If you have a serious problem with your housekeeper, ending the employment may be inevitable, whether it is voluntary on your housekeeper's part or involuntary. When such a problem arises, you should prepare yourself for that possibility. One of the most productive things you can do at this point may be to identify where you went wrong in hiring this person, so that you don't make the same mistake twice. While Kim's problem would have been difficult to identify during hiring, most serious problems originate as hiring problems.

Teresa had a nagging feeling while interviewing Mona for a house-keeper/nanny position, but she brushed it aside because she was uncomfortable with how she described the feeling to herself: The term that came to Teresa's mind was that Mona was not "subservient." Teresa scolded herself for expecting an employee to act servile and convinced herself that what she had witnessed was high self-esteem, so she hired Mona.

Unfortunately, soon after Mona accepted the position, she began putting restrictions on the task assignments that she would accept from

Teresa. Things came to a head several months into the job when Teresa asked Mona to weed the garden. "I did it last time," Mona replied. "This time it's your turn."

Whether she should be expected to weed the garden is an issue that should have been negotiated during the hiring process. Teresa's "nagging feeling" during the interview was a reading of Mona's reluctance to do certain kinds of tasks. In retrospect, Teresa should have been more careful when selecting her new housekeeper/nanny. But in the meantime, what was she to do about Mona?

After several conversations, it became clear that Mona was not going to back down, and, in fact, was likely to set down even more restrictions in the future. Worse, as Mona reacted badly in some of their conversations, Teresa began to wonder about her stability and worried about the wisdom of leaving her children in Mona's care. It was time to end Mona's employment—delicately. How it was done is addressed in the section titled "Firing Your Housekeeper."

When to Let Problems Go

After many years of employing housecleaners or cleaning services, and almost never needing to correct my employees (housecleaning is, after all, fairly straightforward), it came as a shock when I hired a 20-hour-per-week housekeeper. She was taking over most of the household tasks that I had been doing; although part of me was eager to delegate them, part of me had developed a strong sense of the "right" way to do them, and it was hard to let go.

I found myself correcting my new housekeeper for style differences that truly didn't matter. (Who cares how the towels are folded when stacked in the linen closet?) While I was helping my housekeeper develop a sense of ownership toward my household, I needed simultaneously to find a way to reduce my own strong investment in the way the chores were being done.

Focusing on my new priorities ultimately helped me emotionally disengage from the housework. Other employers of household help have similarly reported that a shift in focus helped them to readjust their perspective with regard to household chores. (Chapter 3 discusses the new opportunities that household help can make possible.)

So if you find yourself making a lengthy list of corrections for your housekeeper, you might ask yourself regarding each item, "Does this matter?" If you're not sure, engross yourself in your new opportunities for a few weeks, then ask the question again.

What about the corrections that *do* matter and *are* needed? If your housekeeper is new and the list of corrections is long, you can avoid overwhelming her by prioritizing them and discussing the most important ones with her, a few at a time. Remember to point out what she's doing well, so that she doesn't get the idea that you don't like anything about her work (unless that's true). As she begins to master the job, you'll have opportunities to fine-tune her job performance.

What if a task seems to be too hard for your housekeeper? Sometimes you might find that your housekeeper simply doesn't have the level of sophistication required for a particular task. Management is not all that different from motherhood, and in such cases I like to use the mother model. What do you do when a task is too difficult for a child—cleaning his room, for example? Besides defining the task very specifically, you help with the parts he can't do, like putting away the toys that are kept on high shelves, or folding the clothes that got pulled out of the drawer and need to be put away.

If certain tasks appear to be beyond an otherwise competent housekeeper's ability, can you find a way to help her be successful? Using the mother model, maybe you can break the task down into steps and delegate some, but not all, of the steps. Or maybe you can provide better tools, for example, a master shopping list like the one in Chapter 7, instead of a handwritten, less descriptive one.

Finally, your otherwise wonderful housekeeper might have a quirk or two that you decide to live with. I once had a fantastic housekeeper, Yelena, who had a habit of opening cupboard doors in the middle of cooking, without regard to the state of her hands, often leaving the door hardware slimy or sticky. Nothing I said to her had any impact on this habit, but we all loved her so much that I decided to drop the subject. If I found door hardware that needed attention, I took care of it myself—a small price to pay, I thought, in exchange for such a gem.

When You Lose Your Housekeeper

You've invested so much in hiring and training your housekeeper that you'd like never to have to do that again. What can you do to ensure that your housekeeper stays with you forever?

The good news is that if you've followed the advice in this book, you've created a very attractive position, and your housekeeper is likely to remain in your employ as long as her circumstances allow. Realistically speaking, though, the average housekeeper's tenure is relatively short, and your housekeeper's longevity may have nothing to do with you.

If your housekeeper is very ambitious, she is likely to aspire to another type of work. Yelena left my employ when she finished her studies and embarked on a career in the computer industry. A position as a housekeeper is not likely to hold much sway if changes in her personal life necessitate a change in her employment; I once lost a housekeeper whose sister was diagnosed with cancer and needed a full-time caregiver.

If (when) you do change housekeepers, all is not lost. Most of the time you've invested has been in planning and organizing, which you won't have to repeat. Even hiring goes smoother the second time around, because you aren't learning the process as you go.

If your relationship with your housekeeper is good, she is likely to give you advance notice before resigning. This will allow you to avoid the stress of interviewing housekeepers while your household is out of control. You may even want your outgoing housekeeper to meet a job candidate or two, as a way of giving *you* a good reference.

I don't recommend, however, having your outgoing housekeeper train your new one. If you want your new housekeeper to feel a sense of ownership toward your household, it's best if the training comes from you. Besides, the time-saving strategy can backfire. Yelena scared off a newly hired housekeeper, Nelia, by overtraining her. Yelena felt so protective toward our household that, in her zeal to make sure Nelia would do a good job, she led her to perceive that my expectations were out of reach. Nelia quit after the week of training was over (Yelena's last week coincided with Nelia's first and only week), complaining that the job was too hard.

Housekeeper Absences

Although not as disruptive as resigning, your housekeeper will periodically need to miss work. She will occasionally get sick, have a doctor's or legal appointment that conflicts with work, or have family obligations. If she is conscientious and has some flexibility in her schedule, she can work longer hours on a different day, or abbreviate her work schedule, performing only the highest priority tasks, and catch up the following week.

Longer absences are more problematic, though. What about a vacation that doesn't coincide with yours? If it's only a week or two, you can make do with a hodge-podge of services, just as you may have done to give yourself some breathing room during the hiring process. Hire a maid service to do the heavy cleaning. Take your laundry to a laundromat that has wash-and-fold service. Eat take-out or buy ready-to-eat meals at your supermarket deli. You'll spend more than you would have on your housekeeper's salary, but it's only for a week or two.

The biggest dilemma may arise if your housekeeper needs to take a leave of absence. Two of my immigrant housekeepers needed time to return to their native countries, one to help her parents put their affairs in order so that they could also immigrate, the other to spend some time with her dying mother. Pregnancy is another reason an employee might need a leave of absence, as well as illness, either her own or a family member's.

You are under no moral or legal obligation to grant leave to your housekeeper, even if it's unpaid. Because you have only one employee, upon whom you depend greatly, it would be unreasonable to expect you to "make do" without her for an extended time.

Yet you may decide, for pragmatic reasons, that you wish to grant your housekeeper's request. Maybe she is so exceptional that it's worth a sacrifice to await her return. Maybe the labor market in your area is such that it would be hard to replace her. Maybe she can recommend a friend or relative to fill in for her. If you decide to grant the leave, you can try to find temporary help, or use the strategies suggested above for briefer absences.

In the two cases where I granted a leave of absence, one was worth the investment and one didn't pay off. In the first case, my housekeeper returned after seven weeks, more loyal and hardworking than ever. In the second case, my housekeeper never really came "back," emotionally speaking. After three months, she asked for another leave of absence, this one without any specific purpose, simply because she wanted some personal time off. I decided not to grant the second leave and hired a replacement, wishing that I had done so in the first place.

Firing Your Housekeeper

If you've kept the lines of communication open, you may be able to avoid actually firing someone who is a bad fit. After hearing repeated correction and complaints from you, your housekeeper may see the handwriting on the wall, find a new job, and resign. If you're lucky, she'll give you a couple of weeks' notice, but chances are she won't, despite any agreements you made at the time of hiring. Consider yourself lucky not to have had to formally fire her.

By the way, some authors recommend declaring the first 30 to 90 days of your housekeeper's employment a "trial period," during which either of you is free to part company without explanation. I recommend against using a trial period for two reasons: First, I think the use of a trial period hinders the emotional commitment that is fundamental to creating your housekeeper's all-important "sense of ownership." Second, I don't think trial periods make rarely needed firings any less painful.

When it *is* necessary to fire your housekeeper, your first priority should be to safeguard the safety and security of your household. If you think she will be very angry and upset, you may want to discharge her with no notice, giving her severance pay instead. (Two weeks is standard, unless she has committed an offense such as stealing or has worked for you for a very short time.) You can avoid inflaming the situation by speaking in vague terms about your reasons. "Things just aren't working out."

Be sure to retrieve your house key before she leaves; if you are unable to do this or suspect she has made a copy of your key, have your locks rekeyed, to be on the safe side. You should also reprogram any electronic keypads for which she knows the codes.

If your relationship is more amicable, you can give her the more traditional two weeks' notice. Avoid interviewing potential replacements in her presence.

If you feel, as Teresa did, that your housekeeper is emotionally unstable, you may want to avoid letting her know that she is being fired. You can give her several weeks' notice and tell her, as Teresa told Mona, that you are making a major lifestyle change and will no longer be employing household help. In Teresa's case, she even gave Mona a letter of recommendation, at Mona's request, to make the charade complete. Although Teresa knew that she was potentially creating problems for Mona's future employers, her first priority was to protect her family—a good example of why written references, without follow-up phone contact, are to be taken with a very large grain of salt.

Don't Create a Problem Employee

Even though it's often possible to solve housekeeper problems, there is no substitute for hiring a great one in the first place. But it would be unfortunate to hire a great housekeeper and turn her into a problem employee. Sound ludicrous? Believe it or not, it can happen. The following list of things *not* to do describes real-life situations that happened to housekeepers I've known.

DON'T give your housekeeper impossible tasks.

One housekeeper was expected to tidy rooms in which the children were playing. Making the task even more difficult was the fact that the children were given a clear message by their parents that they were not responsible for cleaning up the toys they played with.

Housekeeper Don'ts

- Don't give your housekeeper impossible tasks.
- Don't add extra tasks to your housekeeper's workload, unless you make appropriate adjustments.
- Don't raise your voice, even (and especially) if you need to blow off steam.
- Don't fail to pay your housekeeper on payday.
- Don't neglect to provide your live-in housekeeper with comfortable and private living quarters.
- Don't allow your children to behave badly or speak rudely to your housekeeper.

DON'T add extra tasks to your housekeeper's workload, unless you make appropriate adjustments.

I know several housekeepers who are regularly asked to add extra tasks to their already full workloads. Their employers don't pay for added work hours, don't subtract any lower priority tasks, and don't even relax their standards for the less critical tasks. This occurs when the family is entertaining, during the holidays, when there are out-of-town visitors, and so on.

If you have slack time built into your housekeeper's schedule, great. If not, set priorities for your housekeeper if you need to add new tasks, and be reasonable in your expectation of what can be accomplished in a given time frame.

DON'T raise your voice, even (and especially) if you need to blow off steam.

When tasks are not done to the expected standards, some employers let their housekeepers have it. A bad day of your own is no excuse to treat an employee discourteously.

DON'T fail to pay your housekeeper on payday.

Don't expect your housekeeper to be flexible if you're a little short of cash one week, or just are too busy or distracted to write her paycheck. Your disorganization might mean that she won't be able to pay her rent.

DON'T neglect to provide your live-in housekeeper with private and comfortable living quarters.

As unbelievable as it may seem, some live-ins are expected to sleep on the couch or the floor. If you can't provide adequate living conditions, don't hire live-in help.

DON'T allow your children to behave badly or speak rudely to your housekeeper.

Even if your housekeeper does not take care of your children, she deserves to be treated with respect. If she does take care of them, it is doubly important that you back her authority with them.

It's possible that the employers guilty of the offenses described above started out with good intentions. But somewhere along the way, they lost sight of the most important management principle of all: that the best way to keep your housekeeper happy while getting the help you need is to focus on creating a mutually rewarding business relationship.

Epilog

Some Final Lessons

As this book goes to press, I've just resolved a minor housekeeper crisis. The feeling is familiar: I have such a crisis every so often. Periodically, I lose my housekeeper for one reason or another, and then panic sets in as I fear that I'll never find a good housekeeper again, and I'll have to go back to life as it used to be.

As time marches on, however, the panics become less and less severe because I inevitably do find a great housekeeper, learning a valuable lesson or two in the process. The question has evolved from "Will I be able to find another housekeeper?" to "What lesson will I learn this time?" It's become a bit of a puzzle that my analytical mind enjoys solving.

My latest crisis began when I gave my beloved housekeeper an ultimatum: she had to commit to working full weeks on a regular basis. For the first year or so, she had been the steadiest of employees. But lately, circumstances (many of her own creation) had caused her workweeks to be frequently shortened, often by two or three days. Although I had initially tried to be flexible, wanting to hold onto a good employee, her absences were highly inconvenient and had become more and more annoying.

I sensed that something had changed in my housekeeper's attitude toward her job. Frankly, I felt that she was viewing her workday as somehow optional. Could I be right? I was sure that a straightforward conversation between the two of us would set things right.

Unfortunately, I learned that my housekeeper did, in fact, view her workday as optional. She informed me that her job now held a relatively low priority in her life. When I explained that I needed someone who could commit to showing up at work five days a week, barring genuine emergencies or previously arranged time off, she resigned, giving me only two days' notice.

The Mad Scramble

The end-of the-year holidays were approaching, so this unpleasant turn of events was ill timed. But I was glad to clarify things between us. Now I was free to hire someone else. But how? It seemed unlikely that in the booming Silicon Valley economy, with "Help Wanted" signs visible in every store window, good housekeepers would be looking to start new jobs right before the holidays.

In the past, I'd weathered extended periods without permanent help by using temporary housekeepers hired through agencies. But the results were often unsatisfactory (because the agencies provided workers who were unreliable or lacked relevant experience) and once nearly disastrous (my husband came home late at night to find a slow-moving car with its headlights off obviously "casing" the house, necessitating an immediate change of locks). This time, I decided that prepackaged services, though expensive, would be the least stressful way to survive the holiday season. So I consulted the Yellow Pages for a nationally known cleaning franchise, booking a team of two to spend two hours each week cleaning the house, and located a local wash-and-fold service to handle the laundry and ironing. That left meals, errands, and daily tidy-up for myself, husband, and kids to handle on our own.

Next, I placed an ad, hoping against hope that someone qualified would respond.

Desperation Enhances Creativity

As the weeks went by, only the poorest-qualified candidates responded to my ad. In an attempt to increase exposure, I placed ads in places I wouldn't normally have bothered, such as in church bulletins, and told everyone I knew that I was looking for help. I consoled myself with the thought that all the best candidates had the luxury of waiting till after the holidays to hunt for a new job. How I hoped this were true.

A few days into the New Year, when the quality of responses to my ad still had not improved, my sense of panic grew. Unemployment in Silicon Valley was close to zero. Did the low response mean that virtually all housekeepers were gainfully employed? Maybe supply and demand had pushed wages higher, but that seemed an unlikely cause for the low response rate because I hadn't mentioned a pay rate in my ad. How could I get the attention of those few housekeepers out there who *were* looking for work?

I looked at the other "domestic help wanted" ads that were running alongside mine. They all sounded so similar. There was little to make mine stand out, other than the possibility that the hours or location might be more convenient for some candidates. My boring ad had produced great results in the past. But apparently the competitive job market demanded something more exciting. So I marshaled my "sales and marketing" brain cells and changed my ad. Instead of:

> **HOUSEKEEPER/Cook M-F,**
>
> **2-6pm, exper'd, refs, own**
>
> **car, Engl. Call 321 555-1234**

I changed the ad to read like this:

> **HOUSEKEEPER/Cook M-F,**
>
> **2-6pm, grt pay, paid hol, need**
>
> **English and refs. 321 555-1234**

The next day, the phone started ringing off the hook. Many of the callers were people who were already employed, but who regularly scan the classifieds looking for something better. Would they have called the first ad? No. But the second one piqued their curiosity.

With all the qualified candidates who called during my new ad's two-week run, I could have started an agency. And I ended up hiring a great housekeeper.

Lessons Learned

What did I learn from this experience? Several things. First, December is the worst possible time to hire. Because I didn't have much choice in the timing, I was smart to engage household services that would see me through the six weeks it took me to find a new housekeeper.

Second, the goal of a help-wanted ad is to entice qualified job candidates to call. Even though my originally worded ad had produced results in the past, times had changed. My new ad distinguished me from the competition (other household employers) and convinced job seekers to dial my number. By viewing the job search from the point of view of the potential candidates and emphasizing the benefits rather than the requirements of the job, I was able to write an ad that was effective even in the most competitive of job markets.

Third, I realized that I should have conveyed my annoyance to my former housekeeper before the situation came to a head. Because I had been so happy with her performance during the first year, and regularly told her so, I didn't want to do anything to jeopardize our good working relationship. But by not being more open with my dissatisfaction, I did damage our relationship. I should have warned her earlier that her repeated absences were consuming the reserve of good will that I had toward her and that she needed to reestablish the reliability that I had so appreciated the first year. By the time I did raise the issue with her, it's possible that she was backed into a corner and felt that the only way she could save face would be to resign.

These lessons all underscore a fundamental principle in hiring household help: that the key to success is to create a mutually rewarding business relationship. The value that the employer and the housekeeper receive must always be in balance. If not, then correction is in order.

Let Us Hear from You

I've been successfully hiring and managing household help for nearly 20 years, yet I continue to learn new lessons. By training myself to hunt for the lesson in every obstacle, I find that the process keeps getting easier.

I've enjoyed sharing *my* lessons by writing this book. Now I'd like to help readers benefit from the wisdom of *your* experience. I plan to incorporate your stories in future editions of this book. Please write to me about the obstacles you've faced and the lessons you've learned. I'd like to hear, too, about the value you've received from employing a housekeeper. Let me know how your life has changed. Send your comments to me in care of:

> Life Tools Press
> PO Box 390220
> Mountain View, CA 94039-0220

Or send email to *comments@LifeToolsPress.com*. The best stories will be posted on our website at *www.LifeToolsPress.com*. I can't wait to hear from you!

Appendix — Housekeeper Instructions

The following are the written instructions that I use with my housekeeper. You may wish to develop a similar set of instructions, making it more or less detailed.

DAILY SCHEDULE

EVERY DAY   Unload dishwasher; flip magnet from CLEAN to DIRTY
Collect recycling and empty kitchen trash
Vacuum kitchen, entry hall, kitchen bathroom, welcome mat in garage, living room carpet in area near kitchen door
Chop fruit—check with Kathy or see note

AS NEEDED   Mirrors, window touchup
Clean metal switchplates with Windex
Dust baseboards, wipe down moldings, etc.
Dust/wash all mini-blinds
Clean top edge of tile in shower
Kitchen floor—extra mopping
Water plants in front and sweep front entry
Knock down cobwebs in front doorway
Wipe mailbox clean
Hose down patio in back
Vacuum kids' bathroom floor
Empty trash baskets around the house
Wipe down/vacuum all upholstered furniture
Wipe down kitchen cupboards with Murphy's Oil Soap
Clean the front, top, and sides of kitchen appliances with Windex; check inside rim of dishwasher
Clean pantry shelves
Vacuum window coverings (or wipe down with damp cloth)

MONDAY SCHEDULE

LAUNDRY First Load: **Lights from Kathy's, Sam's, and Leslie's closets**
Add clothes to washer
Add detergent
Select NORMAL
Set water level
Set temperature level to WARM (middle)
Press START

Dry on LOW HEAT, MORE
Set ironing aside
Fold and put away clothes

Second Load: **Drip-dry clothes from Kathy's closet**
Add clothes to washer
Add detergent
Select GENTLE
Set water level
Set temperature level to COLD (bottom)
Press START

Lay flat on racks in upstairs tub to dry

GROCERIES Wait for delivery from Webvan or Peapod
Check groceries to make sure everything is correct
Return bins to delivery person
Sign receipt
Wash produce
Clear refrigerator of any food that has spoiled
Wash out vegetable containers, if needed
Put food away

CLEANING Dust

TUESDAY SCHEDULE

LAUNDRY First Load: **Darks from Michael's closet**
Add clothes to washer
Add detergent to tub and to detergent cup
Select PREWASH then select NORMAL
Set water level
Set temperature to HOT (top)
Press START

Add one sheet of Bounce to dryer
Dry on MED HEAT, More
Fold and put away clothes

Second Load: **Towels from Kathy and Michael's bathroom**
Add towels to washer
Add detergent
Select NORMAL
Set water level
Set temperature to WARM (middle)
Press START

Dry on MED HEAT, MORE
Fold towels and put away in bathroom cabinet
Hang alternate set of towels on towel racks

ERRANDS Dry Cleaning: Retrieve dry cleaning and hangers from
basket in closet
Pick up clean clothes at cleaners, drop off
dirty ones, return hangers
Hang up clean clothes, remove tags, save
hangers
Sunnymount Produce and/or Nob Hill Foods: Buy items
from list

IRONING Iron whites from Monday; hang clothes
Put away drip-dry clothes from Monday; iron if needed

CLEANING Vacuum downstairs only

COOKING Cook dinner

WEDNESDAY SCHEDULE

LAUNDRY First Load: **Darks from Kathy's closet**
Add clothes to washer
Add detergent
Select NORMAL
Set water level
Set temperature to WARM (middle)
Press START

Dry on LOW HEAT, MORE
Set ironing aside
Fold and put away clothes

Second Load: **Miscellaneous towels**
Collect hand towels from kids' bathroom, kitchen,
  powder room, upstairs bathroom, and Lifecycle
Get other dirty towels from basket under powder
  room sink
Add towels to washer
Add detergent
Select NORMAL
Set water level
Set temperature to WARM (middle)
Press START

Dry on HIGH HEAT, MORE
Fold towels and put away

CLEANING Bathrooms—mirrors, sinks, shower/tub, floors, etc.
Kitchen—sink, counter, floor, refrigerator, toaster oven,
  microwave, stove, etc.
NOTE *Never* mop kitchen floor with water.
Vacuum first, then clean with Pergo floor cleaner, using
  special mop or nylon scrub brush.
Entry hall—mop
Empty trash throughout house
Bag newspapers for recycling

THURSDAY SCHEDULE (Week 1)

LAUNDRY First Load: **Sheets and pillowcases** *only* **from Sam's & Leslie's beds**

Strip beds, leave comforter covers on
Add sheets to washer
Add detergent
Select PERM PRESS
Set water level
Set temperature to WARM (middle)
Press START

Dry on MED HEAT, MORE
Remake beds

Second Load: **Darks from Sam's and Leslie's closets**
Add clothes to washer
Add detergent to tub and detergent cup
Select PREWASH then select NORMAL
Set water level
Set temperature to WARM (middle)
Press START

Add one sheet of Bounce to dryer
Dry on MED HEAT, MORE
Set ironing aside
Fold and put away clothes

CLEANING   Dust

IRONING   Do as much as time permits: darks from Wednesday, darks from Thursday. Hang clothes.

COOKING   Cook dinner

THURSDAY SCHEDULE (Week 2)

LAUNDRY First Load: **Sheets and pillowcases only from Michael and Kathy's bed**
Strip bed, leave comforter cover on
Add sheets to washer
Add detergent
Select PERM PRESS
Set water level
Set temperature to WARM (middle)
Press START

Dry on MED HEAT, MORE
Remake bed with same sheets

Second Load: **Darks from Sam's and Leslie's closets**
Add clothes to washer
Add detergent to tub and detergent cup
Select PREWASH then select NORMAL
Set water level
Set temperature to WARM (middle)
Press START

Add one sheet of Bounce to dryer
Dry on MED HEAT, MORE
Set ironing aside
Fold and put away clothes

CLEANING Dust

IRONING Do as much as time permits: darks from Wednesday, darks from Thursday. Hang clothes.

COOKING Cook dinner

THURSDAY SCHEDULE (Week 3)

LAUNDRY First and
Second Load:
Sheets, pillowcases, and comforter covers from Sam's and Leslie's beds
Strip beds, remove comforter covers
NOTE This will require two loads
Add sheets to washer
Add detergent
Select PERM PRESS
Set water level
Set temperature to WARM (middle)
Press START

Dry on MED HEAT, MORE
Iron comforter covers if needed
Remake beds and replace comforter covers

Third Load:
Darks from Sam's and Leslie's closets
Add clothes to washer
Add detergent to tub and detergent cup
Select PREWASH then select NORMAL
Set water level
Set temperature to WARM (middle)
Press START

Add one sheet of Bounce to dryer
Dry on MED HEAT, MORE
Set ironing aside
Fold and put away clothes

CLEANING Dust

IRONING Do as much as time permits: darks from Wednesday, darks from Thursday, comforter covers if needed. Hang clothes.

COOKING Cook dinner

THURSDAY SCHEDULE (Week 4)

LAUNDRY First Load: **Sheets, pillowcases, and comforter cover from Michael and Kathy's bed**
Strip bed, remove comforter cover
Add sheets to washer
Add detergent
Select PERM PRESS
Set water level
Set temperature to WARM (middle)
Press START

Dry on MED HEAT, MORE
Remake beds using opposite color sheets and
  comforter cover
Put clean sheets in closet

Second Load: **Darks from Sam's and Leslie's closets**
Add clothes to washer
Add detergent to tub and detergent cup
Select PREWASH then select NORMAL
Set water level
Set temperature to WARM (middle)
Press START

Add one sheet of Bounce to dryer
Dry on MED HEAT, MORE
Set ironing aside
Fold and put away clothes

CLEANING Dust

IRONING Do as much as time permits: darks from Wednesday, darks
from Thursday, comforter cover. Hang clothes,
put comforter cover in closet.

COOKING Cook dinner

FRIDAY SCHEDULE

LAUNDRY First Load: **Towels from Kathy and Michael's bathroom**
Add towels to washer
Add detergent
Select NORMAL
Set water level
Set temperature to WARM (middle)
Press START

Dry on MED HEAT, MORE
Fold towels and put away in bathroom cabinet
Hang alternate set of towels on towel racks

Second Load: **Whites from Michael's closet**
Add detergent to tub and detergent cup
Add bleach to tub (not to cup)
Select NORMAL
Select SOAK
Set time to 30
Set water level
Set temperature to WARM (middle)
Select NORMAL
Press START
Let tub fill, then add clothes

Add one sheet of Bounce to dryer
Dry on MED HEAT, MORE
Fold and put away clothes

CLEANING Vacuum upstairs and downstairs

IRONING Iron anything left over from Thursday. Hang clothes, put comforter cover in closet.

COOKING Cook dinner

Appendix — Housekeeper-Friendly Recipes

The following are the recipes used for the sample meal plan described in Chapter 7. Note that a shopping list can be easily developed from the ingredient list. The instructions are laid out in a step-by-step manner, so that the recipes can be followed by non-native English speakers.

CHOCOLATE CHIP COOKIES

Groceries Needed:

2 eggs	(Safeway Grade AA Eggs/Large)
2 sticks butter or margarine	(Land O Lakes Salted Butter/4 Qtrs)
1 cup white flour	(Gold Medal All-Purpose Flour)
1 cup whole wheat flour	(Pillsbury Whole Wheat Flour)
1 cup bran flakes	(Kellogg Complete Bran Flakes)
½ teaspoon salt	(Morton Salt)
1 teaspoon baking soda	(Arm&Hammer Baking Soda)
½ cup white sugar	(C&H Granulated Sugar)
1 cup brown sugar	(C&H Golden Brown Sugar)
1 teaspoon vanilla	(Schilling Pure Vanilla Extract)
1 bag chocolate chips, 12 ounces	(Nestle Semi Sweet Morsels)

Cooking Instructions:

1. Remove eggs and butter from refrigerator at least an hour before baking to bring to room temperature. Do not microwave or melt butter.
2. Preheat oven to 375.
3. Get out mixer, large glass mixing bowl, and one other large bowl.
4. Into large bowl (not glass mixing bowl), measure white flour, whole wheat flour, bran flakes, salt, baking soda. Stir together.
5. In glass mixing bowl, cream together butter, eggs, white sugar, brown sugar, and vanilla.
6. Gradually add flour mixture to glass mixing bowl.
7. Add chocolate chips. Mix until chips are distributed evenly throughout batter.
8. Drop medium-size spoonfuls of batter onto cookie sheets. Bake 8 to 10 minutes. Remove from cookie sheets and let cool on racks.

SPAGHETTI WITH MEAT SAUCE

Produce Needed:

2 green bell peppers
2 large yellow onions
¼ pound mushrooms in bulk
3 cloves garlic

Groceries Needed:

1 pound 93% fat-free ground beef	(Whole Foods Market)
2 tablespoons olive oil	(Star Extra Virgin Olive Oil)
1 can tomato paste, 12 ounces	(Contadina Tomato Paste)
2 cans tomato sauce, 28 ounces each	(Contadina Tomato Sauce)
2 cans crushed tomatoes, 28 ounces each	(Progresso Crushed Tomatoes)
2 tablespoons parsley	(Spice Island Parsley)
2 teaspoons oregano	(Spice Island Oregano Leaf)
2 teaspoons basil	(Schilling Basil Leaves)
1 teaspoon thyme	(Spice Island Thyme)
1 package thin spaghetti, 16 ounces	(DaVinci Thin Spaghetti)
1 loaf garlic bread	(Colombo Garlic Bread)

Cooking Instructions:

1. Dice onions and green peppers. Slice mushrooms. Mince garlic.
2. Sauté ground beef in frying pan until brown and crumbly. Drain fat, if any.
3. In large stainless steel soup pot, heat olive oil over medium heat. Sauté garlic about 1 minute. Add onions, green peppers, and mushrooms. Cover pot and cook until vegetables are softened, stirring occasionally, 5 to 10 minutes.
4. Open canned tomato products and add to pot.
5. Add spices: parsley, oregano, basil, thyme.
6. Add meat to pot, stir everything to mix, and bring slowly to a boil.
7. After mixture comes to a boil, lower heat to "LOW," and cook with cover tilted slightly for about two hours. Stir every 15 minutes to prevent burning. (Be sure nothing is sticking to bottom of pot.)
8. Break the spaghetti into pieces and cook it for 10 minutes.
9. Preheat the oven to 400 degrees. Heat the garlic bread for 8 to 10 minutes. Cut into 1-inch slices.

GREEN SALAD

Produce Needed:

½ head iceberg lettuce
1 cucumber
1 small tomato
¼ red onion

Groceries Needed:

Salad dressing   (Good Seasons Italian Dressing Mix)

Instructions:

1. (Iceberg lettuce has been previously cleaned.) Tear—don't cut—lettuce into bite-size pieces. Place in salad bowl.
2. Cut red onion into thin slices. Add to salad bowl.
3. Peel cucumber. Cut in half lengthwise. Cut into ¼-inch slices. Place in a separate bowl. (Sam doesn't like cucumbers or tomato.)
4. Cut tomato into wedges. Place in bowl with cucumber.
5. Just before serving, toss with Good Seasons Italian salad dressing. Use what is in dispenser or, if not enough, make using seasoning packet.

TACOS

Produce Needed:

¼ head iceberg lettuce
1 small tomato

Groceries Needed:

1 pound 93% fat-free ground beef	(Whole Foods Market)
1 packet taco seasoning	(Old El Paso Taco Seas. Mix/Less Salt)
½ brick mild cheddar cheese	(Mild Cheddar Chunk/Deli)
1 can sliced olives, 3.8 ounces	(Early California Ripe Olives Sliced)
2 packages taco shells	(Townhouse Taco Shells)

For burritos, add:

1 package tortillas	(Mission Flour Tortilla Soft Taco Size)
1 can refried beans, 15 ounces	(Rosarita Refried Beans/Traditional)

Cooking Instructions:

1. Sauté ground beef. Add spices to beef according to package directions.
2. Grate cheese using hand grater. Shred lettuce by cutting lettuce into fine pieces with a knife. Dice tomatoes. Open and drain can of olives.
3. Put each ingredient in separate small serving bowl.
4. Heat taco shells in oven.
5. For burritos: Warm beans in pan on stove. Warm tortillas in microwave.

CHICKEN FRICASSEE

Produce Needed:

6 large potatoes
1 yellow onion
6 carrots
6 stalks of celery

Groceries Needed:

1 lb. boneless, skinless chicken breasts	(Foster Farms Bnls/Sknls Breast Flts)
2 bouillon cubes, chicken flavor	(Herb-Ox Chicken Bouillon Cubes)
1 tablespoon dried parsley	(Spice Island Parsley)
½ teaspoon sage	(Spice Island Sage)
½ teaspoon thyme	(Spice Island Thyme)
¼ teaspoon salt	(Morton Salt)
¼ teaspoon pepper	(Crown Colony Ground Black Pepper)
white flour	(Gold Medal All-Purpose Flour)
Kitchen Bouquet browning sauce	(Kitchen Bouquet...)
milk	(Lactaid 100 Calcium Fat-Free Milk)
butter	(Land O Lakes Salted Butter/4 Qtrs)

Cooking Instructions:

1. Peel carrots and dice. Dice onion and celery.
2. In large stockpot, lightly brown chicken with 1 tablespoon butter.
3. Add vegetables to pot. Cover with water.
4. Add spices: bouillon cubes, parsley, sage, thyme, salt, pepper.
5. Bring to a boil and let boil gently for 1½ or 2 hours. Add water periodically, if necessary.
6. Peel potatoes and cut into quarters.
7. Boil potatoes for 30 to 45 minutes.
8. Drain (and save) chicken stock.
9. Shred chicken.
10. Make gravy with chicken stock, flour, Kitchen Bouquet, bouillon cube.
11. Mash potatoes with milk and butter.

GREAT AMERICAN BEAN SALAD

Produce Needed:

1 red bell pepper (substitute green if red not available)
¼ red onion
fresh basil (a few leaves needed, buy one bunch)

Groceries Needed:

1 can tuna, 6 ounces	(Bumble Bee Chunk Albacore Tuna/Wtr)
1 can olives, 2 ¼ ounces	(Early California Ripe Olives Sliced)
1 can kidney beans, 15 ounces	(S&W Lite Slt Kidney Beans Drk Red)
1 can garbanzo beans, 15 ounces	(S&W Lite Garbanzo Beans Less Salt)
½ cup walnuts	(Diamond Shelled Walnuts)
¼ cup salad dressing	(Good Seasons Italian Dressing Mix)

Instructions:

1. Open all cans and drain liquid. Combine ingredients in salad bowl.
2. Cut several leaves of fresh basil into small pieces.
3. Cut red onion into thin slices. Cut half the red pepper into thin rings.
4. Chop walnuts in Braun chopper.
5. Combine all ingredients and toss with salad dressing.

Resources

The resources listed in this section offer further help with some of the issues raised in this book. They are organized by "issue," in the order that the issues were raised.

Understanding the Problem

The Second Shift by Arlie Russell Hochschild with Anne Machung. New York: Avon Books, 1989. This groundbreaking book defined the problem of women's double day.

Chore Wars: How Households Can Share the Work and Keep the Peace by James Thornton. Berkeley, CA: Conari Press, 1997. Providing an updated definition of the problem, this book was written by a man who was able to "get" this women's issue. Although Thornton proposes sharing as the solution to the problem, much of the set-up work that he outlines is necessary whether chores are to be shared or delegated.

Motherhood Stress by Deborah Shaw Lewis with Gregg Lewis. Dallas: Word Publishing, 1989. If motherhood overwhelms you and you don't know why, this is the book to read.

Overcoming Guilt

I've Done So Well, Why Do I Feel So Bad? by Celia Halas and Roberta Matteson. New York: Ballantine Books, 1978. Chapter 9, "Guilt," demonstrates how our irrational feelings of guilt can keep us stuck, whether or not we have the power to make changes in our lives.

Clarifying Daydreams

Wishcraft: How to Get What You Really Want by Barbara Sher with Anne Gottlieb. New York: Ballantine Books, 1979. This classic book explores the two key components of getting what you want in life: desire (wishing) and technique (craft).

Do What You Love, the Money Will Follow: Discovering Your Right Livelihood by Marsha Sinetar. New York: Dell Publishing, 1987. This inspirational book is worth reading just for the lift it will give your spirits.

Finding Your Perfect Work: The New Career Guide to Making a Living, Creating a Life by Paul and Sarah Edwards. New York: Jeremy P. Tarcher/Putnam Books, 1996. This comprehensive career guide focuses on four alternative paths to your perfect work: harvesting a gift, pursuing a passion, following a mission, and capitalizing on your assets.

First Things First: To Live, to Love, to Learn, to Leave a Legacy by Steven R. Covey, A. Roger Merrill, and Rebecca R. Merrill. New York: Simon & Schuster, 1994. This meaty book takes time management to a new level by encouraging you to examine your effectiveness in the context of your values.

Negotiating with Your Spouse

You Just Don't Understand: Women and Men in Conversation by Deborah Tannen. New York: Ballantine Books, 1990. This book is a good place to begin understanding why men and women seem to speak different languages.

Men Are from Mars, Women Are from Venus: A Practical Guide for Improving Communication and Getting What You Want in Your Relationships by John Gray. This is a humorous but helpful look at the psychological differences between men and women.

Brain Sex: The Real Difference Between Men and Women by Anne Moir and David Jessel. New York: Dell Publishing, 1991. Originally published in Britain, this book thoroughly analyzes the biological differences between the brains of men and women.

When Talking Makes Things Worse! Resolving Problems When Communication Fails by David Stiebel. Dallas: Whitehall & Nolton, 1997. This book outlines a simple, four-step strategy to resolving disagreements instead of just talking about them.

If Only He Knew and *For Better or for Best* by Gary Smalley with Steve Scott. Grand Rapids, MI: Zondervan, 1979. These are companion books written, respectively, for husbands and wives. Although Gary Smalley is a Christian who writes from a Biblical perspective, these books would benefit any couple who wanted to understand each other better.

Psycho-Cybernetics by Maxwell Maltz. New York: Pocket Books, 1960. This is a generation-old but still-valid guidebook on gaining confidence through "synthetic experience."

Getting Organized

How to Get Control of Your Time and Your Life by Alan Lakein. New York: Signet, 1973. This classic time-management how-to book asks the now-famous question, "What is the best use of my time right now?"

Don't Do. Delegate! by James M. Jenks and John Kelly. New York: Ballantine Books, 1985. This is an easy-to-read guidebook on the art of delegation.

How to Get Organized When You Don't Have the Time by Stephanie Culp. Cincinnati: Writer's Digest Books, 1986. This excellent primer on getting organized is divided into two parts: "Organizing Your Time" and "Organizing Your Space." The second part includes several chapters on how to make your household run more smoothly.

Make Your House Do the Housework by Don Aslett and Laura Aslett Simons. Cincinnati: Writer's Digest Books, 1986. A housecleaning expert and his interior designer daughter suggest hundreds of ways to make cleaning and maintenance easier through techniques ranging in complexity from rearranging the furniture to redecorating, remodeling, or building a custom-designed home.

The Sidetracked Sisters Catch-Up on the Kitchen by Pam Young and Peggy Jones. New York: Warner Books, 1983. This entire book focuses on making the kitchen more workable—from menu planning to cupboard organization.

Clutter Control: Putting Your Home on a Diet by Jeff Campbell. New York: Dell Publishing, 1992. Also, *Clutter's Last Stand* by Dan Aslett. Cincinnati: Writer's Digest Books, 1984. If clutter is a major problem in your house, either of these books might help. It takes much longer to clean a house that's full of clutter. So, besides creating a more pleasant living environment, if you declutter, you'll also save money on household help.

National Association of Professional Organizers (N.A.P.O.) If you're desperate, you might want to hire a professional to help you get organized. For the phone number of an organizer near you, contact N.A.P.O at (512) 206-0151 or *www.napo.net*. You might also check the Yellow Pages under "Organizing Services."

On-Line Grocery Shopping

An application well suited for the Internet, on-line grocery shopping is a rapidly growing industry. Services operate one of two ways: either by maintaining their own warehouses and delivering product straight to you, avoiding the retail middleman, or by forming liaisons with retail stores, purchasing product from those stores, and then delivering to you. A few large companies have established service in several geographic areas, but most are smaller operations committed to serving one local area.

The following list of on-line grocery-shopping services contains but a few of all of the choices available today. To augment this list, try conducting an Internet search using the keywords "online grocery shopping." (Try it using "on line" and "on-line", too.) You can also contact your local supermarkets and ask them about their plans to offer such a service.

Many of the following companies are growing rapidly. Check the websites for recently added service areas.

Webvan operates in Atlanta and the San Francisco Bay Area, and will open in Chicago and Seattle during 2000. It plans to open in 26 markets in total over a three-year period. Contact Webvan at (800) 799-4999 or *www.webvan.com*.

Home Grocer serves Seattle/Puget Sound; Portland, OR; and Orange, San Bernardino, and Los Angeles Counties in Southern California. Contact Home Grocer at (800) 688-0201 or *www.homegrocer.com*.

Peapod is currently available in Austin, Boston, Chicago, Columbus, Dallas/Fort Worth, Houston, Long Island/Nassau County, and San Francisco/San Jose. The "Peapod Packages" program offers national services for nonperishables. Contact Peapod at (800) 5-PEAPOD or *www.peapod.com*. As this book goes to press, Peapod Inc. is up for sale. Call or check the website to make sure information listed here is still accurate.

GroceryWorks currently offers service in Dallas, Fort Worth, and Houston. As this book goes to press, they have signed a letter of intent with Safeway, which will significantly expand their service area. Visit their website at *www.groceryworks.com* for more information.

Pink Dot offers service in the Los Angeles and San Fernando Valley areas. Contact Pink Dot at (800) PINKDOT or *www.pinkdot.com*.

Streamline serves suburban Boston and Washington DC. Contact Streamline at (877) STREAMLINE or *www.streamline.com*.

Shoplink provides service in communities in Massachusetts, Connecticut, and New York. Contact Shoplink at (888) YOUR TIME or *www.shoplink.com*.

Bag Boy Express serves the Minneapolis/St. Paul area. Contact Bag Boy Express at (612) 862-5365 or *www.bagboyexpress.com*.

PC Foods serves customers in Austin, Texas. Contact PC Foods at (512) 335-9806 or *www.pcfoods.com*.

Food Town Supermarkets offer on-line grocery shopping to customers in Toledo, Ohio. Contact Food Town Online at (800) 999-8355 or *www.foodtownonline.com*.

HomeRuns serves customers in the Boston area. Contact Home Runs at (800) 882-7867 or *www.homeruns.com*.

Grocery Shopping Network has formed an alliance of local grocery stores, which collectively provides on-line grocery shopping. Visit its website at *www.groceryshopping.net* and click on "store locator" to find a comprehensive, nationwide list of local grocery stores that are network members or call (888) 673-4663.

eGrocer also provides on-line grocery shopping through a variety of high-end grocery stores throughout the country. Contact eGrocer at (408) 795-1540 or *www.egrocer.com.*

Net Grocer ships nonperishables to customers in the 48 contiguous United States via Federal Express. Contact Net Grocer at (888) 638-4762 or *www.netgrocer.com.*

Offering Insurance as a Benefit

Eisenberg Associates offers individual medical, dental, life, and disability insurance and can set up IRAs, mutual funds, or other investments, to help your employee save. Contact Eisenberg Associates at (800) 777-5765 or *www.eisenbergassociates.com.*

Pacific Benefit and Health Options provides individual medical, dental, and vision insurance at group rates for California clients only. Contact Pacific Benefit and Health Options at (800) 472-2236 or *www.pacifichealthinsurance.com.*

Background Checking

The ChildCare Registry provides national background checks for a fee and reports back within 96 hours. Contact The ChildCare Registry at (925) 846-5327.

Trustline supplies background checks for California employers of in-home childcare. It will check the California criminal history system and a database of documented child abusers, and perform a nationwide background check. It reports back in six to eight weeks. Contact Trustline at (800) 822-8490 or *www.trustline.org.*

Equifax (for credit checking) can be reached at (800) 685-1111.

Experian, formerly TRW, (for credit checking) can be reached at (888) EXPERIAN or (800) 682-7654 or *www.experian.com/product/consumer/index.html.*

Trans-Union (for credit checking) can be reached at (800) 888-4213.

Help with Payroll Tax Paperwork

Nanitax-Home/Work Solutions has a one-time service called Quick Start, which helps employers understand and organize their tax obligations. The company will also complete relevant tax forms for ongoing subscribers, as well as provide weekly or semi-monthly payroll services. Contact Nanitax at (800) NANITAX or *www.4nannytaxes.com*.

GTM Associates also provides payroll services for household employees. Besides EasyPay, its nanny tax and payroll service, its website offers a "Nanny Tax Resource Center," including a tax calculator, a tax calendar, and downloadable tax forms. Contact GTM Associates at (888) 4-EASYPAY or *www.gtmassoc.com*.

Local bookkeeping or accounting services may also provide payroll and tax services for household employers. Look in the Yellow Pages under "Bookkeeping Services."

Communicating with Your Housekeeper

Household Spanish by William C. Harvey. Hauppage, NY: Barron's, 1995. If your housekeeper is a native speaker of Spanish, this book might help you communicate better with her. The most useful section may be the last one, which suggests ways that you can help her improve her English.

Bridging Cultural Barriers for Corporate Success: How to Manage the Multicultural Work Force or *Profiting in America's Multicultural Marketplace: How to Do Business Across Cultural Lines* by Sondra Thiederman. Both New York: Lexington Books, 1991. Either of these would be a good sourcebook for understanding cultural differences that when misunderstood create obstacles to effective workplace communication and harmony.

Establishing Boundaries with Your Housekeeper

Boundaries: When to Say YES, When to Say NO to Take Control of Your Life by Henry Cloud and John Townsend. Grand Rapids, MI: Zondervan, 1992. Although the advice in this book is Biblically based, the material is extremely valuable for those of any religious belief. The book, which defines a boundary as a "personal property line," will be useful for those who want to establish a warm but professional relationship with their housekeeper.

And don't forget to visit *www.LifeToolsPress.com* for downloadable forms and checklists, useful links, frequently asked questions, and much more.

Notes

Chapter 1

1 Daniel Evan Weiss, *The Great Divide: How Females and Males Really Differ* (New York: Poseidon Press, 1991), p. 29.

2 Anne Chappell Belden, "Don't Sweat the Small Stuff: An Interview with Best-Selling Author Richard Carlson, Ph.D.," *Bay Area Parent* (January 1999), pp. 30-34.

3 "Report Card on the New Providers: Kids and Moms Speak," *Whirlpool Foundation Study* (May 1998), p. 56.

4 Scott Coltrane, *Family Man: Fatherhood, Housework, and Gender Equity* (New York: Oxford University Press, 1996), p. 161.

5 Jessie Bernard, *The Future of Motherhood* (New York: Dial Press, 1974), p. 116.

6 Debra Wierenga, "Mysteries of the Fourth Dimension," *Juggle Magazine* (www.jugglezine.com), p. 2.

7 Carol Tavris and Carole Wade, *The Longest War: Sex Differences in Perspective* (New York: Harcourt Brace Jovanovich, 1984), p. 285.

8 Bernard, p. 120.

9 Donna Britt, "Superwoman? Give Me a Break!" *San Jose Mercury News* (October 2, 1994), p. 2H.

10 Arlie Hochschild, "The Second Shift: Employed Women Are Putting in Another Day of Work at Home," *Utne Reader* (March/April 1990), p. 66.

11 Weiss, p. 29.

[12] Pepper Schwartz, *Peer Marriage: How Love Between Equals Really Works* (New York: The Free Press, 1994), p. 123.

[13] Beth Anne Shelton, *Women, Men and Time: Gender Differences in Paid Work, Housework and Leisure* (New York: Greenwood Press, 1992), p. 153.

[14] Mary C. Hickey, "The Exhausted Woman," *Ladies' Home Journal* (March 1994), p. 90.

[15] Hochschild, p. 69.

[16] Hickey, p. 90.

[17] Amy Rock Wohl, Hal Morgenstern, and Jess F. Kraus, "Occupational Injury in Female Aerospace Workers," *Epidemiology* (March 1995), pp. 110-114.

[18] NHTSA's Drowsy Driver Research Program, "Fact Sheet" (January 1997).

[19] Hickey, p. 90.

[20] Carolyn Hagan, "Is Motherhood Good for Your Health?," *Child* (May 1995), p. 71.

[21] Ann Reeves, "Work and Family: The Delicate Balance," *Bay Area Parent* (July 1995), p. 22.

[22] Hagan, p. 71.

[23] Schwartz, p. 122.

[24] Rosalind C. Barnett and Caryl Rivers, *She Works/He Works: How Two-Income Families Are Happier, Healthier, and Better-Off* (New York: HarperSanFrancisco, 1996), p. 185.

[25] Anne Cassidy, "What Pushes Your Stress Button?," *Working Mother* (July/August 1996), p. 21.

[26] Lucie Young, "Current: Housecleaning Survey; Till Dust Do Us Part," *The New York Times* (January 29, 1999), p. 3

[27] Arlie Hochschild with Anne Machung, *Second Shift* (New York: Viking Penguin, 1989), p. 260.

[28] Marilyn Lewis, "Think Tank Disputes Idea of Bias in Women's Wages," *San Jose Mercury News* (December 14, 1995), p. 1A.

[29] Terri Apter, *Working Women Don't Have Wives* (New York: St. Martin's Griffin, 1993), p. 165.

[30] Virginia Woolf, *A Room of One's Own* (New York: Harcourt Brace Jovanovich, 1929).

Chapter 2

[1] Anne Cassidy, "What Pushes Your Stress Button?," *Working Mother* (July/August 1996), pp. 18-22.

[2] Stephanie Coontz, *The Way We Really Are: Coming to Terms with America's Changing Families* (New York: BasicBooks, 1997), p. 20.

[3] Ladies Home Journal Staff, "Special Report: American Women: Where We Are Now," *Ladies Home Journal* (September 1997), p. 131+.

[4] Mary C. Hickey, "The Exhausted Woman," *Ladies Home Journal* (March 1994), p. 90.

[5] Anne Moir and David Jessel, *Brain Sex* (New York: Dell Publishing, 1989).

[6] Beth Anne Shelton, *Women, Men and Time: Gender Differences in Paid Work, Housework and Leisure* (New York: Greenwood Press, 1992), p. 146.

[7] Margaret Ambry, "At Home in the Office," *American Demographics* (December 1988), p. 33.

[8] Carol Tavris and Carole Wade, *The Longest War: Sex Differences in Perspective* (New York: Harcourt Brace Jovanovich, 1984), p. 283.

[9] Rose L. Glickman, *Daughters of Feminists* (New York: St. Martin's Press, 1993), p. 23.

[10] Sheila Himmel, "Chore Leave," *West* (May 14, 1995), p. 10.

[11] Michael Walsh, "Think Smaller: There Are Many Advantages to Having a Modest-Sized Home," *San Jose Mercury News* (March 13, 1999), p. 1F.

[12] Bradley Inman, "The Village That It Takes Has Moved Inside the Home," *San Jose Mercury News* (October 19, 1996), p. 4E.

[13] W. Michael Cox and Richard Alm, "The Good Old Days Are Now," *Reason* (December 1995), p. 23.

[14] Jonathan Gershuny and John P. Robinson, "Historical Changes in the Household Division of Labor," *Demography* (November 1988).

[15] Jill Wolfson, "Busier Than Thou," *West* (October 1, 1995), p. 25.

[16] Jessie Bernard, *The Future of Motherhood* (New York: Dial Press, 1974), p. 125.

[17] Delia Blackler and Caroline Sorgen, "Pages from the Past: 100 Years of Homemaking," *Good Housekeeping* (July 1999), p. 176.

[18] Susan Strasser, *Never Done: A History of American Housework* (New York: Pantheon Books, 1982), p. 186.

[19] Cox and Alm, pp. 20-27.

[20] Cox and Alm, pp. 20-27.

[21] A talk given by Arlie Russell Hochschild at Printers Inc in Palo Alto, California, on May 27, 1997.

[22] Ann Reeves, "Work & Family: The Delicate Balance," *Bay Area Parent* (July 1995), p. 22.

Chapter 3

1   Jacqueline Cutler, "Alison Owings," *San Jose Mercury News* (July 21, 1996), p. 4 (Books).

2   Marilyn Gardner, "How to Find More Family Time," *Working Mother* (February 1996), p. 19.

3   Laurence Zuckerman, "Job? Kids? A Sad Route to a Happy Balance," *The New York Times* (January 12, 1997), p. 1.

4   Adrienne Rich, *On Lies, Secrets, and Silence* (New York: W.W. Norton, 1979), pp. 233-234.

5   Harold J. Leavitt, *Corporate Pathfinders* (Homewood, IL: Dow Jones-Irwin, 1986), p. 69.

Chapter 4

1   Phyllis Palmer, *Domesticity and Dirt: Housewives and Domestic Servants in the United States, 1920-1945* (Philadelphia: Temple University Press, 1989), p. 75.

2   Palmer, p. 83.

3   Penny Colman, *Rosie the Riveter: Women Working on the Home Front in World War II* (New York: Crown, 1995), p. 31.

4   Tia O'Brien, "Domestic Workers Get Their Voice," *West* (May 19, 1996), p. 14.

Chapter 6

1   Elizabeth Rapoport, "Mother's Daze," *Child* (May 1995) Adventures in Parenting supplement.

2   James Thornton, *Chore Wars: How Households Can Share the Work and Keep the Peace* (Berkeley, CA: Conari Press, 1997), p. 12.

3   Arlie Hochschild with Anne Machung, *The Second Shift: Working Parents and the Revolution At Home* (New York: Viking Penguin, 1989), p. 7.

4   James Dobson, "Dr. Dobson Answers Your Questions," *Dr. James Dobson's Focus on the Family Bulletin* (May 1995).

5   Maxwell Maltz, *Psycho-Cybernetics* (New York: Pocket Books, 1960), p. xii.

6   Rhona Mahony, *Kidding Ourselves: Breadwinning, Babies, and Bargaining Power* (New York: BasicBooks, 1995), pp. 90-91.

7   John Gray, *Men Are from Mars, Women Are from Venus: A Practical Guide for Improving Communication and Getting What You Want in Your Relationships* (New York: HarperCollins, 1992).

8   Gray, p. 269.

[9] Pepper Schwartz, *Peer Marriage: How Love Between Equals Really Works* (New York: Free Press, 1994) pp. 11-12.

[10] Gray, p. 55.

Chapter 7

[1] "Your Household Management Search," Starkey International, (www.starkeyintl.com), 1998.

[2] "Terms or Titles for Household Staff," Professional Domestic Services, (www.professionaldomestics.com), 1991.

[3] Tim Seldin, "Maria Montessori: An Historical Perspective," *Who Was Maria?* (www.montessori.org/mariawho.htm), The Montessori Foundation, 1996.

Chapter 8

[1] "Child File," *Child* (June/July 1996), p. 24.

[2] "Household Employer's Tax Guide for Wages Paid in 1998," Internal Revenue Service, *Publication 926*, p. 2.

[3] David Cay Johnson, "Millions Ignoring Nanny Tax," *San Jose Mercury News* (April 5, 1998), p. 1A.

[4] Chad R. Turner, *Employing Household Help: How to Avoid Tax and Legal Problems* (New York: John Wiley & Sons, 1995), p. vii.

[5] "Tighter Immigration Rules Due," *San Jose Mercury News* (July 1, 1997), p. 8A.

Chapter 10

[1] Jeff A. Schnepper, *How to Pay Zero Taxes* (New York: McGraw-Hill, 1995), pp. 37-38.

Chapter 11

[1] Andrew Hacker, *Money: Who Has How Much and Why* (New York: Scribner, 1997), p. 180.

[2] Sondra Thiederman, *Profiting in America's Multicultural Marketplace: How to Do Business Across Cultural Lines* (New York: Lexington Books, 1991).

[3] Deborah Tannen, *That's Not What I Meant! How Conversational Style Makes or Breaks Relationships* (New York: Ballantine Books, 1986).

[4] Thiederman.

[5] *El Norte* (American Playhouse, 1983).

[6] Thiederman, *Bridging Cultural Barriers for Corporate Success: How to Manage the Multicultural Work Force* (New York: Lexington Books, 1991).

Chapter 12

[1] Carol Kleiman, "Attention College Students: Take Time to Read This Article," *San Jose Mercury News* (October 2, 1994), p. 2PC.

[2] Sherwood Ross, "Best Motivational Tool Costs Nothing," *San Jose Mercury News* (February 17, 1995), p. 1G.

[3] Richard Carlson, "Book Bonus: Don't Sweat the Small Stuff with Your Family," *Working Mother* (November, 1998), pp. 34-38.

Index

A

Absences, housekeeper, 127, 201-202, 206, 208
  see also Time off, housekeeper's
Accidental breakage
  see Breakage, accidental
Accidents, 27, 85
Ads, for housekeepers, 64, 76-77, 136, 139-141, 145, 158, 206-208
  rates, 140
  four-line ad sample, 140, 141
  three-line ad sample, 140, 141, 207
Advance earned income credit
  see Earned income credit
Advantages and Disadvantages of Recruiting Methods, *figure*, 137
Advertising, 33, 44
  see also Ads, for housekeepers
Affordability, of household help, 16, 41-44, 79-91
  see also Costs
African-American (women), 58
Age Discrimination in Employment Act, 174
Agencies
  government, 161, 162
  housekeeper, 77, 128, 129, 136-138, 139, 145, 152, 206, 208
Alice (from *The Brady Bunch*), 121, 158
Alison, *anecdote,* 138
American Dream, 59-60
Americans with Disabilities Act, 153-154, 174
Amy, *anecdote,* 139
Anger, 25, 27-28, 33, 53, 88, 93, 196, 197, 202
Antidiscrimination laws, 174
Appliances, household, 25, 36-37, 41-43
Aristotle, 30
Attitude, of housekeeper, 196-197, 206

B

Babysitters, 18, 71, 129, 139, 173, 193
Background checking, 141, 151-153, 155, 234
Battered women
  see Domestic violence
Baird, Zoe, 128
Barb, *anecdote,* 90
Beecher, Catherine, 40-41
Benefits
  job, of employer, 176
  job, for housekeeper, 56, 121-133, 155, 156, 173, 193, 208
  of hiring help, 21, 79-87, 91, 92
Benefits You Can Offer, *figure,* 122
Berra, Yogi, 63
Bertila, *anecdotes*, 73, 194-195
Bill-paying, 70, 103
Biology, and housework, 33-34
Blood pressure, 27
Bob, *anecdote*, 53
Bonding, 152
Bonuses, 127
Boundaries, 189-190, 235-236
  see also Friendship, with housekeeper
Brady Bunch, The, 121, 158
Breakage, accidental, 152
Breaks, 174, 182
Budget, 14, 16, 78, 79, 87-92
Burn-out, housekeeper, 72
Business relationship,
  see Mutually rewarding business relationship

C

Calculations
  of amount of help needed, 17, 63-65
  of housework to be done, 103-104
  of whether to hire help, 21, 79-91, 94
  tax, 162, 168-171, 175-176
Capability, of housekeeper, 192, 196-197
Cardiovascular disease, 27

Car expenses
  see Expenses, car
Car keys, 103
Carlson, Richard, 24, 193
Charitable acts, 158
Charlene, *anecdote*, 42
Chauffeuring, 39, 71, 88, 151
Cheryl, *anecdote*, 64
Child and Dependent Care Expenses
  (IRS), 175
Child and dependent care expense tax
  credit, 175-177
Childcare, 15, 18, 25, 29, 43, 50, 65,
    71-72, 129, 150, 152, 153, 159,
    176, 188
Child labor, 173
Childrearing, 25, 32, 35, 91
Children
  and household supplies, 108
  and meal planning, 112
  effect of housework on, 29
  housework and presence of, 25, 33
  household tasks for, 75, 105
  older, 71-72
  teaching to do housework, 32
  younger, 71-72
Cholesterol, 27
"Chore wars", 51
Christine, *anecdote*, 49
Circular E, Employer's Tax Guide (IRS),
  169
  see also, Publication 15
Civil Rights Act, 58, 174
Clarity, 52-54
Claudia, *anecdote*, 57, 61
Cleaning products, 192
Cleaning services, 19, 49, 65, 71-72, 76,
    78, 84, 89, 124, 125, 126, 129, 136,
    138, 152, 158, 198, 200, 207
Clinton, Bill, 128
Closets, 105, 107-108, 192
Clothing, identification of, 110
Clutter, 101-102
Collectibles, 152
Columbus, Christopher, 30

Commitment, 52-54
Communication
  tone of, 194
  with housekeeper, 123, 182-183, 235
Communication Tips, *figure*, 184
Compassion, 158, 197
Conflicts over housework, 25, 28, 30, 31,
    51, 85, 105
Conflict, work/family, 50
Confrontation, avoiding, 185
Consumption, 38-39
Contract of employment
  see Employment contract
Convenience foods, 25
Coontz, Stephanie, 32
Correction, of housekeeper, 198, 201, 208
Cost Justification Formula, *figures*, 80, 86
Cost-justification, of housekeeper
  expense, 17, 78, 79-94
Cost Justification Worksheet, *figure*, 81
Cost Justification Worksheet (Completed),
  figure, 82
Cost of living, 193
Costs
  of hiring help, 16, 21, 63, 64, 75-78,
    79-87
  of not hiring help, 16, 26-30, 80-82,
    85-87
Credit check, of job candidate, 151
Creeping consumerism, 44
Criminal background check, of job
  candidate, 151
Cronkite, Walter, 46
Cultural differences
  see Differences, in culture
Cultural myths
  see Myths, about hiring household help
Cultural restrictions, 197

D

Daily Kitchen Tidy-Up, *figure*, 73
Dana, *anecdote*, 154
Daydreams
  see Dreams

Days off, housekeeper's
    paid, 193
    unpaid, 173, 195
Deanna, *anecdote*, 41-42
Debbie, *anecdote*, 54
Decision-making
    repeated, in household, 74-75, 97-98,
        103-104, 111-112, 119
    whether to hire a particular candidate,
        153, 155, 159
    whether to hire household help, 17, 21,
        44, 79
Deductions, tax
    see Paycheck, housekeeper's,
        adjustments to
Delegation
    of housework to children, 32, 75, 99
    of housework to family members, 66,
        68, 69
    of housework to worker, 21, 23, 31, 34,
        48, 56, 64, 66, 68, 70, 71, 74-75,
        98, 102, 104, 107, 110, 113, 118,
        175, 181, 192, 198-199
    of tax and payroll paperwork, 162, 235
"Deminimus fringe benefit exclusion",
    125
Department of Justice, 166
Department of Labor, 172
    see also Labor, state department of
Dependent care assistance program, 176
Depression, 28
Differences, 183
    in culture, 17, 65, 175, 185-187
    in language, 19, 175, 183-185
    in personality, 187
Directing, of housekeeper, 56, 95,
    179-190
Disability, 76, 132
Disability insurance, 127, 131, 167, 169
Discretionary spending, 88
Discrimination, 30, 58, 59, 154, 174-175
    see also Antidiscrimination laws
Dismissal,
    see Firing
Diversity, 187
Divorce, 28-30, 50, 53, 85

Dobson, Dr. James, 91
Domestic violence, 28, 60, 150
Don't Sweat the Small Stuff, 24
*Don't Sweat the Small Stuff with Your
    Family*, 193
Doris, *anecdote*, 69
Dreams, 45-54, 230
Driving record, of job candidate, 151
Duties, of housekeeper, 56, 121, 123, 124,
    149, 156, 181

E

Earned income credit, 130, 167, 168, 169,
    172
Economy, market-driven, 57
    see also Free market
Education, 57, 59, 60
Effective Household System Ground
    Rules, *figure*, 102
Effectiveness, personal, 14, 15, 16, 19, 46,
    192
Egalitarian
    attitude toward housekeeper, 186
Eldercare, 143, 173
Elena, *anecdote*, 48
Eligibility for employment, 166
Elitism, and hiring household help, 40, 57
El Norte, 185
Emergencies, housekeeper's, 206
Emotional caretaking, 34
Employee (vs. independent contractor),
    78, 128-129, 164, 165
Employer Identification Number, 167
Employer's Supplemental Tax Guide
    (IRS), 129
*Employing Household Help: How to
    Avoid Tax and Legal Problems*, 132
Employment contract, 157
Employment letter, 156-157
Employment Tax Checklist, *figure*, 163
Employment taxes
    see Taxes, employment
Employment terms, 156-157

English
language skills, 60, 76, 77, 141, 147, 149, 154, 175, 183-185
Pidgin, 185
Entitlement, sense of, 31
Entropy, 105-106
Environment, working, 57, 60, 136, 189, 192
Equal Pay Act, 174
Errands, 110, 141, 182
Estimates of time spent on housework, 65, 72-73
Evaluating, of housekeeper, 56, 95, 191-204
Exercise, 27
Exercise, Roles and Tasks, 66
Expectations, 90
of employer, 105, 123, 180, 181, 191, 192, 193, 200, 204
of housekeeper, 147, 157
Expenses, car, 118, 125
Exploitation, of housekeepers, 57-61

F

Face, saving
see Saving face
Fair labor requirements, 58, 124, 162, 172-177
see also Legal requirements
Fair Labor Standards Act, 172-173
Family size, 39
Fatigue, 25-27, 53
see also Sleep deprivation
Feedback, to housekeeper, 56, 127, 183, 191-204
see also Directing, of housekeeper
see also Evaluating, of housekeeper
FICA (Federal Insurance Contributions Act), 167-171
Figures
Advantages and Disadvantages of Recruiting Methods, 137
Benefits You Can Offer, 121
Communication Tips, 184
Cost Justification Formula, 80, 86

Cost Justification Worksheet, 81
Cost Justification Worksheet (Completed), 82
Daily Kitchen Tidy-Up, 73
Effective Household System Ground Rules, 102
Employment Tax Checklist, 163
Four-Line Ad Sample, 141
Household Tools and Supplies, 109
Housekeeper Don'ts, 203
Laundress (Sample Task List), 68
Master Shopping List, 115-116
"Nanny Tax" Myths, Misperceptions, and Realities, 128
Opportunities and Benefits, 83
Other Informative Government Publications, 166
Phone Screen Worksheet, 146
Reference Check Worksheet, 148
Reminder List, 117
Residual Cost Formula, 87
Roles and Tasks Exercise, The, 70
Sample Employment Letter, 156-157
Sample Pay Stub, 170
Sample Roles and Sub-Roles, 67
Three-Line Ad Samples, 141, 207
To Be Answered During Screening, 142
Weekly Meal Plan, 113
Which Forms to Request from Which Agencies, 164-165
Finances
see Affordability, of household help
Firing, of housekeeper, 195, 198, 202-203
Flexible time off, 126
see also Time off, housekeeper's
Florence, *anecdote*, 40
Focus on the Family, 91
Food management, system for, 112
Form 2441 (IRS), 176
Forms and publications
ordering information, 163
tax-related, 162, 163, 164
Four-Line Ad Sample, *figure*, 141
Frank, *anecdote*, 23-24
Free market, 57, 59

Free time
   see Leisure time
Friendship, with housekeeper, 187
FUTA (Federal Unemployment Tax Act),
   169-171

G

Gardener
   see Lawn care
Gender-based division of labor, 25-26, 35
   see also Roles, traditional
Gender conflicts
   see Conflicts over housework
Geographic differences in labor market
   see Labor market, geographic
     differences
GI Bill, 41
Ginny, *anecdote*, 64
"Going rate" to pay housekeepers
   see Pay rate, for housekeepers,
     "going rate"
Good Housekeeping, 40
Gray, John, 93-94
Greg, *anecdote*, 90
Groceries, delivery of, 39
Grocery shopping lists
   see Shopping lists
Grocery shopping services, 117-118,
   232-234
Grocery store layout, 114
Gross National Product (GNP), 25
"Growing" your own (housekeeper), 136,
   139
Guilt, 15-16, 19, 28, 57, 60, 186, 189, 192,
   230

H

Hale, Sarah Josepha, 40
Handy Reference Guide (Department of
   Labor), 172, 173
Harassment, sexual, 174, 188
Health
   financial, 29-30
   physical, 27-28, 85
Healthcare, 39, 127

Hiring, 17, 56, 119, 135-159, 197, 200,
   202-203, 206
   see also, Staffing
Hiring tips, 158-159
History
   of American working women, 36, 43
   of domestic workers, 39-41, 57-61
   of housework, 35-36
Hochschild, Arlie, 26, 28, 43, 85
Holidays, 73, 141, 158, 182, 204, 206
   paid, of housekeeper, 126
   see also Time off, housekeeper's
Home-based work, 35
Homemaker/homemaking, 15, 16, 17, 21,
   35, 37, 39, 91, 103
Hours, working, of housekeeper, 123-124,
   139, 140, 156, 173, 195
   see also Schedule, work
Housecleaners, 129, 138, 147, 152, 159,
   179, 189, 198
   see also Cleaning services
Household Employer's Tax Guide (IRS),
   162
   see also Publication 926
Household labor, unpaid, 24-26, 65-70, 88
Household routine, 99, 103-105, 107,
   188-119
Household Tools and Supplies, *figure*, 109
Housekeeper Don'ts, *figure*, 203
Housekeeper, traditional, 19, 71
Housework, magnitude of, 14, 21, 24-25,
   72

I

I-9 (INS), 166
"I" messages, 92, 187, 194-196
   see also, "You" messages
Illness, housekeeper
   see Sick leave
Immigrants/immigration, 41, 58, 64, 76,
   132, 133, 167, 183-185, 196, 201
Immune system, 26
Income taxes
   see Taxes, income

Independent contractor, 78, 128-129, 164, 165

Individual Taxpayer Identification Number, 167

Industrial Revolution, 35, 37, 38

Injuries, 27

INS (Immigration and Naturalization Service), 133, 166, 167

Insomnia, 27
 see also Sleep deprivation

Instructions
 for housekeeper, 56, 114, 123, 147, 175, 182, 185, 193, 195
 manual, 107, 110, 123, 154, 181, 211-220

Instructions for Household Employers (IRS), 171

Insurance, 127
 as benefit for housekeeper, 234
 homeowner's, 152, 174
 renter's, 152, 174
 required/government, 127, 128, 131, 132, 167, 174
 theft, 152
 see also Bonding
 see also Disability insurance
 see also Medicare
 see also Social Security
 see also Unemployment insurance
 see also Worker's compensation insurance

Insurance benefits, 122

Interviewing, 63, 65, 106, 126, 141, 144, 149, 153-157, 197, 200, 202

Investigators, private, 152

Investment, in household help, 14, 15, 101, 107, 118

(IRS) Internal Revenue Service, 125, 128-130, 132, 161-162, 167-173, 175

J

Jackie, *anecdote*, 48-49

Janitorial services, 35

Jill, *anecdote*, 42

Jim, *anecdote*, 191

Job boards, 136, 138-139, 145

Job description, 17, 66, 72, 123, 124

Job duties
 see Duties, of housekeeper

Job market, for housekeepers, 207

Job offer, 156

Job performance
 see Performance, job

Job requirements, 57, 145, 153, 159

Jones, Judy, *anecdote*, 100-103

Julia, *anecdote*, 88

Juliana, *anecdote*, 188

Justice, Department of
 see Department of Justice

K

Kathryn, *anecdote*, 47-48

Kidding Ourselves: Breadwinning, Babies, and Bargaining Power, 92-93

Kim, *anecdote*, 196-197

L

Labor market, 201
 geographic differences, 76, 183

Labor, Department of
 see Department of Labor

"Labor-saving devices", 38, 41

Labor, state department of, 167, 169, 171-173

Language differences
 see Differences, in language

Laundress (Sample Task List), *figure*, 68

"Laundry emergency", 100

Laundry services, 39, 50, 158, 201, 206

Laundry, systems for, 100-101, 111

Lawn care, 54, 74, 88, 99, 129

Leavitt, Harold J., 53

Legal requirements, 17, 56, 76, 127, 132, 161-171, 201

Leisure time, 15, 27, 28, 32, 33, 89

Leo, *anecdote*, 47-48

Letter of employment
 see Employment letter

Letter of recommendation
   see Recommendation, letter
Leverage, 55-56
Lifestyle, 43-44, 74, 88-89, 90, 144, 202
Life Tools Press, 17, 209, 236
Live-in housekeepers, 169, 172-173,
   188-189, 204
Love, the meaning of housework as, 33
Loyalty, of housekeeper, 57, 58, 181
Luxury, household help as, 14, 15, 40, 41,
   91, 92

M

Mahony, Rhona, 92-93
Maid services
   see Cleaning services
Maltz, Maxwell, 92
Management, 19, 55-61, 95, 199
   skills, 14, 77
Maria, *anecdote*, 64
Marjorie, *anecdote*, 53
Marriage, 14, 28, 85
   see also Conflicts over housework
   see also Divorce
Marriage counseling, 82, 85, 92
Master Shopping List, *figure*, 115-116
Maternity leave, 35
Meals and lodging, 169, 173
   see also Room and board
Meal planning, 99, 110, 112-113, 117-118,
   182
Medicare, 127, 130, 131, 167
Melanie, *anecdote*, 86
*Men Are from Mars, Women Are from
   Venus*, 93-94
Michael, *anecdotes*, 23, 28, 33, 34, 88,
   113, 194
Michaelangelo, 30
Miller Time, 32
Minimum wage, 172, 173
Mona, *anecdotes*, 197-198, 203
Money-management, 44
Monique, *anecdote*, 154
Montessori, Maria, 102
Moral reasons for not hiring help, 41, 57

Motherhood, 199
"Motherhood Myopia", 17-19, 21, 51, 93
Mothering, 17, 50
   see also Parenting
"Mother model", 199
Mother Nature, 33
Motivation
   of housekeeper, 17, 192
   of working women, 36
Mutually rewarding business relationship,
   57, 61, 158, 189-190, 208
Myths
   about the "nanny tax", 128-131
   about hiring household help, 14, 17,
   21, 41

N

Nannies, 50, 71-72, 123, 126, 128, 138,
   143, 154, 159, 197, 198
"Nanny tax", 49, 128-133, 137, 161, 162
"Nanny Tax" Myths, Misperceptions, and
   Realities, *figure*, 128
National Guard, 32
Negotiation
   with housekeeper, 57, 124, 188, 198
   with spouse, 92-94, 230-231
Nelia, *anecdote*, 200
Nora, *anecdote*, 50
Nutrition, 85

O

Objections, to hiring help, 54
Okin, Susan Moller, 38
On-line grocery shopping
   see Grocery shopping services
"On the books" payments, 133
   see also "Under the table" payments
Opportunities and Benefits, *figure*, 83
Opportunities, made possible by
   household help, 21, 45-54, 198
Organizing, 24, 49, 56, 75, 95, 97-119,
   182, 192, 200, 231-232
Other Informative Government
   Publications, *figure*, 166

Overtime, 173
  unpaid, 124
Owings, Alison, 46
Ownership
  sense of, 34, 180, 181, 182, 189, 198,
    200, 202
  pride of, 179

P

Paige, *anecdote*, 40
Paper handling, 108
Paperwork, tax-related, 130, 132, 161,
  162, 235
Parenting, 14, 15, 40
  see also Mothering
Part-time work, 25, 30, 35, 48, 50, 60, 101
Pasteur, Louis, 30
"Pathfinders", 53
Paula, *anecdotes*, 48, 51, 99
Pavlov's dogs, 44
Paycheck, housekeeper's, 124, 162, 169,
  204
  adjustments to, 131, 167, 168, 169, 173
Payday, for housekeepers, 173, 204
Pay period, for housekeepers, 169, 173
Pay rate, for housekeepers, 76-78, 84,
  136-137, 147, 207
  "going rate", 77, 121
  see also Wages, of housekeepers
Pay stub, 169, 170
Peer Marriage, 94
Performance, job, 199
Performance reviews
  see Reviews, of housekeeper
    performance
Personality differences
  see Differences, in personality
Personal time off, 126
  see also Time off, housekeeper's
Pets, 47-48, 144, 155
Phone screening, 141, 145-149, 151, 153
Phone Screen Worksheet, *figure*, 146
Placement services, 136
Planning, 49, 56, 63-78, 90, 92, 95, 97,
  107, 192, 200

Praise, 191-193
Pregnancy
  of employer, 34
  of housekeeper, 201
Pride of ownership
  see Ownership, pride of
Priorities
  for tasks to be done, 72, 123, 124, 181,
    182, 198, 200, 204
  of employer, 90, 91, 198, 202
    see also Values, interests, and
      priorities
  of housekeeper, 193, 206
  of IRS, 130
Private investigators
  see Investigators, private
Professional Domestic Services, 97
Professional (women), 16, 18, 44, 48, 55,
  88
Psycho-Cybernetics, 92
Publication 15 (IRS), 169
Publication 15-A (IRS), 129
Publication 503 (IRS), 175
Publication 926 (IRS), 162, 165, 166, 169

Q

Qualifications
  see Job requirements
Quality
  of housekeeper's work, 19, 149, 150, 181
  of life, 26, 43-44, 89, 91
    see also Standards, living
  of products, 42
"Quality time", 29, 40, 51
Questionnaire, author's
  see Survey, author's

R

Raises, housekeeper, 127, 193
Reasons for hiring help, 17
"Recharge your batteries", 14, 27
Recipes, 64, 76, 110, 112, 114, 118, 149,
  154, 182, 221-227
Recommendation, letter, 202
Records, employment, 170, 173

Recruiting methods, 135-141
Recycling, 104-106
Reference checking, 65, 141, 149-151, 153
Reference Check Worksheet, *figure*, 148
References, 63, 140, 143, 144, 147, 151, 159, 200
Referrals, 136, 138, 145, 151
Relationship
  with housekeeper, 200
    see also Mutually rewarding
      business relationship
  with spouse
    see Marriage
Reliability, of housekeeper, 149, 150, 153, 158, 196, 208
Reminder List, *figure*, 117
Reprimands, of housekeeper, 186
Requirements
  see Job requirements
  see Legal requirements
  see Tax requirements
Resentment, over housework 14, 85-86
Residual Cost Formula, *figure*, 87
Resource centers, 136, 138-139
Resources, 46, 99, 108, 122, 130, 151, 162, 187, 190, 229-236
Reviews, of housekeeper performance, 127
Rich, Adrienne, 52
Rita, *anecdote*, 91
Roles and Tasks Exercise, 66-70
Roles and Tasks Exercise, The, *figure*, 70
Roles, traditional, 32, 90-91
Room and board, housekeeper's, 169, 172
Room of One's Own, A, 30
Routine, household
  see Household routine
Ruth, *anecdote*, 139

S

Sam, *anecdote*, 52
Sample Employment Letter, *figure*, 156
Sample Pay Stub, *figure*, 170

Sample Roles and Sub-Roles, *figure*, 67
Sandra, *anecdote*, 139
San Francisco Bay Area, 77
Sanger, Margaret, 30
Saving face, 185, 187, 195, 208
Savings, of hiring help, 80-82, 84-87
  see also Costs
Schedule, housework, 65, 104, 107, 121, 123, 124, 126, 181, 182, 200, 204
Schedule H, 1040 (IRS), 168, 171, 172
Schwartz, Pepper, 94
Screening, of job candidates, 141-157
  see also Background checking
  see also Interviewing
  see also Phone screening
  see also Reference checking
"Second shift", 29, 36, 39
Second Shift, The, 26, 28, 85
Selling, idea of housekeeper to spouse, 17, 92-94
Sense of ownership
  see Ownership, sense of
Servants, 40, 41, 105
Severance pay, 202
Sex, 28
Sexual harassment
  see Harassment, sexual
Sharing of housework
  with spouse, 15, 24, 32, 94, 99
Shopping lists, 112-118, 182
Sick leave, 73, 126, 201
  see also Time off, housekeeper's
Sister Gratia, *anecdote*, 50-51
Sistine Chapel, 30
Slavery, 58
Sleep deprivation, 15, 26-27, 85
  see also Fatigue
Smith, Sharon, *anecdote*, 100-103
Social Security, 127, 130, 131, 132, 167, 176
Social Security Administration, 171
Spock, Dr., 39
Spring cleaning, 125
SS-4 (IRS), 167
SS-5 (SSA), 167

Staffing, 56, 95, 121-177
   see also Hiring
Standards
   housework, 19, 25, 49, 56, 73, 91, 105,
      181, 204
   living, 38, 42-44, 53, 89
Starkey International, 97
State department of labor
   see Labor, state department of
Stealing
   see Theft
Steve, *anecdote*, 91
Stowe, Harriet Beecher, 40
Stress, 27, 28, 32, 85, 105, 200
Studies, surveys, and statistics, 14, 15,
     24-26, 28, 38, 39, 46, 58, 126, 131
   see also Survey, author's
Style, working, 181, 198
Supermarkets, 201
Superwoman, 19, 26, 49
Supplies, household
   see Tools, for housekeeper
Survey, author's, 18, 29, 41
Susan, *anecdote*, 23-24
"Synthetic experience", 92
System, household, 99-118

T

Taboos, against hiring help
   see Myths, about hiring household help
Take-out food, 73, 158, 201
Tannen, Deborah, 185
Task list, 66, 68
Tax credits, 175-176
Tax deductions
   see Paycheck, housekeeper's,
     adjustments to
Tax forms
   see Forms and publications, tax-related
Taxes
   employment, 77-78, 128, 130, 161-172
   income, of housekeeper, 118, 125, 164,
     167, 168
   income, withholding, of employer, 172

income, withholding, of housekeeper,
   131, 168, 169, 171, 172
   personal, of employer, 172, 176
   see also "Nanny tax"
Tax liability, employer's, 170-172
Tax payments, estimated, 172
Tax refunds, 168
Tax requirements, 19, 161-172
   see also Legal requirements
Tax return, employer's personal, 172
Ted, *anecdote*, 88
Temporary help, 136-137, 152, 201, 206
1040 (IRS)
   see also Schedule H, 1040
1040-ES (IRS), 172
Teresa, *anecdote*, 197-198, 203
Terms of employment
   see Employment terms
That's Not What I Meant!, 185
Theft, 152, 195, 202
Three-Line Ad Sample, *figures*, 141, 207
*Time Bind, The: When Work Becomes
   Home and Home Becomes Work*, 43
Time estimates
   see Estimates of time spent on
     housework
Time-management, 14, 41, 44, 92
Time off, housekeeper's, 206
   paid, 126
   unpaid, 126
   see also Absences, housekeeper
   see also Flexible time off
   see also Holidays
   see also Personal time off
   see also Sick leave
   see also Vacations
Tired
   see Fatigue
To Be Answered During Screening,
   figure, 142
Tomlin, Lily, 44
Tools
   for housekeeper, 106-110, 199
   for job success, 180
Toys, 108, 154, 199, 203

Tradition, and housework
  see History of housework
Training, of housekeeper, 16, 17, 19, 56,
  123, 181-182, 193, 195, 200, 209
Turner, Chad R., 132

U

"Under the table" payments, 76, 144
  see also "On the books" payments
Unemployment, 76, 125, 127
Unemployment insurance
  see FUTA (Federal Unemployment
  Tax Act)
Unpaid household labor
  see Household labor, unpaid
U.S. Treasury, 131

V

Vacations, 182
  of employer, 125, 126, 200
  of housekeeper, 126, 200
  see also Time off, housekeeper's
Valuables, 152
Values, interests, and priorities, 17, 19, 46
Volunteering, 45, 91

W

W-2 (IRS), 133, 171
W-3 (IRS), 171
W-4 (IRS), 168, 169, 172
W-5 (IRS), 168
W-7 (IRS), 167
Wage, minimum
  see Minimum wage
Wages, 42-43
  of housekeepers, 56-60, 71, 86, 122,
  124-125, 127, 131, 140, 156, 159,
  169-173, 189, 207
    cash, 169
    non-cash, 172
Wash-and-fold services
  see Laundry services
Way We Really Are, The, 32
Wealth, 14, 41-44, 46, 61, 91, 140, 142

Weekly Meal Plan, *figure,* 113
Welfare, 76, 132, 144, 167, 183
Wendy, *anecdote,* 51
Which Forms to Request from Which
  Agencies, *figure,* 164-165
Withholding
  see Taxes, income, withholding
Women, professional
  see Professional (women)
Women's work, housework as
  see History, of housework
Woolf, Virginia, 30
Word of mouth, 136, 152
Work environment
  See Environment, working
Worker's compensation insurance, 174
Work/family conflict
  see Conflict, work/family
Work hours
  see Hours, working
Working Mother, 28, 31, 46
Working women
  see Professional (women)
Work schedule
  see Schedule, work
Work style
  see Style, working
Workweek, of housekeeper, 205
World War II, 36, 41, 59
World wars, 36, 58

Y

Yardwork
  see Lawn care
Yelena, *anecdotes,* 123, 199, 200
Yellow Pages, 138, 139, 152, 153, 162,
  206, 232, 235
"You" messages, 92, 194-195

Z

Zisman, Mike, *anecdote,* 50

Give the Gift of Time to Your Loved Ones, Friends, and Colleagues

Check your favorite bookstore or order...

- From our website at *www.LifeToolsPress.com*
- Toll-free by phone at (877) LIFE-TLS or (877) 543-3857
- By fax at (650) 960-0338
- By mail at Life Tools Press
  PO Box 390220
  Mountain View, CA 94039-0220
- By email at *orders@LifeToolsPress.com*

Non-U.S. orders: request ordering instructions by fax or email.

Name: _____

Company Name: _____

Address: _____

City: _____ State: _____ Zip: _____

Phone (recommended for credit card purchase)

    Day: _____ Evening: _____

Email Address: _____

Amount Enclosed:

_____ copies of *A Housekeeper Is Cheaper Than a Divorce* at $19.95 each   _____

    California residents please add 8.25% sales tax at $1.65 per book   _____

        Please add your shipping choice:

           Standard shipping (1-2 weeks) $3.50

           Priority shipping (2-3 days) $5.00   _____

      Please add $1.00 in shipping for each additional copy   _____

                               Total   _____

Payment: ☐ Check/Money Order   ☐ Visa   ☐ Mastercard

Card Number: _____

Name on Card: _____ Exp. Date: _____

Signature: _____